GUIDE TO
NEVADA CORPORATIONS

THE SECRET MILLIONAIRE

GUIDE TO
NEVADA CORPORATIONS

JOHN V. CHILDERS, JR.

Lighthouse Publishing Group, Inc.
Seattle, Washington

Lighthouse Publishing Group, Inc.
Copyright © 1998 by John V. Childers, Jr.

Library of Congress Cataloging-in-Publication Data
Childers, John V., Jr.
The Secret Millionaire
Guide to Nevada Corporations/John V. Childers, Jr.
p. cm.
1. Corporation law--Nevada--Popular works. 2. Incorporation--Nevada--Popular works. I. Title.
KFN813.Z9C48 1998
346.793'066--dc21 98-15610
ISBN (cloth) 0-910019-57-6

This book is sold with the understanding that neither the author nor the publisher is engaged in rendering legal, accounting, or professional services. Questions relevant to the specific tax, legal, and accounting needs of the reader should be addressed to practicing members of those professions.

The information, ideas, and suggestions contained herein have been developed from sources, including publications and research, that are considered and believed to be reliable, but cannot be guaranteed insofar as they apply to any particular taxpayer or individual desiring to form a corporation. Moreover, because of the technical nature of the material and the fact that laws are never static, but ever changing, the assistance of a competent, qualified lawyer or accountant is recommended when implementing any plans of ideas discussed in this book.

The Author and the Publisher specifically disclaim any liability, loss, or risk, personal or otherwise, incurred as a consequence directly or indirectly of the use and application of any of the techniques or contents of this book.

Lighthouse Publishing would like to acknowledge the following people for their hard work on the creation of this book:
Book Design by Judy Burkhalter
Dust Jacket by Angela Wilson
Layout by Brent Magarrell
Art Direction by Mark Engelbrecht
Editing/Proofing by Connie Suehiro, Bethany McVannel, Vicki Van Hise, and Liz Lake

Published by Lighthouse Publishing Group, Inc.
14675 Interurban Avenue South
Seattle, WA 98168-4664
1-800-706-8657
206-901-3100 (fax)
www.lighthousebooks.com

Printed in the United States of America
10 9 8 7 6 5 4 3 2 1

To: Jill

ACKNOWLEDGMENTS

A lot of work is involved in undertaking a task as large as writing a book. There is no way I could have done it all on my own. Without the support of others, you wouldn't be reading this right now. There are several people who I want to recognize for making this book a reality. First of all, I'd like to thank Jon Baxley whose assistance really got things going and made all of this possible. Also, I'd like to thank Alison Curtis and the rest of the folks at Lighthouse Publishing for keeping on me every step of the way. It may not have seemed like it at times, but I really do appreciate it. Lord knows I needed it. Along those lines, I want to thank Kathy Voorhees for keeping me on track throughout the project and helping me see a light at the end of the tunnel. I also want to thank Wade Cook for inspiring me to actually do it rather than just talking about it. Kent Mangelson, Katheryn Biel, and Larry Ogden were also very supportive when things got stressful; thanks for your support. Special thanks also go to Steve "Stevie Wall Street" Wirrick and Scott Lamm for their encouragement and assistance.

I need to give special thanks and praise to my parents, John and Brenda Childers, who have taught me many of the most important things I know, including Nevada Corporations. Your continued guidance and support throughout my life is appreciated more than I could ever express. You are my heroes.

Last by not least, I want to thank my wife, Jill, who has put up with me through it all. Without your support I would not be where I am today. I know that I am truly blessed to have someone who always believes in me, even when there's not much to believe in.

CONTENTS

CHAPTER
HIGHLIGHTS

FOREWORD

"If you want to make over $100,000 a year, why are you talking about making money with anyone who makes under $100,000 a year? To whom are you listening?"

WADE B. COOK

E very so often, a book comes along which can help people to accomplish great things. I read a lot of books and I am always searching for new ways to not only accumulate wealth but to preserve it as well. Occasionally, I'll come across a book which offers keen insight into how to accomplish these key objectives. *The Secret Millionaire Guide to Nevada Corporations* is just such a book.

I have had the opportunity over the years to work closely with the author, JJ Childers, and one thing I have learned about him is that he has an amazing ability to take difficult legal and tax-related concepts, and present them in straightforward, no-nonsense terms so that anyone can learn and implement these powerful secrets. In *The Secret Millionaire Guide to Nevada Corporations*, he presents exactly how anyone, who has the desire and interest, can apply the high-powered strategies used by today's secret millionaires to overcome some of the devastating forces at work in today's society.

I often point out to people that there are basically three financial Goliaths at work today: 1) lawsuits, 2) income taxes, and 3) death taxes. One of the great things about *The Secret Millionaire Guide to Nevada Corporations* is that it continues where most books leave off. Not only does it give the legal benefits of utilizing a Nevada Corporation, it outlines exactly how to implement those benefits. It shows you how to take advantage of highly effective strategies to help protect your assets and reduce your taxes.

In my books and seminars, I often tell about an important lesson I learned many years ago. A very wise man told me, "If you really want to get rich in this country, watch what poor people do and don't do it." I've taken that to heart. I've watched poor people all over the country. What they do, simply put, is not going to make them a lot of money. The other side of that coin, if you want to make a lot of money, is to watch rich people and do what they do. *The Secret Millionaire Guide to Nevada Corporations* offers a look at what some of this country's most successful individuals and companies are doing to generate vast amounts of wealth and how they protect it. If you plan on being involved in any type of money-making endeavor, I highly recommend that you study *The Secret Millionaire Guide to Nevada Corporations*.

Wade B. Cook
New York Times Best-Selling Author,
Wall Street Money Machine
Stock Market Miracles
Business Buy The Bible

PREFACE

"To be a success in business, be daring, be first, be different."

MARCHANT

Why write a book teaching people how to protect themselves? It seems that people would already know how to protect themselves. But, is that the case? Not hardly.

When I first decided to write this book, I wanted to cover exactly how people could protect their hard-earned assets. This is not something I wanted to do for those individuals alone, but also for their families. The problem is that there is a lack of good information on this important subject. It was with this thought in mind that I decided to undertake the project.

In my life, I have been extremely fortunate in that I have had the opportunity to learn from some of this country's brightest financial minds. Growing up, the thought never entered my mind that I couldn't achieve anything I set my mind to. I've had the opportunity to not only meet, but also to develop great relationships with a vast number of multi-millionaires. Having this access has enabled me to learn some very valuable lessons.

From an early age, I began to realize that making a lot of money wasn't the hardest thing to do. What I learned is that the hardest thing to do is to keep that money. In the world we live in today, that is much easier said than done.

Protecting assets is something which has been very important to me. I have been blessed to be a part of a moderately wealthy family. As such, I stand to benefit immensely from this wealth. For this reason, I have a bit of incentive to learn the intricacies of asset protection.

When I first started learning about this subject, I decided to go to law school. In law school, I learned a lot about how the law works. Through the study of case precedents, I developed an understanding of how the legal system as a whole operates. But law school, in and of itself, did not teach me all that I needed to know about asset protection. None of the courses offered the nuts and bolts of protecting your assets that I was really looking for. Simply put, I needed more.

I gained a greater understanding of how things worked when I went to work in state government. Through my work in the Office of the Attorney General, I was able to see firsthand how regulatory agencies play a part in the legal world. By seeing things from that point of view, I was able to develop a better insight into how businesses must deal with our legal system. Working on consumer protection issues helped me to learn some of the safeguards people implement to protect their money from unscrupulous individuals and businesses. This was a major breakthrough for me.

One of the most eye-opening experiences of my life was when I went to work for a private plaintiffs' law firm. There, our objective was to seek compensation for our clients who had been adversely affected by tortuous actions. Many of the lawsuits we were involved with were against insurance companies. We were suing the insurance companies so that our clients could collect for their various injuries. The typical lawsuit often works this way. Do you suppose that the insurance companies were happy to pay these claims? Not hardly. The fact is, they would go to great lengths to keep from paying these claims.

Do I tell you this to beat up on insurance companies? Not at all. The point I am making here is that insurance alone will not protect you in every situation. If the insurance company doesn't pay these claims, who do you suppose the plaintiffs' firm will go after? You better be ready!

That experience helped me learn a lot about the mentality and the tactics utilized by the people going after your assets. Let me tell you, these people are good. They're smart, and they're tenacious. If you do not have a plan on how to deal with these lawsuits, they will absolutely eat you alive!

I learned a great deal in each of these positions, but there are two more areas that I gained experience in which have helped me develop a better insight. These two areas are my work for a federal judge and my work in the state legislature. My work in the federal judge's office showed me in greater detail how case precedents factor into judicial policy. This helped me to understand things much better because it was real world information.

Perhaps the best experience I had was in working with the state legislature. There, I saw firsthand how laws are actually made and the process through which they occur. This showed me how and why laws turn out the way they do. I learned full well that individual state's laws can differ markedly from those of other states. This had a significant impact on the direction I needed to head in.

Through this blend of legal experiences, I have been able to develop a unique approach to the area of asset protection. In writing this book, I am able to pass on the information which I've learned, as well as that developed by those much smarter and much more experienced than I am.

Folks, there is a financial war going on. You didn't ask to be a part of this war, but you are involved nonetheless. We are all faced with bombs which can absolutely destroy us. The trick is to install safeguards and shields to protect ourselves. This book is about techniques utilized by veterans of this war. *The Secret Millionaire Guide to Nevada Corporations* teaches the strategies which helped those veterans reach elite status. You too, can achieve this status and earn the title "Secret Millionaire."

I THE SECRET MILLIONAIRE

*"An infallible method of conciliating a
tiger is to allow oneself to be devoured."*

KONRAD ADENAUER

Now, more than at any other time in this
country, you must become a "secret millionaire." Financial war has been declared on the people of this country and if you are
not prepared, it will devour you. To prepare yourself, you must understand the importance and the
seriousness of the situation.

Imagine that the year is 1969. You are nine-
teen years old and in the prime of your youth.
You have your entire life ahead of you. Unfortunately, you are thrown into a situation which you
feel ill-equipped to deal with. Your dreams are on
hold as you find yourself in a foreign country
thousands and thousands of miles away from
your home. The country is Vietnam. You didn't
ask to come here. You haven't done anything to
cause yourself to be put in this predicament. You
have no choice. You must deal with the situation.

Today is one of the worst days of your life. It's unbearably hot and humid. The atmosphere is miserable and you have been chosen to lead your troop through the jungle. Your judgment may very well determine your future. It is your responsibility to do the things which will protect not only you, but others as well. If you fail to implement protective safeguards, the consequences can be catastrophic.

Does this sound pretty grim? Does it scare you to think of yourself involved in a war such as I just described? The problem is, today we are in a situation that can be every bit as devastating. There is a money war in this country and the chief enemy is lawsuits.

In the lawsuit crazed world we live in today, people can easily find themselves in a financial and/or legal crisis that can destroy their estates and even their lives in many instances. Lawsuits can and will take a large chunk of everything that they have worked so hard to accumulate unless they *learn* how to do something to protect themselves.

Lawsuits are certainly not the only things that can devour finances, destroy estates and ruin all that people have built for their children. Other forces are at work today which can be every bit as devastating. You need to know what these forces are, and how to overcome them. It was with that thought in mind that this book was written.

WHAT IS THIS BOOK ABOUT?

This book is designed to teach you all you need to know about one of the greatest financial protection entities available in the United States today, the corporation. More specifically, this book will teach you how to understand and use *Nevada Corporations*.

The material in this book is laid out in a question and answer format so that you can use it as both a guide for protection and as a general reference source on incorporating. That way, if you have a particular question about Nevada Corporations, you can thumb right to the answer.

The main thrust of this book is to help you understand why the state of Nevada has become the preferred jurisdiction for those desiring to establish corporations. There are a lot of reasons for doing so, and you need to understand them all. Then you can use that information to protect yourself, your family and your estate from potential catastrophic financial loss. Most importantly, by studying this material, you will develop a firm understanding and appreciation for the corporation as a tool for achieving important financial goals. As the title implies, you need to be implementing the secrets applied by today's secret millionaires.

While working with investors, small business owners, and others over the years, I have constantly encountered those in need of the protection offered by Nevada Corporations. The problem was that these people did not know where to find the necessary information, and even when they did, they could not understand it. This book has been formatted to explain what you need, where to find it, and exactly how the Nevada Corporation concept can work for you and your particular situation. This is explained in plain, ordinary language instead of legal jargon. This book will be of great importance to you regardless of your current situation or experience level.

FINANCIAL GOALS

The Nevada Corporation is one of the best tools available for accomplishing your personal financial goals, whatever they may be. Most of the concerns people have about their financial futures fall within three main categories. By focusing your attention on these three areas, you can make a big difference in the place you would most like to see improvement, your bank account!

The first area that you need to look at is asset protection. The second is estate planning and the third is tax reduction, an area of immense interest to most business people. These three areas can mean a great deal in accomplishing whatever it is that you want to achieve, financially, in your business as well as personal life.

ASSET PROTECTION

In the area of asset protection, it is really important for you to understand what a litigious society we live in. That means, in plain language, that a lot of folks are suing a lot of other folks, and often for very frivolous reasons.

The best way to illustrate this is by taking a look at a few key statistics on lawsuits. Actual numbers will usually open your eyes to something that you really need to take to heart. The following statistics should do just that.

Studies show that a new lawsuit is filed in this country every 30 seconds on average. That's two a minute, people! To make this point hit home, think about what that really means. In the short time that it's taken you to read this first chapter, several lawsuits have already been filed somewhere against somebody. Lives have been changed, forever! Financial pictures have been altered, irrevocably. Entire family futures have been put in jeopardy. The worst part of this is that it could often be avoided by taking a few simple steps. But that is just the beginning.

One out of four people will be sued this year in this country. Even worse, the average number of lawsuits over an individual's lifetime is five, and of these five, one will be what is known as a "devastating" lawsuit. The term devastating means that it wipes someone out completely, costing them everything they own. It's a horrible sight to see somebody ruined by this kind of litigation, but it *does* happen. By studying this book carefully, you can go a long way toward making sure it does *not* happen to you.

As you begin to see, rampant litigation is a big problem in this country. Everyone needs to learn what to do to help eliminate this problem.

This becomes particularly important when you consider that of all the lawsuits filed in the entire world, 94% are filed right here in the good old United States. 94%! We're the world's leader in filing lawsuits. Now, I don't know about you, but that's not an area I would prefer to lead the world in.

Combine these statistics with the fact that there are currently more law students in law school than there are practicing attorneys and it becomes downright scary, doesn't it? Why is that? Why are law degrees in such high demand these days? Is it because we have a shortage of lawyers in this country? I don't think so!

Flip through your telephone book and see how many attorneys there are in your area alone. There is certainly no lack of membership in the legal profession. The number of lawyers is constantly growing, not because there is a larger need, but because there is more opportunity out there for someone to file and win a lawsuit.

With this in mind, which way do you think the number of lawsuits is going in this country, up or down? Up, up, up, of course! Now more than ever, asset protection needs to become a central concern in your financial planning. You absolutely must have a plan to protect your assets, and the use of Nevada Corporations should be an essential element in that plan.

ESTATE PLANNING

A consideration of equal importance to asset protection is estate planning. Too many times, families unexpectedly discover that enormous amounts of their wealth are being consumed by estate taxes, fees, and other expenses upon the death of a loved one. The worst part of these tragedies is that many of these situations could have been avoided by implementing simple estate plans using the tools you are learning right now.

Unfortunately, people fail to utilize these tools because they do not believe the tools are necessary. It is sad but true that most people spend more time planning their vacations than they do planning their estates. Studies have indicated that the average person will spend over 90,000 hours working to accumulate wealth (40 hours a week times 50 weeks a year for 45 years of their working lives), but less than three hours learning how to preserve that wealth. These people simply fail to plan their estates. It is a well known axiom that *if you fail to plan, you plan to fail.*

Part of the reason for this failure to plan is that historically, estate planning has been an area reserved only for the truly wealthy. If your bank account and assets didn't total into the six figure range, at a minimum, the traditional line of thinking was that you need not worry about estate planning. People have had the mindset that if they were not from a family whose last name conveyed enormous wealth, they did not need any estate planning. As you well know, that is certainly not the case any more. Everyone needs an estate plan. You need to ask yourself a question. Would you like to have the estate plan of the average person, or the estate plan used by many of today's millionaires?

The simple truth is, everyone needs to be concerned about estate planning, even if you live from paycheck to paycheck. You are dealing with forces, right now, that can destroy everything you have worked all your life to accumulate. It can happen in the blink of an eye! The Nevada Corporation is a great tool to help you prevent that from happening to your family or estate.

TAX REDUCTION

The third key area of concern in this book is one which is near and dear to all of our hearts. That is the area of tax reduction. No matter where I go or who I talk to, it seems that this area is of primary importance. It sure seems that everyone I speak with says they are paying too much in taxes.

Whether in a seminar, on an airplane, in my business, or even at church, I hear the same old refrain about how bad a person's tax situation has become. When I hear this story, I always ask the same question: *so what are you doing about it?*

It seems that everyone wants to reduce their tax bill but very few are willing to do what that requires. The simple fact is *you* have got to *learn* to reduce your tax bill. Nobody is going to do it for you. If you doubt me on this, ask yourself a question. When was the last time you got that letter from the Internal Revenue Service (IRS) stating that you could have paid a lot less in taxes if you had done things differently? You see, the IRS will not teach you how to reduce your taxes, you must do it yourself. Nobody cares about reducing your taxes more than you do. Since that's the case, *you* must learn how to do it. It's up to you!

Having control over your tax bill can mean a great difference in your life. The hard part in all of this is convincing people that they are indeed in control. It seems too hard a pill to swallow that they may in fact be the problem. It's much easier to blame the problem on someone else.

Think about that for a minute. What have you done this year to reduce your tax bill?

Let me take time out right now to commend you for taking the time out of your schedule to read this book. That's a real step in reducing your taxes, and nobody made you do it. This information can make a tremendous difference in your financial future, if you will just apply it once you've learned it. To reduce the amount you pay in taxes, you have to *do* something about it.

The key is knowledge. You must accumulate as much knowledge as you can about understanding your tax situation. Read tax newsletters, books, the Tax Code, IRS publications, and anything else that you can get your hands on to increase your knowledge base. Go to the bookstores and/or libraries and devour their tax material. Continually gain more and more tax knowledge. This is an investment that can provide exponential returns in the form of increased tax savings.

While knowledge is certainly the key, the implementation of that knowledge is the most crucial step. It does you no good whatsoever to learn the information if you fail to do anything with it. The use of a Nevada Corporation can help you to significantly reduce your tax bill, if not eliminate certain taxes. However, it only works for those who are willing to exert the effort required to implement the strategies. You must take control over your situation, or your situation will take control of you.

SUMMARY

The landscape is dangerous out there. A war is taking place which will require a great deal of knowledge and savvy in order to survive. The areas of asset protection, estate planning, and tax reduction need to be on your mind constantly. You need to continually build upon your knowledge base and develop a greater understanding of how to best address these concerns. Read this and other books over and over again to familiarize yourself with the contents and implement the information contained herein. There are excellent ways to structure your affairs, but the responsibility for their implementation lies with you. *You are in control!*

II DECIDING ON INVISIBILITY

"Nothing will come of nothing. Dare mighty things."

S hould I form my own corporation? What will it help me to accomplish? How can it assist me with my particular situation? Should I do it now or later? Do you know the answer to these questions? If not, you better learn them.

These are but a few of the many questions I hear from people across the country when I speak to them about corporations. The decision to incorporate is one of the most important ones you will ever make. And it's one you *must* make in order to deal with the three areas that were covered in Chapter I.

If you do not know the answers to those questions, rest assured that you are not alone. The fact is, most people do not know the answers. However, if they can't answer those simple questions, how on earth can they consider actually forming and operating a corporation? To many people, the

9

thought of ever having their own corporation seems like a task far too complicated. As you will see, that is certainly not the case. It's not difficult, it's just different.

The key to answering the questions lies in gaining a full understanding of exactly what it means to become incorporated. You must truly understand corporations before you decide to form one.

As you begin your endeavor of fully understanding Nevada Corporations, I believe you must first begin with the absolute basics. While studying the basics may be quite elementary for some, it has proven to be essential in gaining an in-depth comprehension of any topic, much less one as complex as a legal entity. Besides that, regardless of your level of experience, you can never get enough of the fundamentals.

Think about it. When you go to watch your favorite sports team play, when they practice before the game, are they practicing the difficult plays or the basics? The basics! If that is what the professionals do, perhaps you should take a hint and do the same thing. If you want to get the best results, you must do things in the best manner possible. Learn from those who are getting the results that you would like in your life. That is the secret applied by today's millionaires.

If you want to know about something, you first need to know what it is. With this in mind, you have to ask the most basic questions first. The most basic question to deal with when it comes to corporations is simply, "What is a corporation?" We will answer this question before going any further.

WHAT IS A CORPORATION?

If you were to ask most people to define the term "corporation," I'm quite sure you would get a myriad of responses, none of which may be correct. I'm convinced, as I travel throughout the country speaking with individuals from all walks of life, that there is a huge misconception as to exactly what it means to be incorporated.

Generally, the term conjures up images of New York City and the vast array of skyscrapers which serve as headquarters to the Fortune 500 companies. While these huge multinational companies may indeed be corporations, it must be realized that the corporation can also be the mom and pop grocery on your local street corner. It's also the real estate agency through which you purchased your home, the insurance agent you play golf with, and the restaurant where you have dinner.

Most people simply don't see these smaller businesses when they envision corporations. But in actuality, it is these smaller businesses that make up the bulk of corporations throughout the world. It is these smaller businesses which mean more to the average person when it comes to benefiting from the use of a corporation. In fact, it is these smaller businesses which belong to many of today's millionaires.

The typical corporation in this country is a small business. In many instances, this small business, this small *corporation*, is owned and operated by families and even friends. This seems strange to many people who tend to think of corporations more in terms of those companies whose shares are traded on Wall Street.

The fact is, the overwhelming vast majority of corporations in this country are privately held. Actually, of the thousands, even millions, of corporations currently operating in the United States, an extremely small number are publicly traded. The chances are, if you are reading this book with the thought of forming a corporation, you are not planning to form this type of publicly traded company. At least not yet, anyway.

This makes it a bit more difficult to explain to someone about corporations because much of what they know comes from what they have learned in conjunction with the stock market. It seems that people all too often tend to associate all corporations with the Dow Jones Industrials.

This really comes as no surprise since a good knowledge of corporations can help one develop a greater understanding of how and why stock is traded on the various exchanges. Considering that some 50 million individuals have brokerage accounts, it is not hard to see why the primary understanding of corporations comes from this arena.

A slight familiarity with corporations is inherent in any investment and/or trading environment. To truly understand corporations, and, more importantly to understand how you can benefit by having a corporation, you need to set aside any preconceptions you have and look at corporations from a whole new perspective. If you can do this, it can mean money in your pocket!

Let's begin by looking at some of the legal definitions of a corporation. Then we'll break those definitions down into language that is more understandable and readily applicable to your daily life. One of the first steps in finding out what any legal term means is to look it up in a law dictionary. The most common dictionary, *Black's Law Dictionary*, defines a corporation as:

> An artificial person or legal entity created by or under authority of the laws of a state or nation, composed, in some rare instances, of a single person and his successors, being the incumbents of a particular office, but ordinarily consisting of an association of numerous individuals, who subsist as a body politic under a special denomination, which is regarded in law as having a personality and existence distinct from that of its several members, and which is by the same authority, vested with the capacity of continuous succession, irrespective of changes in its membership, either in perpetuity or for a limited term of years, and of acting as a unit or single individual in matters relating to the common purpose of the association, within the scope of the powers and authorities conferred upon such bodies by law.
>
> Dartmouth College v. Woodward, 17 U.S. (4 Wheat.) 518, 636, 657, 4 L.Ed. 629; U.S. v. Trinidad Coal Co., 137 U.S. 160, 11 S.Ct. 57, 34 L.Ed. 640.

There it is. Now, does that clear everything up for you? That is the official definition of what it means to be a corporation, straight from the Supreme Court. After reading this definition, I have a question for you: what is a corporation?

Seriously! I learned this lesson the hard way. Early on, when I was first studying to be an attorney, I met with a lady who wanted to know about a corporation. I did what I thought at the time to be the best thing which was to draft a memorandum outlining this legal definition of a corporation. Her response was certainly not what I expected but it taught me a valuable lesson. Her response was, "Everything I need to know about what it means to be a corporation is written right there in plain English but I still don't have a clue what it means." Talk about an enlightening experience. I learned right then and there that people want real world answers rather than a lot of technical legal jargon.

While this may be the legal definition of a corporation, it does little to shed light on the issue of what a corporation means to the average person. Too many times, this is exactly the case. You can go to an attorney and he can give you page after page of information on a subject and you leave the office more confused than you started, despite the fact that you actually have the "appropriate" documentation purportedly answering your questions. With this in mind, let's take a little different approach to defining exactly what it means to be a corporation.

Basically, a corporation is a separate and legal, artificial person. That's right, a separate person from you. The corporation is not you and you are not the corporation. It is completely separate, a distinct entity separate and apart from you. It has the same rights as a person but it is more of a legal entity than a person. This point needs further attention.

A corporation is a separate legal entity. It is an entity separate and apart from its members, stockholders, directors and officers. While it is indeed a separate entity, it is still dependent upon others in order to take any action. This is the best news of all.

That is great news for you because you are the person upon whom the corporation is dependent. The corporation can act only through its members, officers and directors or agents thereof. Although it is separate, the best part of this is that it can have no knowledge or belief on any subject independent of the knowledge or belief of those who control the corporation. This works very well since you are going to be the person(s) in control. It can do nothing unless you tell it to.

You are in control over this entity in the same way that a parent is in control of their children (ideally). Some of you may be thinking that this is not necessarily a good thing. You may be thinking that you've got enough on your hands with your kids without having another one when you form your corporation. The difference is that the corporation always minds you, no matter what the situation. Wouldn't that be nice? Do you understand the power in that? Let's take a closer look.

The corporation is an artificial person. Its rights, duties and liabilities do not differ from those of a natural person under like conditions. The only difference between a corporation and those directing it is that it lacks the ability to think for itself. That is the purpose of the officers and directors. These individuals do the thinking for the corporation.

To evidence this fact, documentation is kept for all decisions made on behalf of the corporation in the form of minutes and/or corporate resolutions. These documents are crucial and will be discussed in later sections in much greater detail. This distinction between the entity and those who control it becomes key in determining exactly what it is that people are searching for when they make the decision to form a corporation.

This also leads to our next question which will really be a bit more telling in understanding what a corporation is all about. It often requires more information than a simple definition of an item before your mind can form a picture of the item. The trick is to understand what that particular item does. What is the function that it performs which makes it of value to you? Knowing what it is that a corporation does will reveal more about the entity and why a person would want to have one.

For example, if someone asked you what a car is, you would be hard pressed to tell them without telling them what it does. Just as you cannot truly understand what an automobile is without knowing what it does, so it is with a corporation. With this in mind, let's take a look at our next question: why do people incorporate?

WHY DO PEOPLE INCORPORATE?

This is the question that really needs to be answered. If you can determine what makes a person decide that they would like to have a corporation, you can more accurately determine what a corporation is all about. Just like the automobile, you need to see why anyone would want this corporation.

As previously outlined, the corporation is an artificial, legal person. It is a citizen of the state wherein it is created. In a later chapter, we will look at the various jurisdictions where you may want to create your corporation. Right now, however, you need to understand that a corporation does not cease to be a citizen of the state in which it is incorporated by engaging in business in another state. Nor does it change its citizenship by acquiring property in another state. These are both great benefits of having a corporation.

Another incredible benefit of being incorporated is that the existence of that corporation is not affected by the death of a shareholder or by the transfer of the shareholder's ownership stake (shares). This is phenomenal with respect to accomplishing estate planning objectives as we will discuss more fully in a later chapter. Further, the corporation's existence is not affected in the event that one of its owners undergoes the unfortunate circumstances surrounding bankruptcy. This makes the entity excellent for asset protection.

The reason for this, once again, is because the corporation is separate. It is separate from its owners. It is separate from its officers and directors. It owns things in its own name, not in the name of the owners, officers, and/or directors. It is *separate!*

As a separate legal entity, a corporation has the same rights and characteristics that we all have. It is considered to have its domicile or home in the state in which it is incorporated and the place where it retains its resident agent or home office in that state. When the corporation is physically located in a different place, the location of the corporation's resident agent is oftentimes referred to as its "statutory domicile." Considering the separate nature of corporations, let's take a look at some of the exciting possibilities presented for those who decide to incorporate.

The way I prefer to think of a corporation is that it functions as more of a twin brother or sister. Most of you have had days when you wished that you could send someone to work in your place so that you could stay home and do as you please. Really, wouldn't it be nice to have someone step into your shoes and deal with undesirable situations that you all too often find yourself in? What if you had this other person that could fill in for you and all you have to do is tell that other person what to do? You could do all of the thinking for that person so that he or she would know what to do for you. Wouldn't that be ideal? That is exactly what a corporation does.

You may be thinking to yourself, "Yeah, right, sounds like just a dream!" Today, you have all sorts of worries and concerns you have to deal with. It sounds almost too good to be true to think that you could have someone that could take care of that stuff for you. It would be great in today's litigious society to be able to associate assets with that other person rather than with yourself personally. Then that person could be sued rather than you, right? Would that be amazing or what? That is exactly how it works when you begin to understand things more fully.

As I explain the benefits of Nevada Corporations to groups, this whole structure at first seems like a farfetched idea that simply doesn't exist. They think, "Too bad I can't send that person to court to risk his assets instead of mine. If only I really did have a person who would do anything I told him. I could have him hold title to those assets so that I could significantly limit my vulnerability to lawsuits in connection with those assets, giving me tremendous asset protection. In the event that the other person lost that lawsuit and a judgment was rendered against him, the worst that could possibly happen is that he would lose his assets, not mine. Best of all, my personal assets would not be attached." Sound pretty incredible? Actually, this is exactly what a corporation is all about.

The reason people decide to incorporate is to create a situation much like what I've just outlined. By setting up a corporation, it is as if you have formed a twin who has all the rights that you do, yet is completely separate and apart from you.

A corporation is indeed a legal person. It is an entity in and of itself with a life and an identity all its own. The corporation is not you and you are not the corporation. It is completely separate from you and under the law, it is treated as if it were a human being.

Basically, a corporation is a form of business entity which is created based upon the laws of a specific state or country. Corporations cannot be established simply by creating a document between parties. All corporations must be set up under the authority of the government of the jurisdiction in which they are created.

Which jurisdiction that will be is of great significance, so much so that we will spend a good deal of time on it later on in this book. But right now, let's discuss an equally important aspect of corporations by answering another key question: when should one incorporate?

WHEN SHOULD ONE INCORPORATE?

A question of primary concern for many is exactly when they should form their corporation. This is certainly a good question, but it is not something that should be a hindrance to your plan. There are a great number of excellent reasons to place your activities within the corporate structure. The vast majority of these reasons are not time sensitive. The only real issue of a timely nature would be the tax consequences. While we all understand that the tax laws change occasionally, the business value of forming a corporation stays constant.

The bottom line in determining whether it is time for you to establish your corporation is if you answer "yes" to any of the following questions:

1. Would you be interested in maintaining flexibility in the management and control of your own business?
2. Would you like to implement a plan whereby you could protect your assets?
3. Are you interested in maintaining privacy over your finances?

4. Do you want to lower your overall tax obligation?
5. Is preserving your estate for your heirs important to you?

If you answered "yes" to any of these questions, *now* is the time for you to form your corporation. One thing you need to understand is that this is contrary to what other professionals are advising. Many attorneys and accountants have a tendency to give the standard answer to the question of when to incorporate. It seems that they think they know the answer to your situation without ever really taking the time to hear about your situation. They just go on giving the same old standard answer. The fact is, the financial and legal environment in which we live simply will not allow for a "standard" answer to this question. Extraordinary results are not "standard."

There are several factors which you must take into consideration in determining whether the time is right for you to incorporate. While this is not a decision to be made lightly, it is also not a decision you need to lose too much sleep over. Too many times, people will fret over their situation for so long that it turns out that the best time for them to have incorporated was a long time ago. The failure to take action may have cost them thousands, or even tens of thousands of dollars. If you are concerned about protecting your assets, planning your estate, or reducing your taxes, the time to take action is *right now*.

I never fail to be blown away by the responses I get from people who tell me about their dealings with so-called "experts" in setting up their business plans. These responses are amazingly shortsighted. Anyone who has dealt much with attorneys and/or accountants will recognize this frustration. I hear stories on a regular basis about how someone went for professional help and was told that they did not need a corporation until their income reached a certain dollar amount. Not only does this strike me as shortsighted, it is actually quite offensive to me as well.

The reason I find this so offensive is that it completely avoids the issue of asset protection. If one of these professionals says that you do not need a corporation unless you have at least a certain dollar amount, aren't they really saying that if you have below that dollar amount that your assets aren't worth protecting? This offends me! Every person reading this book has worked very hard to get where they are today. For a professional to say that what you've accomplished is not worth protecting is a slap in the face.

Really, if someone told you that you don't need a security system you would think that it must be because there is no need for one due to a low crime rate, right? Does a new lawsuit being filed every 30 seconds sound like a low level? Think about it, if there was an epidemic in criminal activity and someone told you not to secure yourself, the only possible reason would be that they don't think that what you have is worthy of security. This is the advice that is often given.

If one of these professionals tells someone that they do not need a corporation until they reach a certain dollar amount, this tells me something about that advisor. It tells me that they have tunnel vision. They are not seeing the overall picture because they have focused all of their attention on just one issue, the money. Let me give you an example to illustrate my point.

I was teaching a seminar one night in Los Angeles and I had a member of the class tell me that their CPA told them that they did not need a corporation until they had at least $50,000 a year in income. The CPA said that the cost of the corporation would be more than the amount of money this individual would save in taxes for that year. According to that CPA, by the end of the year, after taxes were calculated and the cost of the corporation had been factored in, this person would end up paying $100 more to have the corporation. Let's take a closer look at this mentality.

It was true, as I understood after talking to this person, that he would end up paying more that first year if he set up a corporation. But my question for his CPA would have been, "What about next year? And the year after that? And the year after that?"

It seems that the CPA never really discussed that with his client. This was yet another example of where the CPA gave a true statement but one which was little more than half a truth. Do you see what I mean about being shortsighted?

This sort of thing infuriates me about some attorneys and accountants who pass themselves off as financial experts. Let me point out right now, in no uncertain terms that I highly recommend for you to build a Mastermind Team, which will consist of an attorney and accountant, to help you with your financial decisions. The point I make here is that you need to be careful in selecting that attorney and accountant. A CPA like the one I have mentioned can cost you a lot of money, and I don't mean just in fees. The worst part about it is that many people take their CPA's word as fact and stop right there.

There is a simple rule which I have learned in my life about how people judge others and their information. The rule is this. "If they are not up on it, they are down on it."

What I mean by that is that if your attorney or accountant is not up to speed on a particular subject, the chances are that they will not have anything particularly nice to say about it. If you hear them speaking negatively about something that you are interested in, the first thing you need to determine is how much they really know about that topic.

The best way to find out is to ask them, point blank. Many times, the problem is that they simply do not have the information, knowledge, or experience to comment on the subject but are afraid to let you know that. Call them on it. A good professional will answer your question, even if the answer is, "I don't know." It's worth a lot more for them to tell you they don't know than to try to advise you by talking about something they know little about.

Okay, now let's get back to the situation with my student in Los Angeles. He also wanted to know where he should form his corporation should he decide to incorporate.

The decision on where to establish your corporation will be one of the most crucial ones you will make in forming your corporate entity. Each state in this country has specific laws which govern the formation of corporations. These laws are fairly easy to locate by simply looking at the statutes of that state. Evaluating those laws is the tricky part.

In many instances, the corporate laws of one state will vary markedly from those of another. These differences can be stated expressly in the statutes with regard to how corporations are formed, how they are operated with respect to their internal controls, and the amount of power granted to those corporations. A firm understanding of the state's corporate statutes can prove highly valuable as you operate your corporation. I advise you to spend time becoming familiar with these laws, even if you have someone else setting up your corporation for you. It is with this thought in mind that I have included a portion Nevada's laws on corporations in this book.

As with all things in life, the time to gain insight into this area is prior to setting up your corporation. I can't tell you the number of times I have talked to people from one part of the country to another who spent little or no time familiarizing themselves with this material before setting up their entity. In each of these instances, the looks on the faces of these people told me they knew they had made a huge mistake. Specifically, these people heard about the phenomenal value of a Nevada Corporation *after* they had already formed a corporation in their home states. They felt like it was too late for them to benefit from their newfound knowledge.

Not to minimize the importance of choosing the proper jurisdiction, but it is often not as big a mistake as they believe it to be. What I mean by that is that even though they may have set up a corporation in their home state rather than in a more advantageous state, there is no reason to completely scrap that first corporation. You will see later how this may actually prove to be a benefit in implementing a tax reduction strategy. The important part is to establish a corporation in a jurisdiction which will give you all of the benefits that you are looking for.

The absolute best jurisdiction in which to form a corporation is the state of Nevada. Throughout the book, the benefits of incorporating in Nevada will be discussed. However, the most specific information relating to establishing your corporation in Nevada is outlined in the chapter comparing the various preferred venues. As will be pointed out, the benefits offered by the state of Nevada far outweigh those of all other locales. While corporate location is extremely important, there are many other considerations which need to be factored in as well. It is important to understand these considerations before you incorporate.

WHAT CONSIDERATIONS ARE MADE BEFORE INCORPORATING?

Prior to any incorporation, there are several things that you need to think through and plan thoroughly. How you handle these various issues can be put forth in a draft of the Bylaws or the Articles of Incorporation well before actually filing for your corporate charter. Some people even use their board of directors to adopt a separate written policy to cover the more significant aspects of their corporation. The following list may be a bit intimidating at first, but this information can be crucial.

The more important pre-incorporation considerations should include:

1. **WHAT WILL THE CORPORATION'S TAX STATUS BE?**

   A. Will your corporation be formed as a C Corporation or an S Corporation for tax purposes?

   B. Will your corporation take advantage of Internal Revenue Code (IRC) 1244 stock treatment or IRC 351 treatment for non-cash assets?

   C. What are the potential tax problems for your corporation, such as debt/equity ratios, personal holding company status, personal service corporation status, or imputed interest problems?

2. **WHERE WILL THE CORPORATION'S INITIAL FINANCING COME FROM?**

   A. Who or what is going to provide the funds, equipment and/or other assets to the corporation? This should include credit considerations, for the corporation's initial borrowing power.

B. What considerations will those people providing the initial financing receive in return?

3. WHAT WILL THE INITIAL CORPORATE SHARES STRUCTURE LOOK LIKE?

A. How many authorized shares will be written into the Articles of Incorporation?

B. What types of shares (voting, nonvoting, et cetera) will be issued?

4. WHAT KIND OF SECURITIES REGULATIONS ARE NECESSARY?

A. Does your corporation have to comply with state securities regulations?

B. Does your corporation have to comply with federal securities regulations?

5. WHAT STATUTORY AGREEMENTS, IF ANY, NEED TO BE IN PLACE FIRST?

A. Stock restrictions

B. Buy/sell agreements

C. Employment contracts

D. Independent contractor agreements

E. Stock subscription agreements

6. WHAT MANAGEMENT AND/OR CONTROL RULES NEED TO BE ESTABLISHED?

A. How much control will the board of directors be given in decisions concerning daily business operations?

B. What rules do you need to govern stockholder meetings?

C. What rules do you need to govern voting rights?

7. WHAT BENEFITS AND/OR PENSION PLANS NEED TO BE IN PLACE?

A. What should the shareholders expect in terms of benefits?

B. What should the employees expect in terms of benefits?

C. How will these benefits be provided?

8. WHAT ABOUT ESTATE PLANNING AND LIQUIDITY FOR SHAREHOLDERS?

A. If your shareholders are investing a significant portion of their estate in the corporation, how can they be assured of liquidity if they die?

B. Will shareholder ownership interests transfer easily to their heirs?

After seeing this list, some of you reading this book may be thinking that you may not be ready for a corporation. Remember, millionaires get the results they get not because they do things the same old way, but because they do things differently. If you have not operated your own corporation before, of course it will look difficult to you because you are not familiar with it yet. This is the way it is with anything in life until you *learn* what it is all about. Keep in mind, this powerful information is not difficult, it's just different.

Every one of these issues (and there are more) should be an important pre-incorporation consideration for you. There are lots of approaches to these issues that can *only* be effective if they are put in place *prior* to your corporation papers being filed.

For example, your Articles of Incorporation may contain any one of a number of provisions that will resolve these issues to the satisfaction of the people involved, but that presumes some thought was given far enough in advance for the provisions to be drafted. You don't want to leave out anything that might be pertinent later. It is much easier to take a provision *out* of your corporate structure if you find you don't need it, than it is to add it *in* after the fact. Keep that in mind.

Many potential incorporators do not want to go through the time, trouble, and expense of filing for incorporation unless they know for sure they can raise enough money to get the business off the ground. That means they have to raise capital for the operation of their prospective corporate entity before they actually incorporate. Although this is not generally necessary for most people, one good method to accomplish this is with a *pre-incorporation stock subscription*. As you will learn, one of the great benefits of incorporating in Nevada is that there are minimal capitalization requirements.

Stock subscriptions can be used either before incorporation, or after. Pre-incorporation stock subscriptions allow the incorporators to get solid commitments from investors to purchase stock in their proposed corporation. These are much like letters of intent, except that any commitment made through a stock subscription cannot be revoked for at least six months, unless the agreement specifically states otherwise, or unless there is unanimous shareholder consent to the revocation by the subscriber.

Subscription offers are almost always formalized in writing. The subscription should firmly establish the specific offer in detail, including the number of shares offered, to whom, and the price to be paid.

You can use various kinds of pre-incorporation agreements to form a working game plan for your business as well as to establish the relationships, responsibilities, and expectations of all the parties involved. You can have an agreement outlining who will serve as the incorporator or on the board of directors. You can have one to cover who will draft the organizational documents or other provisions.

These agreements can also be drafted to include provisions affecting third parties working with or on behalf of the corporation. Such things as lease arrangements for office space, computer systems, or primary business equipment can be covered, but be very careful about committing to contractual obligations with third parties prior to incorporation. If a third party contracts with an unformed entity, problems can arise in the event the corporation ends up *not* being formed, or if the corporation does not subsequently fulfill its contract for whatever reason.

The question then becomes, "With whom did the third party contract?" They could not have contracted with an *unformed* corporation. The case can then be made that the third party contracted with the organizers, who are still considered individuals. The organizers can then find themselves personally liable for fulfillment of that contract. These pre-incorporation considerations are not intended to be an all-inclusive list of everything imaginable. The point is, to provide you with a good checklist of items that you may want to review prior to forming your Nevada Corporation. Understand, also, that not all of the above stated considerations will apply in all situations.

HOW DO I GO ABOUT INCORPORATING?

Surprisingly enough, becoming incorporated (invisible) is a relatively simple process. You may find this hard to believe after reading the preceding section, but it really is rather uncomplicated. All it amounts to is filing a set of papers with your state, or the state you're filing in, that lay out a few facts about your company. This set of papers is called the *Articles of Incorporation*. These papers are an integral part of the entire incorporation process.

Your Articles of Incorporation must clearly indicate the business purpose of your corporation. Many attorneys like to draft Articles that are extremely specific and restrictive. Others use broader language that provides for any lawful business activity. There is a *Model Business Corporation Act* which allows for a corporation to engage in any legal business activity except for banking or insurance. That gives the incorporators more levity in their business future.

For example, if the Articles you use initially restrict your business activity to just "real estate investment and management," or "an Italian Restaurant," or "speculation on the stock market," you might have a problem down the road. If you decide to branch out into other activities, then your corporation might have to amend its Articles of Incorporation to a broader spectrum of business. In general, I find it best to be more broad in order to allow for a greater amount of options down the road.

The flip side of that situation occurs when a corporation is applying for a loan, and the lender requires it to have more restrictive language in its Articles. This is done to prevent the company from using any loan proceeds for a purpose other than what was represented to that lender. The most important thing for you to remember is that the corporation should be tailor-made for your specific needs.

WHAT IS REQUIRED TO INCORPORATE?

Once you decide to form your corporation, the process is really quite simple. There are only a few things initially required to begin the process.

The first important issue in setting up your corporation is the corporate name. The name of your corporation should include the words "corporation," "company," "incorporated," "limited" or an abbreviation of one of these. Such terms, or their abbreviations, in the name serve notice to people dealing with your company that they are not dealing with an individual. Instead, they are dealing with an entity for which no individual may be held personally liable.

Deciding on a company name is one of the most fun parts of the incorporation process. Have fun with it. Don't get so worried about the name that you take any of the enjoyment out of it. Many people who have decided to form their corporation have expressed their concern that they may decide later that they don't like the name they initially chose. Remember, once you choose the name, this does not mean that it is set in stone never to be changed again. If you get to a point down the road where you would like a different name, a change can be made rather easily.

Your company name should accurately represent the nature of the business, and cannot resemble too closely the name of another corporation that does business in the same state. Every state has its own definition of what constitutes a "resemblance" to another company's name, so familiarize yourself with these statutes before settling on a name. In the state of Nevada, these laws are found in Nevada Revised Statutes (NRS) Section 78.039.

Some people even get pre-incorporation approval for their company name by paying a small fee to the state to reserve the use of the corporate name for a specified period of time. This is particularly true in jurisdictions that have a lot of corporate activity. Good corporate names that are applicable to your type of business can sometimes be very hard to find. When you find what you want, protect it until your corporation is established. I think it's wise to reserve a corporate name, even if you have no plans to use it right away.

Once a corporate name has been reserved, it can only be used by the individual(s) who signed the official request. Don't lose that reservation, or you will not be able to file for your corporation under the reserved name until after the protection has expired.

Federal registration and protection of a corporate name costs around $200 and can be obtained under either of two circumstances:

1. The company has used the name in interstate commerce in marketing goods or services, or
2. The corporation intends to use the name in interstate commerce.

If you have a trademark application based on the second ground, the corporation must file an affidavit within six months that states that the name has been used. It costs an additional $100 to file such an affidavit. It is important to note that in this instance, that can be money well spent.

After you have your corporate name determined, the next thing you need to do is file your Articles of Incorporation. These usually require the notarized signature of the incorporator or initial director. The original, along with two copies of "duplicate originals" are submitted to the state along with the appropriate filing fees. From a privacy point of view, a phenomenal benefit comes from the understanding that you do not have to be the incorporator or the original director.

After processing them, the state keeps one copy of the Articles of Incorporation, and returns the other two copies to the incorporator. Usually, one copy is then kept in the corporation's record book, and the other is retained by the Agent for Service of Process. Within a couple of weeks, the incorporator will receive the processed Articles, with the official stamp of the state, and a file number that is used by the state to reference that company.

Your corporation will also receive a nicely decorated Certificate of Incorporation for the wall, which is more for show than anything else. It has the file number that created your corporation, and that number is important. When that file number was issued, your corporation was born. At that point, many of your personal liabilities and obligations ceased. This is essentially the birth certificate of the corporation.

Now, you already know the premise of this book is that Nevada Corporations are the only way to fly when it comes to starting a corporation. The exact formalities necessary to establish a Nevada Corporation are listed below. Consider these your ABC's of incorporation in Nevada.

This is, by no means, a comprehensive list of all the organizational and corporate formalities or operations you need to understand, but more of an overview of the basic formalities and minimum requirements for the State of Nevada. Every one of these is important for your corporation to follow in order to maintain and protect that Nevada "corporate veil." We will discuss the term corporate veil in more detail later.

A. Draft proper Articles of Incorporation. Include a clause taking full advantage of the Nevada law that limits the liability of corporate officers and directors.
B. Have the signature of the incorporator on the Articles notarized.
C. Appoint a Resident Agent.
D. File your Articles of Incorporation with the Secretary of State.
E. File your Certificate of Acceptance of Resident Agent with the Secretary of State.
F. File certified copies of your Articles and Acceptance of Resident Agent with the County Clerk (only in some counties).

G. Draft a set of Bylaws.

H. Hold organizational meetings.

I. Appoint additional directors, if needed or desired.

J. Formerly adopt your Bylaws.

K. Issue your stock.

L. Issue your stock certificates.

M. Record stock issuance in your corporate record book.

N. Elect your officers.

O. Have your officers sign an acceptance of their appointment.

P. Record *all* minutes of organizational meetings.

Q. Have your corporate Secretary certify the minutes of meetings and your Bylaws.

R. Draft proper resolutions (or minutes) for all acts of Directors.

S. File a copy of your certified Bylaws with the Resident Agent.

T. Send a statement to your Resident Agent disclosing the name and address of whoever is the custodian of the stock ledger.

U. File a "Sixty Day List of Officers, Directors and Agent" with Secretary of State within 60 days of the date of incorporation.

V. Get your Federal Tax ID number from the IRS. *(You obtain this number by filling out Form SS-4, Application for Employer Identification Number, which is available at any IRS office. It is also available on the internet at www.ustreas.gov.)*

W. If a Subchapter S election is desired, file a US Treasury Department Form 2553 with the IRS.

X. Open up your corporate bank account. *(It is necessary to obtain your Federal Tax ID number before you can establish your account.)*

Y. File for whatever state and local business licenses are needed.

Z. Notify all clients and suppliers that the business is now a corporation, especially if you have already been operating as a business.

These are many of the essential organizational and corporate formalities which you need to become familiar with. Understanding these and other corporate requirements will be an important part of achieving the type of results you wish to achieve with your Nevada Corporation.

SUMMARY

The decision to form a Nevada Corporation can prove to be one of the most important decisions of your life. It is a decision to take charge of your financial situation by implementing one of the most powerful tools used by today's millionaires. Gaining a good working knowledge of the formalities and requirements of this *amazing* tool will enable you to accomplish things which most people believe to be unachievable. *It is a decision that will change your life.*

III Top Secret Strategy vs. Other Types of Business Formats

"The essence of success is that it is never necessary to think of a new idea oneself. It is far better to wait until somebody else does it, and then to copy him in every detail, except his mistakes."

—Aubrey Menen

Perhaps the most common question posed at the seminars I teach throughout the country is: why should I have a corporation rather than another form of entity? While a short and simple answer to this question would be great, it's not quite that easy. It would certainly be nice to merely point out all of the benefits of Nevada Corporations and pay no attention whatsoever to other options. However, for you to truly understand what makes the entity so attractive to today's millionaires, you need to see the alternatives as well. This chapter will outline the primary entities people use to conduct business successfully in the United States. As the quote above indicates, the key is to learn what is successful out there and then do it.

Each of the various business forms has its own strengths and weaknesses. These must be weighed out before deciding on your proper structuring

33

plan. It's important for you to realize that no single type of business entity, including the Nevada Corporation, is the "best" solution for every possible business scenario. Although Nevada Corporations are the best for a wide variety of situations, there simply isn't only one entity that is best for everyone in every business environment. An important thing for you to understand however, is that the Nevada Corporation can offer tremendous benefits in nearly every situation.

The key is being able to identify those circumstances where a corporation is the right entity for the people involved. Anyone can learn about these circumstances, but most people are best advised to seek the opinion of someone who knows more than they do about their particular situation. That's where this book, and the guidance it offers, will pay off for *you* in understanding how a Nevada Corporation can best suit your needs.

There are a host of reasons to take a long, hard look at the legal structure of the business you are wanting to form. The complicated nature of conducting a successful enterprise in today's business environment makes your choice of structure more important than it has ever been before. Federal and state tax laws change with every wind shift, sometimes favoring one type of entity, sometimes another. Additionally, today's litigious society makes it essential to protect yourself through privacy and secrecy.

So, your first decision in business must be what type of business entity you want to adopt. And the first question there should be: why use a corporation rather than a sole proprietorship, or some other form of business?

A corporation can provide you with better financial privacy, more favorable tax treatment, significantly increased business deductions, enhanced retirement options, and much greater flexibility when it comes to ownership and management. Because of this, the corporation remains the most important form of business entity in use today. Even though other forms of business may outnumber them, most business transactions, both here and abroad, are conducted by corporations.

That is perhaps the strongest reason I can think of for considering a corporation as your business structure of choice. By default, you gain the power and influence of the nation's entire business community, including powerful lobbyists in government, by setting up your business as a corporation from the start. You also gain all of the case history that has been used to protect businesses who have operated as corporations over the years. That is a *lot* of protection. That is the kind of protection utilized by many of the world's millionaires.

Corporations generally provide greater flexibility than any other type of business entity, but are more complicated to set up. To use a football analogy, a draw play (short run) is easier to design than a long passing play. But which one is more likely to make good yardage and get you closer to the goal? And which one is going to help you win the game faster? You must run the plays which will give you the best overall results.

The following is a quick listing of the major advantages and disadvantages of incorporating. Keep these in mind as you study the other types of business entities in this chapter, as we compare and contrast the advantages of each. I think the clear winner for most of you will be the corporation, and specifically the Nevada Corporation.

In later chapters, each of these aspects of a corporation will be discussed in greater detail both as they relate to general business, and in setting up your Nevada Corporation. For now, just make a mental note of them.

Advantages Of Corporations

1. Shareholders' liability is limited to investment in the corporation.
2. In most situations the Federal Income Tax rates are lower.
3. There is better centralized management and ease of doing business.
4. More tax deductions are available than to other forms of businesses.
5. The separate legal existence is clear and distinct.

6. THERE IS LONG TERM STABILITY AND PERMANENCE OF BUSINESS.
7. FULL FRINGE BENEFITS ARE AVAILABLE AND DEDUCTIBLE.
8. THERE IS AN EASIER TRANSFER OF ASSETS AND OWNERSHIP.
9. WELL ESTABLISHED CASE LAW FOR PROTECTION.
10. THERE IS TREATER FLEXIBILITY IN BORROWING MONEY OR RAISING CAPITAL.

DISADVANTAGES OF CORPORATIONS

1. THEY ARE GENERALLY MORE COMPLICATED TO FORM.
2. THEY CAN BE EXPENSIVE TO SET UP AND MAINTAIN.
3. THERE IS A POSSIBILITY FOR INVESTORS TO BE DOUBLE-TAXED.
4. THEY ARE SUBJECT TO EXTENSIVE GOVERNMENT REGULATIONS.
5. THEY ARE REQUIRED TO FILE LOCAL, STATE, AND FEDERAL REPORTS.
6. COMPANY ACTIVITIES CAN BE LIMITED BY THE COR-PORATE CHARTER.
7. CORPORATE RECORDS AND FORMALITIES MUST BE MAINTAINED.

While there are always disadvantages to anything that you analyze in life, the key is to strike the proper balance between those disadvantages and the advantages which it has to offer. As you will see, the disadvantages (and understand that I am trying to paint an overall picture for you by showing you the perceived disadvantages) of forming your own Nevada Corporation can be easily overcome. The Nevada Corporation will be your most powerful business partner by simply learning how to use it effectively. In order to do that, it is important for you to consider it in comparison with other popular business entities.

WHY USE A CORPORATION RATHER THAN A SOLE PROPRIETORSHIP?

The first entity to look at in drawing our comparisons is the one which is used most often. The sole proprietorship is the simplest and most common form of ownership for those establishing a business entity. Why do you suppose it's the most common form of business entity? The answer to that question should be quite obvious. It's the most common because it is the simplest to set up. What you need to be aware of though, is that in most instances, the simplest option in business is sometimes the most costly because the only real benefit is the ease of start-up that it offers.

For sole proprietors, there is no difference between them and their businesses. Business liabilities automatically become personal liabilities for sole proprietors. The company's bills are their bills. If the business is sued successfully, proprietors may get a judgment levied against their personal assets. And a sole proprietorship cannot survive the owners, if they die. Their ownership interest ends with death. For these reasons, the sole proprietorship is certainly not the best tool for asset protection or estate planning.

On the other hand, since a proprietor is a boss, he or she gets to do pretty much as they please with their business. For some people, that is the greatest single attraction to the sole proprietorship form. For some, there is great value in not having to answer to anyone else. In the proprietorship, there are also few formalities to keep track of, no meetings to conduct, and no formal documents to have to draft or file, even though the business must still adhere to all federal, state, and local guidelines.

For tax purposes, sole proprietors don't even have to file a separate business tax return. They can simply attach a Schedule C to their IRS 1040 form where they report their business income. Sole proprietors pay taxes based on whatever income level applies to them personally as individuals. Any gain or loss in income from the business is combined with other taxable items, and can make for a significant disparity in what one person will pay in taxes, as compared to another in a similar business or even in the same business from one year to the next.

Additionally, sole proprietors are not required to withhold federal income tax on their own business income (as opposed to salary income). However, if the proprietorship has employees, there is a responsibility for collecting and paying withholding taxes out of their employee paychecks.

Most sole proprietors will likely be required to make quarterly estimated tax payments, and will be subject to the 15.3% self employment tax the IRS imposes on business income. We get this figure by understanding how the tax is figured. In the common employment situation out here from a Social Security standpoint, the employer pays 7.65% and the employee pays 7.65%. With the sole proprietorship, you are serving in both capacities. Hence, you pay both sides essentially. This is to offset what the government views as a proprietor's ability to save in Social Security and Medicare taxes.

Since there is no distinction made between business and personal assets for sole proprietors, they risk virtually everything they own by conducting business every day. If a judgment is placed against their business, most personal assets of the owner can be used to satisfy payment of that judgment. Do you understand how significant this could be?

This can include homes, property, automobiles, and even furniture. Cash on hand, checking and savings account funds, investments, and personal effects can also be seized for payment. Additionally, a sole proprietor will often find it more difficult to raise capital or borrow money, since that can only be accomplished if the individual can qualify for a personal loan based on normal loan criteria.

Most local taxing authorities (cities and counties) require sole proprietors to file a fictitious name certificate, sometimes known as a business alias or "DBA" (doing business as) in order to conduct business in their jurisdictions. A fictitious name certificate allows a sole proprietor to function publicly as a business enterprise under a name other than that of the individual owner (as, for example, The Dew Drop Inn instead of as JJ Childers' Inn). Banks routinely require copies of these fictitious name certificates from the city or county in order to allow sole proprietors to open checking accounts in the name of the business. It is important to note though, that, as far as the legal world is concerned, JJ Childers and The Dew Drop Inn are still one and the same.

Historically, sole proprietors have been limited in their ability to participate in such things as federally qualified pension plans and medical reimbursement plans that are available to all kinds of other business entities. For example, sole proprietors can only deduct 25% of the cost of medical insurance for themselves and their dependents, where other business entities can write off up to 100%.

Many sole proprietors may also have trouble getting full deductions for other types of normal business expenses. The IRS has a habit of disallowing expenses if there is any question as to whether a certain expenditure was for business or personal use. Where there is no clear and definable legal separation between individuals and their businesses, this area of deductions gets a little vague at times, and that is an open invitation for the IRS to deny such deductions. When a separate legal entity is formed, this presents a stronger likelihood that an expenditure is business related.

Sole proprietors have a number of basic planning considerations to deal with that are unique to proprietorship status. If proprietors intend to pass their business on to their heirs, for example, there are a number of estate planning and taxation issues that have to be considered well in advance of any deaths in the family. From a practical perspective, there is often no one for sole proprietors to rely on in case of sickness, disability or financial trouble. These are significant concerns which must be dealt with.

If you weigh all these factors, I think you will conclude that a sole proprietorship is certainly not a stable, long-term business solution. I can think of almost *no* cases where a proprietorship would make an appropriate entity for a serious business person. But that is contrary to what is traditionally taught by the "professionals." Too often, they tend to focus only on the perceived costs associated with the entities. This is a shortsighted approach and can end up really costing you a lot more in the long run in the form of taxes and potential lawsuits.

Virtually every type of business has associated risks and liability exposure of some kind, but proprietors usually don't recognize this. As a result, they often face catastrophic loss that they can't possibly comprehend.

Establishing a sole proprietorship, for most people, is often the result of a general lack of planning and foresight at the outset. If you are currently operating your business as a sole proprietorship, you are not only gambling that you will not incur any major business liability, now or down the road, but you are also throwing away a myriad of tax benefits that would be available to you in some other form of business. This is not the way that millionaires typically handle things.

The best way to evaluate the overall effectiveness and value of this entity is by taking a look at the list of advantages and disadvantages associated therewith.

ADVANTAGES OF A SOLE PROPRIETORSHIP

1. IT IS THE SIMPLEST FORM OF DOING BUSINESS.
2. IT REQUIRES LESS FORMALITY AND FEWER LEGAL RESTRICTIONS.
3. IT NEEDS NO GOVERNMENTAL APPROVAL (EXCEPT LOCAL LICENSING).
4. IT IS LESS EXPENSIVE THAN A PARTNERSHIP OR CORPORATION TO FORM.
5. IT ALLOWS SOLE OWNERSHIP OF PROFITS.
6. IT ALLOWS FOR SIMPLIFIED PROFIT TAKING.
7. IT REQUIRES LITTLE EFFORT OR EXPENSE TO FORM OR MAINTAIN.
8. IT PAYS TAXES AT ONLY ONE LEVEL (YOUR INDIVIDUAL RATE).
9. ITS CONTROL AND MANAGEMENT RESTS IN ONE OWNER'S HANDS.

DISADVANTAGES OF A SOLE PROPRIETORSHIP

1. OWNER HAS FULL AND UNLIMITED LIABILITY FOR ALL BUSINESS ACTIVITIES.
2. LIABILITIES MAY INCLUDE DEBTS THAT EXCEED TOTAL INVESTMENT.
3. POTENTIAL LIABILITY EXTENDS TO ALL OF THE OWNER'S PERSONAL ASSETS.

4. Death or disability of the owner could force the business to close.
5. Owner's business and personal assets are commingled.
6. Income is taxed at personal tax rates.
7. There are additional self-employment taxes.
8. Certain expenses are only partially tax deductible, or not at all.
9. There are significant limitations on benefits.
10. Raising money can be very difficult.

In balancing the advantages and disadvantages of the sole proprietorship, and considering them as they compare to Nevada Corporations, it becomes quite clear what is needed. Nevada Corporations once again win out. Let's consider it in comparison to another commonly used business format, the general partnership.

Why use a corporation rather than a general partnership?

In most jurisdictions, general partnerships are almost as easy to form as sole proprietorships. The difference is that a partnership needs at least two involved parties. If two or more people agree to start some business enterprise, but make no effort to set up a specific business entity, by default, they become general partners in all business matters.

General partners are co-owners of the business and its assets. Essentially, they are sole proprietors in a partnership entity. Their ownership interests may not necessarily be identical, but each general partner usually has the same legal powers in relation to their business. Like the sole proprietorship, it is simple to form.

General partnerships can be formed as simple oral agreements. The law in most jurisdictions deals with informal or oral business ventures, such as joint ventures, as if they were a general partnership. General partnerships are usually not even filed with the Secretary of State because there are no uniform standards for limiting the liability of any of the partners involved.

What this means is that asset protection associated with general partnership is minimal. This is a significant drawback.

As with a sole proprietorship, a general partnership must file a fictitious name certificate with the city or county clerk to conduct business by any name other than the given names of the individual partners. As with the sole proprietorship, this acquisition of a fictitious name certificate creates no legal distinction between the partners and the business itself. Once again, there is no asset protection.

Once a general partnership is formed, it has its own identity for most purposes and can own property, make contracts, and conduct business in the name that the partners are using for the general partnership (their fictitious name certificate). The IRS considers a partnership to be any ordinary partnership, syndicate, group, pool, joint venture, or other unincorporated organization that is carrying on a business and that may not be classified as a trust or estate.

General partnerships are not a taxable entity, per se. However they must figure out their profits and losses and file an informational tax return (Form 1065) within $3\frac{1}{2}$ months of their year end. This informational return reports to the IRS the income tax obligation of each partner, who is then responsible for filing his/her own return.

Many states have adopted some version of the Uniform Partnership Act. This is a statute that provides basic rules for deciding the rights of general partners and persons who have transactions with general partnerships. This law provides rules for determining the rights, powers and responsibilities of each individual partner in relation to the partnership and/or its other partners. However, the internal rules used to govern partnerships can be changed by formal, written partnership agreements.

Most general partnerships can exist without a formal agreement, so it is a good idea for partners to get together and draft some sort of a written partnership agreement to govern and control their partnership relations. It is important to understand what needs to be included in the agreement. This kind of agreement should cover at least the following points:

1. The name of the partnership,
2. The state of the partnership domicile,
3. The amount of cash or property to be contributed to the general partnership by each partner, along with a schedule for making the contributions,
4. The duties of each partner in conducting the business and the scope of authority of each partner to make decisions and/or incur obligations for the partnership, (which may be useful in settling legal disputes between the partners, but will not necessarily protect any one of the partners from liability exposure because of partnership activity),
5. Procedures for handling separate debts, including tax obligations,
6. Procedures for changing the partnership agreement,
7. Operational procedures, such as maintenance of books and accounting, employee management, et cetera,
8. Procedures for sharing the profits and losses of the general partnership among the partners, and
9. Any events that could cause the partnership to be dissolved, including procedures for winding down the business, discharging all debts, and distributing the available assets among the partners.

Even though general partnerships are often formed by default, not all joint business activities can be automatically classified as general partnerships. As an example, if two business people agree to share such business expenses as a computer or photocopier, that does not create a general partnership. However, if they then charge customers or clients to use that computer or copy machine, a general partnership can be deemed to exist.

General partnerships are subject to the same limitations as sole proprietorships as far as their ability to participate in certain pension plans and medical reimbursement plans are concerned. Certain business expenses are not always fully deductible, and partners are subject to the same 15.3% self-employment tax as sole proprietors. These are all serious shortfalls of the general partnership.

Each of the individual partners must include the income or loss from a general partnership on their own tax return. In that way, the corporation passes its income or loss directly to the individual partners. This avoids the problem with "double taxation" issues associated with drawing profit out of other forms of business. The way the IRS looks at it, it's your money to do with as you please, as long as you report it and pay taxes on it on time.

Partners in general partnerships have responsibilities to each other that are often compared to those found in civil marriages. Though the partners may have given themselves specific roles and responsibilities in their relationship, including written agreement, they are, nevertheless, jointly and severally liable to the rest of the world for the activities of the business as a whole.

In other words, the actions of one partner in the name of the business are binding on all of the other partners. The effect of this can be devastating. A general partner must realize that every personal asset may be attached to fulfill a legal obligation created by another general partner. Essentially, all of the assets of all of the partners are in constant jeopardy from the actions of all concerned.

Theoretically, it's possible for one general partner (without the knowledge of the others) to go out and sign a million dollar business loan in the name of the partnership, and then fly to Tahiti with the funds, never to return. That would leave the other partners liable for the debt, and could force the sale of the remaining partners' personal assets to repay the loan to the bank. Anyone considering a general partnership has to realize what a horrible situation could result from this.

A general partnership is different from a limited partnership (which will be discussed later) in the following ways:

1. General partners can legally bind the partnership by their actions.
2. General partners are fully liable for all business activities of the partnership.
3. General partners must have the unanimous consent of all other partners before being admitted into the partnership.

As you should have determined by now, general partnerships rely heavily on the element of trust between partners. And smart people know that, when it comes to business, trust alone is just not good business.

History is full of examples of partners whose talents allowed them to get a business off the ground, but were not sufficient to manage the enterprise over the long term. The choices that must be made in these situations can be extremely painful and highly expensive.

General partnerships provide a blueprint for the worst of business conditions. In addition to all of the problems that are inherent with a sole proprietorship, evolutionary changes in the management of a general partnership often result in a forced dissolution of the enterprise when the partners no longer trust or agree with one another. Here is a list of advantages and disadvantages to be factored in when making your decision.

Advantages Of General Partnerships

1. They are the simplest form of business for more than one person.
2. They require little effort or expense to form or maintain.
3. They incur only one rate of taxation.
4. Partners are motivated by rewards resulting from their efforts.
5. Partners have someone else to help operate the business.

Disadvantages Of General Partnerships

1. Partners are liable for debts or judgments against the business.
2. The acts of one partner can be binding on all other partners.
3. It is more difficult to dispose of partnership interests.
4. There is no differentiation between business and personal assets.
5. Partners are required to pay additional self-employment taxes.

6. CERTAIN BUSINESS EXPENSES ARE ONLY PARTIALLY TAX DEDUCTIBLE.
7. THERE ARE LIMITATIONS ON AVAILABLE OWNER/EMPLOYEE BENEFITS.
8. IT IS DIFFICULT TO RAISE CAPITAL, OR BORROW MONEY.

The general partnership becomes far less appealing when we compare it to the power of a Nevada Corporation.

WHY USE A CORPORATION RATHER THAN A LIMITED PARTNERSHIP?

Another form of business entity used by many people is the limited partnership. These entities have the same basic features as general partnerships, except for one very significant difference. Limited Partnerships, by definition, have one or more *limited* partners, who generally have neither liability for business activities nor management responsibilities. Limited Partnerships also have one or more *general* partners who exercise the same rights, responsibilities, and status as partners do in general partnerships.

The entity is based on a principle that attempts to preserve the interests of the public good by requiring the existence of at least one general partner in the organization. The general partner takes on all of the responsibility and/or liability for the activities of the partnership. Essentially, there is no asset protection provided for the general partner.

The liability of the limited partners, however, is limited to the amount they individually have invested in the partnership. Because their status in the partnership is passive, they cannot be held accountable for partnership activity. They can lose their partnership investment, but cannot be held liable beyond that. The problem there however, is that they have no control whatsoever over the activities of the business.

One of the benefits of the Limited Partnership is that it is somewhat easy to establish. You form a Limited Partnership by filing a Certificate of Limited Partnership with the state. This certificate establishes a formalized partnership agreement within the laws of that state and is legally binding. The partnership agreement specifically details the powers and responsibilities of all the partners, as well as any factors that will decide how the partnership will be run.

All limited partnerships are not created equal. They can be as complex in design as the creators wish, as long as they stay within state guidelines. The ability the Limited Partnership will assume in trying to accomplish any specific goals depends to a great degree on the skill and knowledge of the people drafting the original agreement. The wording of that agreement can affect all aspects of the partnership, including tax consequences and liabilities incurred by the different partnership activities. It should be quite obvious from this information, that it is crucial to get a good document drafted.

One of the more common uses of a Limited Partnership is to shield assets from judgments or creditors in the event of a catastrophic lawsuit. However, the ability of the partnership to accomplish that goal is almost entirely dependent upon the original partnership agreement stipulating any eventuality that an adverse lawsuit or judgment could create. That's not easy to do without having an agreement that is longer than the Dead Sea Scrolls.

Another problem is that not all partnership agreements are written with asset protection as a central goal. Even the ones that are focused on asset protection, end up focusing on it in such a way that there is no protection at all. There are poorly drafted partnership agreements written every day. The average person can't tell the difference until it is too late. Even a qualified attorney or expert in the field of asset protection can inadvertently set up a Limited Partnership that results in exposing clients to the unlimited liability associated with being a general partner. This makes it extremely important to find someone who is familiar with limited partnerships and the laws which govern them.

Every state now has a version of either the Uniform Limited Partnership Act (ULPA) or the Revised Limited Partnership Act (RLPA). It is not necessary that you know the difference between these two acts, since individual states have adopted several different forms of these acts. But you should at least be familiar with the version of the law being used in your state if you intend to pursue the formation of a Limited Partnership, or use a qualified attorney or company which is familiar with it.

Most states require that such partnership agreements, or at least a condensed version of them, be filed with the Secretary of State. This is to protect individuals or businesses who may ultimately be dealing with the partnership. This allows creditors access to information for communicating with all of the partners and for determining, among other things, the potential liability of the respective parties in a lawsuit. This requirement also eliminates potential conflicts between the general and limited partners regarding their individual powers and limitations.

There is also an entity that many states recognize now called the Family Limited Partnership. This arrangement has been found to be a suitable device for dealing with a lot of family and estate matters that would not otherwise be of concern in a normal business. For the most part, these Family Limited Partnerships perform their function quite well. However, they are still limited partnerships, and as such, are subject to the limited partnership laws in the state of their origin.

In most cases, it is significantly more complicated and expensive to form effective Limited Partnerships than it is to form the more simplified general partnerships. This is mainly due to a host of legal fees and state filing fees that apply. As with most other business entities, there are annual reporting and maintenance requirements that add to these costs.

Now, as for tax concerns, limited partnerships are not, in themselves, taxable. They are what is known as a "pass through" entity. Basically, the income passes through the partnership into the name of the individual partners. The partnership must file an annual federal tax return on IRS Form 1065, and also provide K-1 schedules to each partner. These K-1s list each partner's share of the income, deductions and credits for the partnership. Many states also require state income tax filings.

One nice benefit that limited partners enjoy is the advantage of dealing with a single level of taxation when it comes to tax filings. Income into the partnership flows directly to the partners according to their individual interests, and is then included on their personal tax returns for the year.

Limited Partnerships can hold almost any asset, except some retirement plans, stocks in professional corporations or shares of S corporations. Retirement plan contributions for limited partnerships are based on "net employment income," (gross income, minus deductions, including the deduction for retirement plan contributions).

Also, there is no double taxation to worry about when taking profits in Limited Partnerships. General partners are, however, still subject to the 15.3% tax on their income from the partnership. Limited partners need not worry about this self-employment tax. This makes this particular entity quite attractive.

So, what are limited partnerships good for? In most states, they are particularly effective in asset protection strategies, where the primary assets are real property. They are effective because neither the Limited Partnership interests, nor the partnership's assets can be attached by a creditor. This protection is usually referred to as a "charging order limitation," which limits a judgment creditor to what, at best, is a lien against partnership income. Those are very difficult to enforce.

To a lot of people, this makes it attractive to own or manage real estate through Limited Partnerships. Many real estate investors and developers form separate partnerships for each property. The problem is that for many people, that even includes transferring ownership of their personal residence(s) into such partnerships, where they lose the advantage of deducting mortgage interest from their personal income tax. That is not a particularly appropriate or effective business strategy, in my opinion.

A well planned, and correctly documented Limited Partnership agreement provides three major legal advantages. The first is that a creditor with a personal judgment against you can only get a "charging order" against your Limited Partnership interests.

In 49 states, that means creditors cannot seize any partnership assets, unless they are creditors to the partnership itself. The charging order gives creditors a right to the income portion of a limited partner's interest in the partnership, and is usually the only means by which creditors can reach a limited partner's interest. Charging orders give creditors no voting rights, and no annual income distribution rights (assuming such provisions were included as part of the original agreement). For all intents and purposes, a charging order is nearly worthless. Anyone looking at this arrangement (who understands how it works) would steer clear of even filing the lawsuit. If they do not understand it, they are the ones hurt, not you.

The second major advantage is that creditors cannot remove the general partner of a limited partnership. That means you can continue to control all partnership activities and assets by controlling the general partner. Once again, you need to remember that the general partner is subject to personal liability.

The third advantage is that a personal creditor has no voting, accounting or inspection rights in the partnership. Thus, creditors are treated as assignees instead of substituted limited partners. So, they are almost completely at the mercy of the other partners. They cannot force the sale of partnership assets to satisfy any personal judgments.

Okay, so much for the good news. The bad news is there are a number of drawbacks in using Limited Partnerships. The first is, limited partners *must* be careful not to attempt to take any active role in management. Nor can they exercise too much control over their investment. If they do, their legal status can be elevated to that of general partners. If this happens, the limited partners lose their limited liability and can become personally liable.

It's not impossible for limited partners to suddenly find themselves exposed to all the personal risk they set up the partnership to avoid. Also, if the partnership has not been filed correctly, the limited status of the partnership can be jeopardized, resulting in full liability exposure to all of the partners. Some courts have even ruled that a limited partnership interest may be sold on foreclosure of a charging order lien at the request of a judgment creditor. That sets a new precedent for liability cases in Limited Partnerships. Fortunately, this has occurred only in a small number of instances.

Unfortunately, this problem is likely to apply to all states as new drafts of uniform statutes on limited partnerships are introduced. In fact, The National Conference of Commissioners on Uniform State Laws has already released a revision to the Revised Uniform Partnership Act that provides for this kind of foreclosure power.

There are still a lot of ways to reduce the impact of creditor attacks on Limited Partnerships, but the key is, the partnership agreement must contain the appropriate provisions *before* this becomes a problem. Most drafters of limited partnership agreements simply do not know how to deal with this eventuality. The sad truth is, limited partnerships are no longer an absolute barrier against judgments or claims. The tremendous asset protection previously available may become somewhat limited.

Courts have also held that any transfer of assets into a limited partnership must *not* be for the purpose of delaying or defrauding creditors, or it is not considered a legitimate transaction. Individuals must be financially solvent both before and after such transactions, and must *not* be facing any claims. So, if a claim already exists against you, it probably won't do you any good to transfer assets into a limited partnership.

Limited Partnerships are a terrific business entity when set up and used properly. Used improperly, they are as dangerous as anything in the business world. People think their partnership protects them from liability, then are sadly disappointed when they find out that their partnership documents are virtually worthless. I view this much as the person who has a security system for their home which doesn't work. It can give a false sense of security.

Attorneys and others who specialize in asset protection concerns, who monitor developments in case law related to that area and who constantly revise their documents to reflect new case law, are a good bet to establish limited partnerships that work long term. Don't go to just anybody to get a limited partnership drafted. That's like going to a barbershop to have a tooth pulled. Yes, a barber can do the job, but boy, the pain afterwards.

I think you will find that the appropriate use of limited partnerships should be confined to four primary concerns:

1. Protecting assets from lawsuits or judgments,
2. Spreading income among family members,
3. Achieving a lower overall family income tax rate, and
4. Planning an estate to lower estate taxes.

By taking a look at the advantages and disadvantages of the Limited Partnership, you will be better positioned to determine whether it is the proper entity for you and your particular situation.

ADVANTAGES OF A LIMITED PARTNERSHIP

1. LIMITED PARTNERS HAVE LIMITED LIABILITY.
2. PARTNERSHIPS HAVE ONE LEVEL OF TAXATION.
3. IT'S A VERY EFFECTIVE TOOL FOR ESTATE PLANNING.
4. IT'S A VERY EFFECTIVE TOOL FOR ASSET PROTECTION.
5. IT'S A VERY EFFECTIVE TOOL FOR TAX PLANNING UNDER CERTAIN CIRCUMSTANCES.
7. PARTNERSHIP INTERESTS ARE GENERALLY NOT ATTACHABLE BY A CREDITOR.
8. PERSONAL CREDITORS CAN'T SEIZE OR FORCE SALE OF PARTNERSHIP ASSETS.
9. THERE IS NO DOUBLE TAXATION FOR PARTNERS WHEN TAKING PROFITS.

DISADVANTAGES OF A LIMITED PARTNERSHIP

1. THERE ARE COMPLICATED AND EXPENSIVE TO FORM AND MAINTAIN.
2. THEY REQUIRE SPECIFIC KNOWLEDGE TO SET UP PROPERLY.
3. A PARTNERSHIP AGREEMENT CAN LEAD TO UNEXPECTED LIABILITY.
4. GENERAL PARTNERS HAVE UNLIMITED LIABILITY.
5. THEE ARE LIMITATIONS ON AVAILABLE FRINGE BENEFITS FOR GENERAL PARTNER.

6. THE GENERAL PARTNER MAY BE SUBJECT TO SELF-EMPLOYMENT TAX.

7. THERE IS NO ABSOLUTE GUARANTEE AGAINST CLAIMS OR CREDITORS.

WHY USE A CORPORATION RATHER THAN A LIMITED LIABILITY COMPANY (LLC)?

More and more frequently, I am asked whether a corporation is necessary with the emergence of the Limited Liability Company (LLC). The LLC is a fairly new concept in American business law, but it is based upon an old European tradition. It is another refinement of the ongoing effort to find a business entity that can provide liability protection to owners and managers, while preserving a pass-through tax status more often associated with partnerships or S Corporations.

This kind of partnership classification can either be good news or bad news, depending upon where you are and the circumstances that can occur *after* the formation of the entity. Properly handled, this entity avoids the double taxation issue, but partners can still find themselves paying tax on company income at the higher personal income tax rate, instead of at a lower corporate rate.

Typically, the LLC is formed by filing articles of organization with the Secretary of State. This document should give the name of the company, the names of all of the members, including their capital contribution schedule, the period of its duration, the purpose for organizing the company, the address of its principal office in the state, and other provisions outlining the rights of the members and the management.

LLC owners are called "members" of the company, and are indemnified by state law from any judgment, debt or obligation of the company, including decrees of the court. Members may exercise direct control over the company, according to their individual percentage of ownership, or may appoint one or more managers. If managers are used, they perform functions commonly associated with corporate officers and directors.

The LLC is basically a hybrid between a corporation and a partnership. It is formed as a legally separate and distinct entity from its members, and, much as a corporation, becomes its own legal person. For tax purposes, though, an LLC is treated like a partnership. An LLC files its informational tax return that details the gain and loss of the individual members, then tax liability flows through to the owners. This tax treatment eliminates the double taxation problems inherent when profits are distributed to the corporation's shareholders. States which have adopted the Limited Liability Company Code have been very judicious when complying with IRS decisions that outline distinctions between the LLC and other business entities. While it is very similar to both the corporation and the partnership, the distinctions must be noted.

A limited liability company is *not* a corporation, although it may look like one on the surface. If it qualified as a corporation, it would be taxed at corporate tax rates by the IRS, of that you can be sure. The LLC is, in essence, a hybrid entity that floats somewhere between the single level of taxation provided by the limited partnership and the liability protection offered by a corporation. When the distinctions are not carefully adhered to by the LLC, it may end up being considered a corporation for federal income tax purposes. This can easily result in catastrophic or even retroactive double taxation.

To be considered an LLC by the IRS, an entity may have no more than two of the following characteristics of a corporation:

1. It is designed to have limited liability.
2. It is designed to have continuity beyond a member's life.
3. It is designed to have centralization of management.
4. It is designed to have free transferability of interests.

Since any properly organized LLC provides limited liability to its members and managers, as well as a form of centralized management, the remaining two characteristics are not normally available. That means the LLC cannot exist beyond the life of its individual members. This makes it markedly different from a corporation. When a member dies, the LLC is automatically dissolved. Remaining members must then reorganize, or have their business entity revert to corporate tax status.

Free transferability of LLC interests is also not available, because the voting rights of ownership cannot be transferred or sold. Only the original members of the LLC have the power to make decisions regarding the operation and administration of the business. If an ownership interest is conveyed or sold to another party, it only carries a right to income, not management. This represents a limitation which must be considered.

In understanding this entity, a little background can prove helpful. The LLC was first allowed in the U.S. in 1977 when Wyoming passed a Limited Liability Company Act. In 1988, the IRS issued a formal opinion on Wyoming's Limited Liability Company Act (Rev. Rule 88-76, 1088 2 C.B. 360), with the conclusion that the LLC formed under that Act should be classified for federal income tax purposes as a partnership, even though none of the members or managers are personally liable for the debts of the company. Since then, there have been over a dozen Internal Revenue Service Rulings that continue to support that original ruling. These rulings make the entity seem quite favorable.

Despite these favorable IRS rulings, the LLC has been slow to catch on in most states. For example, Nevada has only allowed for the creation of the LLC since October, 1991, but the public response has been less than overwhelming. Instead of the expected rush to form these entities, there has been mixed reaction. In the first eight months of availability in Nevada, fewer than 50 LLCs were formed. Since then, the number has increased as attorneys and accountants have had a chance to attend educational seminars that promote the LLC concept. The interest in the entity has grown substantially as a result.

One key advantage these attorneys have found in the LLC is the lack of restrictions on the type and number of stockholders. The S corporation, the LLC's biggest competitor for new business, has severe limitations on shareholders. The LLC may have more than the 35 members allowed to an S corporation, and trusts, estates, corporations, partnerships, and other LLCs may also have ownership interests. This helps to provide a bit more flexibility.

The LLC concept has a lot to offer, depending upon the state, and may become the entity of choice for some people in the future. It may even replace the S Corporation concept eventually. But there are still a lot of questions that have to be resolved. Until this happens, there remains a slight degree of uncertainty.

The biggest problem with the LLC used to be that only a few states recognized them as legal entities. This made conducting interstate business with an LLC a bit risky. For example, can states with dissimilar LLC statutes determine another state's LLCs to be corporations or partnerships for state tax purposes? Many such questions are beginning to be resolved as more states embrace the LLC concept. The major question then becomes: will the courts view the LLC in the broader spectrum of business law?

For example, will the courts allow for a creditor who wins a judgment to foreclose on a member's interest in a limited liability company, as has been the case in some states with limited partnership interests? Right now, personal creditors of a limited liability company member may charge the member's interest with payment of the judgment, but this only provides the creditor with the rights of an assignee of the member's interest. That functions very much the way a "charging order" limitation functions in a limited partnership, and thus is almost worthless. Will this continue to be the case?

Then the question arises, if one member's interest in an LLC is attached, will the LLC, by default, be forced into the IRS definition of a corporation? If that happens, all of the LLC's members will have serious negative tax consequences, and that is simply not equitable under the law. Also, state statutes frequently limit the life span of an LLC to less than 30 years. If an LLC is maintained beyond that, will the IRS suddenly consider it to have become a corporation or what?

As you can see, there are a number of complex legal issues with LLCs, for which there is not yet sufficient case law to predict what will happen with these business entities. But, you can certainly count on this litigious society we live in to resolve them over time. It's just not a good idea to be one of the test cases!

Another major drawback to the LLC, for some people, is the lack of financial privacy it provides for members. Since the members are usually listed in the articles of organization, which are then filed with the Secretary of State, they become public record. The LLC's resident or registered agent is also required to keep a current list of the names and addresses of all the members and managers, along with tax returns and financial statements for the last three years. That kind of information could then be made available to someone serving the resident agent with a subpoena for company records. For this reason, it simply cannot compete with the Nevada Corporation as the secret weapon of today's millionaires.

The long and the short of LLCs is that you may want to wait for the concept to develop further before setting one up for your business, unless you are opening a particular kind of business. Some types of businesses that are natural platforms for LLCs include research and development firms, oil and gas exploration companies, and real estate development operations. The reason these work so well is that these types of businesses usually have a planned limited life span from the outset. In the gas drilling business, for example, you drill a well, pump it dry, and eventually shut it down. Limited life span there is an advantage, rather than a future problem to worry about.

The LLC concept may someday replace S Corporations as the standard entity for flow-through tax options, making S corporations obsolete. It may also supplant limited partnerships in some states, and some uses, but not entirely. But one thing the LLC will never replace is the C Corporation. Besides double taxation considerations, there will always be some income tax advantages for people qualifying for the lower corporate tax rates. In addition, the free transferability of ownership interests that a corporation offers will always be a necessity in the majority of business circumstances. Also, perhaps the biggest drawback is the lack of privacy and secrecy which can be devastating in today's lawsuit-crazed society.

As it becomes more widely accepted, the Limited Liability Company is destined for popularity in the business world. When the legal systems of the individual states finally establish enough case law to frame the foundation of the LLC concept, it will become more of a working standard for a lot of people. The Nevada Corporation, however, is now and will remain the business concept of choice for the "secret millionaire."

ADVANTAGES OF THE LIMITED LIABILITY COMPANY

1. THERE IS NO LIMITATION ON TYPE OR NUMBER OF OWNERS.
2. THERE IS NO LIMITATION ON CLASSES OF MEMBERSHIP INTERESTS.
3. THERE IS NO LIMITATION ON OWNERSHIP OF OTHER CORPORATIONS.
4. THERE ARE NO CITIZENSHIP REQUIREMENTS FOR MEMBERS OR MANAGERS.
5. IT HAS GOOD LIABILITY PROTECTION FOR MEMBERS AND MANAGEMENT.
6. THERE IS SIMPLIFIED PROFIT TAKING.
7. PERSONAL CREDITORS TREATED LIKE ASSIGNEES.
8. PERSONAL CREDITORS CANNOT FORCE SALE OF THE COMPANY.

DISADVANTAGES OF THE LIMITED LIABILITY COMPANY

1. THERE ARE VARIED LIMITATIONS ON USAGE IN SOME STATES.
2. TAXATION ISSUES ARE UNRESOLVED AT THE STATE LEVEL.
3. THE TAX FLOW-THROUGH STATUS OF A ONE PERSON LLC IS QUESTIONABLE.
4. CASE LAW BACKING UP THE CONCEPT IS LIMITED.
5. OPERATIVE LIFETIME CAN BE LIMITED BY STATUTE.

WHY USE A CORPORATION RATHER THAN A BUSINESS TRUST?

Every once in a while, I speak with someone who is absolutely convinced that they have found the secret entity through which they can accomplish completely unbelievable things. My response to their comments is that their theory is correct; it is *unbelievable.* The claims they make with regard to this entity simply cannot be substantiated. The entity that they tell me about is what is known as a business trust.

Business trusts have been promoted for years under various names and concepts. These include the "Massachusetts Business Trust," "The Pure Trust," "The Equity Trust," "The Liberty Trust," "The Business Trust Organization (BTO)," the "Common Law Trust," and a dozen others. Most of these trust entities use evolutionary documents that are based on precepts long accepted in English Common Law.

While properly constructed business trusts do exist and have been around for a long time, the concept of the business trust has quite possibly, and sadly, been forever damaged as a viable business entity. Worthless claims made by promoters of a dozen different fraudulent tax schemes have turned the business trust idea into a nightmare for the legal community. The claims have ranged anywhere from borderline dishonest to downright criminal. In recent history, no other business concept has been promoted with such hype and inflated promises as those applied to the business trust, and no other has achieved so many bad results in the process.

As an example, one of the biggest promises made by trust promoters was that the Trustor (the person who transfers assets into the trust) could be provided with such things as free housing, vehicles, and even medical care with no tax consequences whatsoever. These promoters also promised that the business trust could eliminate income, gift and estate taxes.

In addition, they promised total asset protection to go along with all the other benefits. Unfortunately, most unsuspecting taxpayers who bought into the concept had no idea of the vast number of case histories that could refute, or destroy, these grandiose claims.

As an example, in 1975, the IRS began to strike down business trusts by issuing Revenue Rulings 75-257 through 75-260. In these rulings, the IRS defined fraudulent business trusts as those that, among other things:

1. Produced an assignment of income;
2. Acted as "Grantor" trusts under the Internal Revenue Code (IRC);
3. Acted as "associations taxable as corporations" under the IRC.

The IRS also ruled that the assets of the trust would be included in the grantor's gross estate for estate tax purposes. Faulty trusts were also deemed to provide no protection against the claims of personal creditors, thereby instantly destroying the primary nature of the trust.

Having stated these aspects of the business trust, it must be pointed out that some of the super wealthy in this country have used business trusts quite successfully to achieve tax savings and asset protection for their vast holdings. Most of those trusts were put in place under a different set of laws during simpler times, and could be attacked in court today, but likely won't be. In some instances, they are simply too expensive to litigate successfully, even for the government. Keep in mind however, there are still some types of business trusts which can be excellent entities. But if someone promises you that you will never pay taxes again, be careful!

The bottom line for business trusts is that they can be used for business purposes only under very unusual and restrictive circumstances. The expense of maintaining these special circumstances is sometimes prohibitive to most people. That transforms the business trust concept the way it has been presented by those out there into a losing proposition all the way around for many people, since it would cost more to set it up and keep it working for you than the money it would save by having it set up in the first place. Again, though, with the law being an evolutionary process, this no-win situation could change. It's just not very likely. Beware the opportunity to never pay taxes again, be completely bullet proof from lawsuits, and the ability to pass everything on to your heirs estate tax-free that the promoters of business trusts promise. If it sounds too good to be true, the chances are it is.

What about other options?

There are a number of other business concepts to choose from when starting up your business, but for comparative purposes, we will only be looking at two more in this final section of the chapter. Most other concepts are in such reduced usage, or are so limited in their scope, that they are just not worth the time to discuss. The two that are worth at least a mention here are joint ventures, and Limited Liability Partnerships (LLPs).

Joint ventures are, in many ways, very similar to general partnerships. Two or more parties agree to enter into a business venture, and to split the responsibilities, risks, and rewards according to whatever internal arrangements they make from the outset.

The biggest difference between general partnerships and joint ventures is that general partnerships are usually set up between two individuals. Joint ventures are normally between two business entities.

Also, joint ventures are rarely set up informally, where many general partnerships are routinely done that way. Most joint ventures entail writing a specific joint venture agreement that outlines every conceivable aspect of the joint venture operation down to the smallest detail.

For tax purposes, joint ventures are considered as partnerships. If one party in a joint venture is a Limited Liability Company, and the second is a limited partnership, the income of the joint venture will be distributed between the parties according to their written agreement, and each entity will pay or report tax obligations accordingly.

The other entity alternative gaining prevalence today is the Limited Liability Partnership (LLP). LLPs are legal in only a few states. They have been established primarily for the purpose of allowing existing professional partnerships, such as accounting firms, to be transformed into LLPs without forcing the dissolution of the existing partnership.

Without an LLP designation and the liability protection it can provide, a professional partnership leaves its partners open to personal liability. The LLP status protects the individual partners to varying degrees, depending upon the jurisdiction. For example, some states allow the LLP to insulate the partners from contractual obligations of the partnership, while others do not.

LLPs are routinely taxed as partnerships. Most even retain the original Taxpayer Identification Number of the existing professional partnership. It is important to note that LLPs are not the same as Limited Liability Companies. This is a common misconception. In fact, most states specifically prohibit LLCs from being established to provide professional services.

SUMMARY

The only way to fully gauge the value of a Nevada Corporation as the best entity for your particular situation is by comparing it to other available alternatives. In order to have a good comparison, you must develop an understanding of what the other choices have to offer. While there are certain advantages available with any entity you choose, the only way to make an educated decision is to also factor in the disadvantages. After carefully weighing out all of these advantages and disadvantages, it is clear that one entity stands far above the rest. It's not difficult to see why the best kept secret of today's millionaires is the Nevada Corporation.

IV THE SECRET MILLIONAIRE'S SECRET LOCATION

> *"A state is better governed which has but few laws, and those laws strictly observed . . ."*
>
> RENE DESCARTES (1596-1650)

One thing which definitely must be looked at when considering a corporation is the state of its location. You will learn quickly that the laws of the state in which you incorporate can make a tremendous impact. Once you do, you will find that there is no better corporate "haven" than the thriving state of Nevada.

So, what exactly do I mean by the term corporate haven? It's a jurisdiction that provides the most favorable climate possible for forming corporations and doing business. It is a state that allows businesses a great range of flexibility in the management and structure of their companies, along with a high degree of favorable tax regulations and other benefits. A corporate haven like Nevada is particularly attractive to businesses located in other states where the business climate is not quite as profit friendly as Nevada. This climate is what attracts many of today's most successful companies to the state.

You can always tell which states are corporate havens by the unusually large number of corporations that are formed there, in comparison to their overall population. That's usually a sure sign that the state is attracting businesses from a much wider population base than just the people who live there.

So why do some states establish themselves as corporate havens? As with most things, money and jobs are the central reasons. The more corporations a state allows to be formed, the more revenue that is brought in through filing fees, annual renewal fees, and other expenses necessary for companies to maintain all those corporate entities. Then, of course, a state with a favorable corporate climate also brings in new economic growth as well, and additionally, the jobs associated with that growth. More people means a bigger tax base, and hence, more revenue for the state.

"What about taxes?" you ask. Most state governments look to tax corporations any way they can. After all, corporations are primarily nonvoting taxpayers, and are targeted first when the state needs revenue. No politician in his right mind is going to suggest taxing actual voters over businesses.

Why? Because voters are the ones who keep politicians in office, and not corporations, right? You might get a lot of argument over that point these days, even if the statement is generally still true.

States, though, have to deal with a whole host of economic consequences during recessions, changes in the political climate, and other factors which lead to lowered revenues from sales and other taxes. They have to live with and within federal mandates to provide services such as health care, while suffering from drastically reduced federal aid that used to be available for those services.

The net result for many states is a serious budget deficit that forces layoffs of state employees and reduced spending in the state across the board. That, in turn, causes states to look for new sources of tax revenue, which inevitably falls on businesses.

In fact, tax reform has had a tremendous impact on state corporate taxation laws in recent years. Most of the 46 states that have state corporate income taxes now use federal corporate taxable income as the starting point for computing their state taxes. When Congress decides to cut allowable business expenses, such as lobbying efforts, or meal and entertainment expenses, it impacts the amount of income tax the corporation will pay at both federal and state levels.

These taxes are rapidly becoming a larger percentage of many corporate tax liabilities than they have ever been in the past. Is it any wonder then, that corporations are looking for a favorable business climate where they can substantially reduce these taxes, or eliminate them altogether? And many are looking toward Nevada for just that kind of climate and the other benefits a good corporate haven can provide. The bottom line is that these corporations are looking for the absolute best state for incorporating.

WHAT IS THE BEST STATE FOR INCORPORATING?

Business people who plan to incorporate generally do so for several reasons over and above cutting their tax burden. Although taxes are typically the number one reason, there are other things people are concerned with as well. Here are four of the top considerations in corporate planning:

1. Tax advantages
2. Protection from personal liability
3. Financial privacy and secrecy
4. Management and control flexibility

Just about any corporate structure will provide these advantages to one degree or another, regardless of where the corporation is formed. However, some states provide them far better than others.

Before we get into a discussion of specific state benefits, I want to point out that for some businesses, setting up a corporation in another state for your local business concern is neither possible nor worthwhile because of all the legal or practical limitations that are required. In many instances, it just makes more sense to incorporate your business in your home state, despite the advantages of doing business in Nevada or elsewhere. However, as you will see throughout this book, a Nevada Corporation can be used in conjunction with that home state corporation rather than in lieu of it.

As an example, small businesses that depend entirely on local markets and have no intention of establishing interstate operations, are the logical candidates for local incorporation. It makes no sense for them to maintain a corporation in another state except, and unless the owners are concerned with total anonymity in their business operations. The great thing about it is that you can have the benefits of a Nevada Corporation and still enjoy the advantages of operating a local business.

Such local businesses generally have a public presence in a mall, strip center or other commercial property. They advertise in the local area, and have one or more employees. In most cases, customers physically come to the store to make their purchases (as opposed to mail order).

All of these criteria mean that the corporation engages in "repeated and successive" transactions (more on this later), and would therefore have to "qualify" as a foreign corporation to do business in most states. It would make more sense for you, if that is your situation, to deal with only one set of state laws, and preferably the laws your attorney or CPA is most accustomed to dealing with at home.

However, when the time comes that state corporate tax burdens become an issue for you and your business, you may find, like so many other companies have, that incorporating in haven jurisdictions like Nevada is a good way to reduce your tax load, personal exposure and liability. At the same time, you will be able to provide yourself with a legal and competitive advantage that will make the cost and effort of setting up a Nevada Corporation well worth considering. In the meantime, it's a good idea for you to become familiar with the various jurisdictions and how they can benefit you down the road. Also, learning about these localities can be a vital key to determining what is best for you and your particular situation.

WHAT ABOUT DELAWARE?

Without a doubt, the biggest question I get in regard to corporate location is: why Nevada rather than Delaware? As a matter of fact, I've been getting this question since before I began speaking on Nevada Corporations. I still remember sitting in one of my first law courses in college, Business Law II. One day, as we began discussing the topic of corporations, the teacher asked the class to name the best state in which to form a corporation. Feeling extremely confident with my legal prowess, I answered, "Nevada." The room fell silent just before the class belted out in laughter at my response. The class in unison then shouted out what the teacher wanted to hear, "Delaware."

As many years as have gone by since that grim day as an undergraduate, I still remember the scene vividly. What a strange twist that all these years later I am traveling the country speaking and authoring a book on the most popular and preferred corporate jurisdiction of today's millionaires, Nevada. To give the subject proper analysis nonetheless, we need to compare the two localities.

For a long time, Delaware aggressively promoted its stature as the incorporating capital of the United States, and for good reason. Many of the Fortune 500 companies are, or were, incorporated in Delaware. The big companies went there for protection, not because they particularly liked the corporate climate Delaware offered, but because it was the only place they could find the kind of protection they needed from government intervention. What they sought most was to protect the interests of their stockholders, their directors to some degree, and the corporation and its officers as a whole.

As a result, almost a quarter of a million companies are incorporated in Delaware, which leads the nation as a major corporate location for American and international corporations. It has been estimated that over 100 new companies file their incorporation papers in Delaware every business day.

What were the key elements in helping Delaware establish its reputation as a corporate haven? There are several:

1. DELAWARE'S TAX LAWS

Delaware does not tax corporate activity that takes place outside the state.

2. DELAWARE'S GENERAL CORPORATION LAW

This is one of the most advanced sets of business specific statutes in the nation, especially on issues related to public corporations.

3. DELAWARE'S COURT OF CHANCERY

With over 200 years of legal precedents, this non-jury court is unique in American law. It has exclusive jurisdiction in Delaware business matters relating to corporate government and operations.

4. DELAWARE'S LEGISLATURE

This body works tirelessly to update or modify the state's statutes relating to the ever changing business environment.

Delaware's corporate law was written from the outset to attract shareholders of the large publicly traded companies in the U.S. Its laws go well beyond other states in protecting the rights of shareholders of public corporations.

Their laws regarding corporate takeovers are the most intricate and detailed in the business world. There are established legal precedents to cover almost any conceivable corporate situation. Because of this, a highly stable legal environment has been created for public companies to use as their base.

Even though Delaware is still a favorite haven for many public corporations, a new problem has arisen for this incorporation leader. Since its laws have been geared primarily to protecting minority shareholders in large corporations, Delaware is finding it increasingly difficult to attract the small, closely held corporations that are growing in number.

The state of Nevada has stepped in to fill that need. In fact, there are several states that are pursuing that part of the incorporation market, but none as aggressively (nor as successfully) as Nevada. These states are all focusing their efforts on the needs of closely held companies who are looking for strong management protection along with the usual corporate umbrellas they've come to expect.

These closely held entities typically are not that concerned with shareholder rights or privileges, since the few shareholders of these corporations are usually the actual owners or managers of the business. What these people want is protection from outside liabilities for themselves and anyone else involved in running their companies, and Delaware's law is simply not geared for that.

That's where Nevada comes in. Nevada is actively soliciting a whole different corporate market than Delaware. Its corporation laws (climate) are designed to protect the rights of small, privately held corporations from the outset and to provide as much protection for corporate officers as possible.

As an example, Delaware has a statute in place that allows a corporation to limit the liability of its corporate directors for monetary damages. Unfortunately, it is far less comprehensive than similar statutes in Nevada law. If you are a director, and being sued, which state would you rather be in?

That answer will be even more clear when you review the following list of acts for which officers and directors are protected under Nevada statutes, but exposed under Delaware corporate law:

1. Omissions or acts not in good faith to the corporation,
2. Violation of a corporate director's duty of loyalty,
3. Undisclosed personal transactions benefiting a director,
4. Acts or omissions that occurred before the date that the statute which provides for indemnification of directors was adopted, and
5. Any acts by officers are exempt from monetary damages.

Most state laws require that a corporate officer act with at least some objective standard of care while operating on behalf of the corporation. Delaware follows the Model Business Corporation Act with regard to how it expresses the standard of care expected of corporate officers. This standard is usually defined as the care of an ordinarily prudent person under similar circumstances.

In essence, what that means is that Delaware requires officers to reasonably believe that they are performing their duties in a manner consistent with, and in the best interests of, the corporation. Nevada makes no such distinction in its laws. By not requiring it, Nevada prevents any judicial review of the actions of corporate officers or directors in all cases except where bad faith is evident or in a manner that the officers actually believe to be opposed to the best interest of the corporation.

There is a substantial body of case law in Delaware that frames the standard of care the state requires of directors. This standard defines such things as gross negligence by directors, which has come to mean any reckless indifference to or deliberate disregard of the whole body of stockholders. With that kind of definition in place, directors in Delaware are open to a vast array of potential litigation that may, or may not be in the best interest of their corporations. In most cases, it certainly is not in the best interest of the individual directors.

Another significant problem with Delaware's definition of a corporate haven is in its administrative procedures governing and regulating corporate dealings. This problem has become so acute that the computer giant, Microsoft, was forced to move its corporate domicile out of Delaware and relocate it into its home state of Washington. Microsoft's justification for the costly move was to avoid the corporate bureaucracy and high corporate taxes they had been dealing with in Delaware.

One of the regulations they were faced with is that all businesses incorporated in the State of Delaware that have not filed a dissolution or merger in the current calendar year, are required to file an Annual Franchise Tax Report and pay the Franchise Tax. A minimum $30 filing fee is required for the annual report.

Now, this Franchise Tax may not seem like a lot, but to a large corporation, it can be quite expensive. The tax can be calculated one of two ways:

1. AUTHORIZED SHARES METHOD

Corporations that have shares with no par value *have* to report with this method. If the corporation has less than 3,000 shares, the tax is the minimum amount or $30. Where there are between 3,000 and 5,000 authorized shares, the tax is $50. The tax for up to 10,000 authorized shares is $90, with an additional $50 for each additional 10,000 shares or portion thereof. Thus, a corporation with 25,000 shares of no par value will pay $190 in franchise taxes every year.

2. ASSUMED PAR VALUE CAPITAL METHOD

To use this method, the corporation must provide detailed figures for all issued shares, including treasury stock, as well as the total gross assets of the company as reported on IRS Form 1120, Schedule L. This information becomes public record with the Delaware Secretary of State. The tax rate under this method is $200 per million or portion of a million dollars of the corporation's gross value. The maximum tax is $150,000. For example, if a corporation has 1,000,000 authorized shares (500,000 are issued) at $1 par value, and a total gross asset value of $1,000,000, then the franchise tax would be $400 per year.

Delaware also has a nasty little item known as a corporate income tax. This is levied on all revenues earned by corporations inside the state. Even though Delaware claims this tax treatment as an advantage, it presents a lot of problems for businesses from other states that want to incorporate in Delaware.

Why is that? Because if the income they earn is not earned in Delaware, it must have been earned somewhere else, where it will most certainly be taxed. Thus Delaware offers little, if any, favorable tax incentives to set up shop in their state.

Corporations are forced to choose between paying Delaware's relatively high taxes, or taxes applicable in some other jurisdiction where the company is actually conducting business. For many companies, the expense associated with making or keeping their corporate domiciles in Delaware, added to the tax burden, makes doing business in Delaware cost prohibitive. These are exactly the kinds of businesses that are looking out west to find the kind of improved business climate they want.

WHAT ABOUT WYOMING?

In recent years, I have heard more and more about the purported benefits of incorporating in the state of Wyoming. Due to the buzz surrounding these corporations, we need to take a closer look. The Wyoming Legislature is one of the more progressive in the country at trying to create this optimum corporate climate we've been talking about. They passed a new set of business statutes in 1989 that revolutionized most of their corporation laws.

The total number of corporations formed in Wyoming to take advantage of these new laws has been small compared to other states, but Wyoming is experiencing a real growth spurt as more companies learn of the state's improved corporate climate. Along with this growth has come significant improvements in the state's economy and tax base. Wyoming has helped develop this economic growth and diversification by making its business climate as user-friendly as possible.

The Wyoming Business Corporation Act is unique in its approach to many key areas. With some aspects of its law, Wyoming has created corporate possibilities that are simply not available anywhere else. Here are some of the more important advantages of incorporating in Wyoming:

1. One person may fill all required officer and director posts.
2. Corporations with fewer than 50 shareholders are not required to have a board of directors.
3. Corporations with fewer than 50 shareholders are not required to conduct meetings, keep minutes, or maintain paperwork associated with having a board.
4. There is no minimum capital requirement.
5. There is no state corporate income tax.
6. There are no taxes on corporate shares.
7. There are no franchise taxes.
8. Annual fees are based on the value of corporate assets physically located in Wyoming, and do not include assets located elsewhere.
9. Stockholder lists are not required by the State.
10. Annual reports are not required until the anniversary of the incorporation date.
11. Articles of Incorporation may provide for unlimited stock without stating a par value.
12. Nominee shareholders are allowed.
13. There is no requirement for issuance of share certificates.
14. Corporate meetings may be held anywhere in the world.
15. Officers, directors, employees, and agents of the corporation are indemnified from personal liability due to their corporate activity.
16. Further indemnification is allowed even after suit is filed by a potential judgment creditor.
17. Continuance procedure is allowed, which permits a corporation formed in another state to change domicile to Wyoming while maintaining its corporate history.
18. The "corporate veil" is more difficult to pierce than other states.
19. "Bearer scrip" can be used when stockholders capitalize the corporation in increments less than the par value of the stock.
20. Scrip holders are treated as stockholders.

Now, let's take a detailed look at some of the more important of these Wyoming advantages. They may not mean much to you at the moment, but as we dig deeper into corporate strategies, these points will begin to shed light on why Wyoming's corporate climate is becoming increasingly more inviting to new companies, not only those in the United States but from throughout the world as well.

Item (9). The fact that shareholders of Wyoming corporations are not disclosed on any public documents assures a high degree of shareholder privacy as compared to most other states. However, "bearer shares" are not provided for under the Wyoming Corporation Act. There are provisions in the Wyoming Act that do allow for shares held by nominee shareholders or by voting trusts. If a nominee shareholder is used, the name of the nominee must appear in the stock ledger of the corporation, but the beneficial owner of the corporation is still not a matter of record.

Item (11). Most states base the amount of the fee required for corporations to file their Articles of Incorporation on the dollar value of the shares the corporation is authorized to issue. That being the case, a corporation with any combination of a large number of authorized shares or with high par values is going to pay a much higher fee to incorporate in some states than it will in a corporate haven like Wyoming. This is especially significant to new corporations anticipating a large public offering at some point in the future.

The annual maintenance fee for corporations is also based on one of those same figures, resulting in expensive annual maintenance costs. For example, a corporation with 10,000,000 shares of no par value stock might have to pay $8,000 to file its Articles of Incorporation, depending upon the state, and the same amount each year to keep that corporation in good standing. This can be cost prohibitive for many.

In comparison, the filing fee for a Nevada Corporation with 10,000,000 shares of 50¢ par value stock might pay only $2,225. A Wyoming corporation may state in its Articles of Incorporation that it is authorized to issue an unlimited number of shares at either a specific par value or no par value. How much more do they pay? Not a penny. There are no extra costs in Wyoming to accomplish this.

Item (17). Continuance is the process by which Wyoming allows a relocating corporate entity to say that it has always maintained its domicile in Wyoming, instead of having to form a new domicile and history to relocate there. In that way, whole new corporations don't have to be created. They just set up shop and act like they have always been a Wyoming company.

Wyoming is one of only two states to provide for true continuance in its corporate climate. Many states provide something similar, called "domestication," but that is not the same thing, nor does it accomplish the same purpose. You might find this concept of the continuance very useful in several circumstances:

1. For taking advantage of Wyoming's favorable tax and business environment,
2. For changing the geographical location of your corporate domicile to meet the needs of a changing business climate,
3. For avoiding hostile government action by another state, including confiscation and expropriation,
4. For taking advantage of Wyoming's statutory regulations on issues such as takeovers, buy-outs, mergers, or hostile shareholder actions, or
5. For obtaining extra consideration on Wyoming public bids and contracts, where resident corporations receive preferential treatment.

Item (18). In some states, the corporate veil is just that—little more than a veil. But in Wyoming, through both its statutes and case law, the state has established stringent criteria required to "pierce the corporate veil" of protection that a corporation is designed to provide.

Wyoming courts have determined that the following factors *must* be considered when determining if a corporate veil can be pierced:

1. The commingling of company funds and other assets,
2. The failure to segregate funds of separate entities,

3. The unauthorized diversion of corporate assets,
4. The use of corporate assets as personal,
5. The unauthorized issue or subscription of shares,
6. Absence of major corporate assets,
7. Failure to maintain minutes or adequate corporate records,
8. Failure to adequately capitalize the corporation,
9. The disregard of legal formalities,
10. Failure to maintain arms-length transactions,
11. Use of a corporation as a subterfuge for illegal transactions, and
12. The holding out by an individual that he is personally liable for corporate debts.

This may seem like a long list of potential ways of piercing the corporate veil. However, it's not compared to most states. In reality, if fraud is *not* present, and a Wyoming corporation does *not* commingle funds while maintaining some semblance of its corporate formalities, including holding meetings of shareholders and directors, then that corporation's veil will be very difficult to pierce.

Item (19). While true "bearer shares" are not provided for in Wyoming law, the statutes do allow for the creation of another type of bearer instrument. That instrument is called "bearer scrip," and is provided for in the revised Model Business Corporation Act of 1984, as well as Section 17-16-604 of the Wyoming Business Corporation Act, which reads:

> "A corporation may issue scrip in registered or bearer form entitling the holder to receive a full share upon surrendering enough scrip to equal a full share."

The concept of scrip was originally developed as a means for dealing with fractional shares that can be created when a corporation splits its stock. The intention, as the statute suggests, is that the scrip be exchanged for full shares when there is enough scrip available to do so. There is, however, no *requirement* that the scrip be exchanged. That can only be done by the scrip holder through the process of redemption of the scrip.

What that means is, if a board of directors of a Wyoming corporation establishes a par value for the company by resolution, any individual who capitalizes the corporation in incre-ments less than the par value could be issued scrip in bearer form. The corporation can then be capitalized with legal, but completely anonymous ownership. If an owner is anonymous, that is a huge benefit when it comes to liability exposure. This gets back to our overall theme of privacy and secrecy.

Item (20). The law even allows a bearer scrip holder the right to vote, receive dividends, and participate in the assets of a liq-uidation, if the scrip specifically provides for it. In short, scrip holders can be treated as stockholders under the Wyoming stat-utes. That means, in a roundabout way, that stockholders of Wyoming corporations can become invisible for all practical purposes. In practice however, this concept is not generally well accepted or used, nor has it been thoroughly tested in court.

After reading about all of the benefits involved in incorpo-rating in Wyoming, you may be wondering why you should bypass the state in favor of Nevada. Well, the time has come for us to take a look at the truly phenomenal benefits offered through the state's corporation laws. Prepare to be blown away by the country's most powerful and exciting legal entity. It's time to answer the question of what is involved in becoming a "secret millionaire": why Nevada?

WHY NEVADA?

Nevada ranks number one in the criteria for establishing as close to a perfect corporate climate as most companies could possibly hope for in today's business environment. The state has spent most of the last 10 years developing and redeveloping the infrastructure to support its desire to become the incorpo-rating capital of the West. They have very nearly succeeded. On average, 1,500 corporations are formed every month in Nevada now. That number is three times what it was in 1985.

A large part of Nevada's success in attracting new corporate business followed the complete revision of the Nevada Corpo-ration Code in 1987 and again in 1991. New laws made the whole incorporation process quicker, cheaper, and more efficient. At the same time, greater liability protection was established for corporate officers than had ever existed before.

Nevada's pro-business attitude has brought tremendous accolades from the nation's business community and even a number one ranking from the media for its favorable business climate. The state has clearly established itself as the "Corporation Capital of the West." Not surprisingly, Nevada's corporate legal system, though not as steeped in tradition as Delaware's, has quickly established a host of legal precedents to support the state's laws.

Some in the legal profession have characterized Nevada's Corporation Code as pro-management, offering too much flexibility in maintaining corporate affairs. These critics have argued that the law in Nevada is not concerned enough about the rights of stockholders or employees (as in the Delaware courts). Despite this, since the 1991 version of the Corporation Code was adopted, Nevada has experienced a whopping 20% increase in the number of corporations filed in the state. With that kind of growth, Nevada *must* be doing something right.

Unlike Delaware, most of the new corporations in Nevada are formed by small companies where the stockholders and management are essentially one in the same. These entrepreneurs generally have very little concern about protecting stockholder's rights, since they have few stockholders besides themselves, and since they manage their own companies and receive all of the benefits of Nevada's liberal code for corporate officers.

To give you a little different slant on how the media views this corporate mentality in Nevada, take a look at this excerpt from the *Reno Gazette-Journal*, Monday, April 29, 1991:

Incorporating Becomes Big Business for Nevada

"They come from all over: the busy streets of New York, the snowy slopes of Colorado, the oil fields of the Yukon, and they all want the same thing: the painless, cheap and anonymous security of Nevada's business world.

Scores of companies fill out a few documents, list a few officers, pay a nominal fee and presto, a new corporation is born.

A New York City cab company has established 50 Nevada Corporations—one for every two vehicles in its 100 taxi fleet. If the company gets sued, its liability is limited to the value of individual properties, just two cabs, unless the plaintiff wants to file lawsuits against 50 different companies.

Some ski resorts have followed the same principle, setting up corporations for each ski lift, lodge and snack bar. A major petroleum company set up Nevada Corporations for each of its 100 Alaska Oil wells. "It's really the idea of making a new basket, every time you have an egg you want to insulate," said one Nevada incorporation expert.

Several entertainers have also started their own corporations. Rock stars Madonna, Prince, Michael Jackson and Paul Simon all reportedly have Nevada Corporations, as do Chevy Chase and Rodney Dangerfield. Some have their big-money salaries paid to accounts in Nevada, where there is no income tax or corporate tax, and the entertainers draw a salary from the corporation. 'They buy boats, cars and take trips to Europe and everything,' said Nevada businessman Brian Foote, who helps out-of-staters set up Nevada Corporations. 'They have the corporation buy for them.'

All of this is made possible because Nevada lawmakers drafted its liberal corporation laws over the past several decades," said Cyndy Woodgate, state deputy secretary for corporations.

Officials didn't want to be hard-nosed about business coming to Nevada," Woodgate said. "And not being restricted here, they're able to come here and do business. We like that fact."

There are several benefits of having a Nevada Corporation. These include low filing fees, minimal information requirements, and no standard corporate tax. Most other states, including California, have a tax.

To make matters even better, Nevada is the only state without a reciprocal agreement with the IRS to exchange tax returns. This is especially attractive to some corporations or individuals who want to legally protect their privacy.

With all these advantages, it's sometimes feasible for a single person or company to set up several Nevada Corporations. The same thing would be a paperwork nightmare in California, where basic individual filing fees are up to $800 or more.

The liberal laws have spawned their own growth industry: businesses that specialize in helping other businesses set up corporations. And business is booming, in part because it's getting more complicated and costly to do business in other states.

At least for now, Nevada remains the second most popular state for incorporating on a per capita basis. The leader is Delaware, but local corporation makers aren't impressed. Nevada, they say, has several benefits Delaware doesn't have, like privacy, no franchise taxes and other benefits."

That article says it all. Low fees, privacy, protection, and ease of doing business are all key elements in building and maintaining that sunny corporate climate you want your corporation to enjoy. Now, let's take a more detailed look at specific advantages of the Nevada laws:

1. One person corporations are allowed,
2. No personal income tax,
3. No state corporate taxes,
4. No franchise tax,
5. No tax on corporate shares,
6. Total privacy of shareholders,
7. No formal information sharing agreement with the IRS,
8. Minimal reporting and disclosure requirements,
9. Low annual fees,
10. Case law that prevents easy piercing of the corporate veil,
11. Officer and director names are public records, but no other information, listings, or minutes of meetings are filed with the State,
12. Corporate officers and directors protected from any personal liability for lawful acts they perform for the corporation,

13. Stockholders, directors and officers not required to live or hold meetings in Nevada, or even be U.S. Citizens,

14. There is no minimum initial capital requirement to incorporate,

15. Corporations may issue stock for capital, services, personal property, or real estate. Directors determine the value of any such transactions, and their decision is final, and

16. Allows for the issuance of "bearer shares".

To gain a better understanding of the significance of these amazing benefits, it is important to take a closer look at some of the specific sections.

Item (2). The people of Nevada have always been conservative, especially when it comes to taxes. Nevadans just don't have a very high regard for taxes of any kind. That is particularly true of personal taxes. Several years ago, the Nevada legislature went so far as to make a state personal income tax unconstitutional.

Even though there is no personal income tax in Nevada, individuals and corporations are still subject to federal income tax liability, just as they are in every other state. There are, however, strategies involving the corporation that may help reduce federal tax liabilities, but the state of incorporation is not a direct factor in accomplishing that. In some situations, the use of a corporation from a specific jurisdiction, like Nevada, may help reduce taxes due to the nature of Nevada corporate law.

Item (3). The first place where tax savings in Nevada become apparent is when you start comparing state corporate tax rates. The rate of taxation among the 46 states that have state corporate income taxes ranges from 1% to over 12%. Added to that are various other state surtaxes, plus some local governments are allowed to assess their own corporate taxes. That can really add up.

California, for example, has a state corporate tax rate of 9.3%. Arizona's tax is 9.3% on all taxable income over $6,000. New York assesses a tax rate of 9% (10% on unrelated income) with a minimum required tax of $800 per year, in addition to taxes levied by local jurisdictions (New York City imposes an 8.85% corporate tax). Even Delaware has a corporate tax of 8.7% and a minimum $40 per year franchise tax. And if you set up shop in Pennsylvania, expect to pay a whopping 12.25% corporate tax. Considering these tax schemes, it's easy to see why Nevada is so attractive.

Items (4, 5). So, now you know one of Nevada's biggest drawing cards for corporations. It is one of only four states in the country with no corporate income tax. Nor does Nevada have any franchise taxes, taxes on corporate shares, nor succession taxes. In certain circumstances, there can be no taxes whatsoever on corporations imposed by the state of Nevada.

How does Nevada provide all the services it does to its citizens and still make ends meet without this revenue from corporations? Nevada's unique tax structure is made possible because of the state's three major industries—gaming, tourism, and mining.

These industries generate an enormous amount of revenue and cash flow for the state through sales, airport, hotel, and other direct use taxes paid for by visitors to the state instead of its residents. These taxes account for a major portion of Nevada's overall budget needs. They allow the state of Nevada to provide services for its people that other states can only envy because of budgetary constraints and federal mandates.

So, just by setting up your corporation in Nevada, you automatically provide your new company with a way to avoid paying excess taxes. Keep in mind, there is a huge difference between tax "avoidance" and tax "evasion." Avoidance will save your company money on taxes, while evasion will save you money on everything, because you will most likely be a guest of the federal prison system. Avoiding taxes is perfectly legal. Evading taxes is not. Tax avoidance is good business. Tax evasion is shady business. *never* get the two confused. The IRS has almost no sense of humor in such matters. When it comes to this area, there is a principle which you must abide by. *It's much easier to stay out of trouble than it is to get out of trouble.*

Let's say for example, that you are contemplating incorporation of a new business in Nevada instead of California, where you happen to live. Done correctly, this move could save, right off the top, $9,300 in California state corporate income taxes on every $100,000 of taxable income. That's *every* year you're in business, people!

By having your corporate structure in total compliance with Nevada laws, you have *avoided* a significant amount of taxation that would otherwise affect your bottom line. And it's all perfectly legal under the Nevada statutes.

Before we move on from taxes, I want to mention one tax that a lot of Nevada businesses pay, that you may *not* have to pay. On July 1, 1991, the Nevada Business License Tax went into effect. This tax is based on the average number of employees your company has on the payroll during each quarter of the year. The tax is paid quarterly by every person, corporation, partnership, or proprietorship that conducts any activity for profit in Nevada. Nonprofit organizations and government entities are the only exceptions.

If you don't have any employees in your company, this tax will not apply to you. Only businesses that have employees actually working in Nevada are subject to the tax. Independent contractors are not considered employees of the company and are liable for their own taxes under this law. What this means to you is that Nevada provides an outstanding environment in which to form your corporation.

New corporations will receive an application for this tax from the Nevada Department of Taxation within weeks of incorporating or securing their local business licenses. The original application has to be sent in with a $25 filing fee, along with a current list of corporate officers and directors, even if you have no employees.

The tax is based on the number of hours worked by employees, instead of the actual number of employees hired. The total hours worked are then divided by the number of hours the state determines that a full-time employee should work each quarter, and the result is the number of employee-equivalents that the business is taxed on. The end result is usually around a $100 per employee per year. In comparison to many other states, even if you have to pay this tax, it is an extremely small amount.

Item (6). Privacy is more of an issue now than it has ever been for people and their financial information. In our society today, the less creditors know about your assets, the better off you are going to be. You need to be a "secret millionaire" or at least follow these powerful principles until you get there.

It's a fact of life that individuals with no significant assets simply don't get sued as often as those who have "deep pockets." Business people with any assets at all have to anticipate the possibility of being sued, sooner or later, in their business lifetime. Incorporating can go a long way toward helping them protect themselves and their business activities from judgment liabilities. Without this protection, specifically the privacy offered through Nevada Corporations, you may as well paint a bull's-eye on your chest.

The real truth is, people are tired of being sued. They are tired of the frivolous nature of most lawsuits and of being drawn into arbitrary legal fights just because they are major stockholders in a corporation or members of a corporate board. Many, in fact, are refusing to serve on the board of directors of local corporations because their exposure to stockholders and the public is so risky for them personally.

Gone are the days when prominent individuals volunteered to serve on corporate boards as directors or vice-presidents. People have come to realize that the liability exposure they produce for themselves in those situations is just not worth the prestige being on such boards used to offer. Now more than ever, people are seeing the necessity of keeping their financial affairs secret. It is time to apply the strategies of the "secret millionaire."

Even if you are not a prominent business person, you still need a specific plan of action to protect yourself from this kind of runaway litigation. You need a plan that essentially isolates your assets from you personally. If there's no reason to think that you have a million dollars, it's not too likely that someone is going to file a million dollar judgment against you. You need to follow in the footsteps of today's "secret millionaires."

You certainly won't have to worry about attorneys working on a contingency basis against you unless they see a way of getting paid in the end. Suing people with no money or assets makes it tough for an attorney to get rich, that's for sure. By keeping your assets private, you will greatly reduce any chances of that happening to you.

In 1987, Nevada took a giant step toward helping business people with this problem. The Nevada Legislature passed a law that allows corporations to place provisions in their Articles of Incorporation to *eliminate* any personal liability of officers and directors to the stockholders of Nevada Corporations. Since then, Delaware and a few other states have adopted similar measures, but Nevada's law stands as the most thorough and comprehensive in the country.

This is what the *Reno (Nevada) Gazette Journal* had to say about this subject on Monday, April 29, 1991:

> Silver State's Regulations Allow For 'Hidden Firms'
>
> "Taking advantage of a new Nevada law, some Silver State corporations now are able to withhold from the public the location of their principal offices.
>
> But a top official in Nevada's Secretary of State's office said that she believes the new law isn't causing problems, although the number of hidden corporate sites is unknown.
>
> Under the previous regulation, corporate papers available to the public were required to list the location of a corporation's principal office. That's not required under the new rule, which mandates only that a corporation list the address of its Nevada resident agent.
>
> The updated law requires that the resident agent keep a record of the corporation's principal office address. But there's no requirement that a resident agent reveal a corporate office site, except under court order.
>
> "However, corporate directors must list their names and addresses—information that sometimes can be used as a clue to the area a principal office is located," said Cyndy Woodgate, Deputy Secretary of State.

Nevada's corporation law remains liberal, and finding a corporation 'is no easier than it was before,' she said. That's partly because a Nevada Corporation doesn't necessarily have to conduct business and its address can be listed as a post office box."

Even though the article above is not necessarily glowing with praise for Nevada corporate law, it should be clear that the state offers more ways to protect your privacy as a stockholder than any state in the union. To understand how this is possible, let's examine the five most common ways of determining who the stockholders are in a corporation:

1. You can depose corporate officers or directors under oath and force them to reveal any *direct* knowledge of the ownership of the corporation.
2. You can call the Secretary of State's office (or its equivalent) where the corporation was formed. In some states, the Secretary of State requires a list of stockholders to be kept on file, including a listing of their capital contribution and the value of their stock. In some states, you can even get this information with a phone call.
3. You can get a copy of the corporation's tax return in that state. Every state that has a corporate income tax or franchise tax requires that the return be filed on a state-approved form. Most state income tax returns require a list of stockholders, especially when that state also levies a personal income tax. This information is harder to get over the phone, but can be sent to you, either through the mail or to anyone who can get a subpoena for the record.
4. You can contact the corporation's resident agent in that state, who is required to have information on file regarding the ownership of all stock. Most of the time, the corporation is required to provide the agent with an actual copy of the stock ledger for file. This is not available to just anyone, but again, a subpoena will get you immediate access to it.
5. You can subpoena the corporation itself, which maintains the original of the stock ledger. The stock ledger contains all of the information regarding amount,

type, and value of stock owned by each stockholder. A proper subpoena can get you just about any corporate record you want.

It stands to reason that if you can subpoena information to find out who owns a corporation or is responsible for its actions, you can then file suit if you have a grievance. That can be difficult or impossible to determine from Nevada Corporations using any of those five methods. Why is that?

Well, to begin with, the only filing to the Secretary of State required from Nevada Corporations is their annual list of officers and directors. This list is the only official information the Secretary of State will have on file regarding the ownership and management of any corporation. This list is due within 60 days of incorporation, and then annually after that.

On this list, only five names need to be reported, even though you could theoretically send in every stockholder's name. The required offices that the Secretary of State must have on file include the president, the secretary, the treasurer, at least one director and the corporation's resident agent. Keep in mind that in Nevada, *one* person may serve in all five capacities, and that person is not even required to be a stockholder. This offers immense flexibility not offered elsewhere.

So, if you were to call the Secretary of State in Nevada and request information on a particular corporation, you could learn several things. You could learn whether or not the corporation is in good standing with the state. You could get the names of the president, secretary, treasurer, and a director, as well as any additional officers that may have been reported, such as a vice-president or some other director.

You might also learn that all of the positions in that corporation are filled by the same person, which usually suggests a one person corporation, or by several different people. You might determine that the officers and directors appear to be U.S. residents, or that they appear to be citizens of a foreign country. And, you might also discover who the resident agent is.

Okay, so what *can't* you learn? That's the real question I want you to focus on. That issue is the heart and soul of Nevada Corporate Law.

First and foremost, the Secretary of State's office can't tell you who the stockholders are, how many there are, or how much stock is issued. That's a lot of information that is readily available in other states. Second, the Secretary of State's office can't tell you what assets the corporation owns, how much capitalization exists, or what their value was. And third, the Secretary of State could not tell you if the officers and directors of a particular corporation have changed from when the last list was filed, since filing the list is only required once a year.

Let's say, for instance that the list of officers and directors of the corporation you are researching was filed on November 1st. That list only represents the officers and directors of the corporation on the date of filing. It's quite possible that the corporation could have had a meeting on November 2nd, where a whole new set of officers and directors was elected. Those new officers and directors wouldn't have to be a matter of public record for a whole year, *if then*.

The corporation could call another meeting the following October and put the original officers and directors back into office in time for their annual filing. So, there's no guarantee that the names you found in your first round of research have any relevance to the current situation for that corporation. This offers a level of privacy and secrecy which can be an enormous benefit given the current legal climate in this country.

All right, what about other filing sources for information? Since Nevada has no corporate income tax, or the bureaucracy required to administer such a tax, there are no state corporate tax returns to look for. The only thing the Department of Taxation has is a filing form for the Nevada Business License Tax. This form is not immediately available as a public record, and even if it were, it would only show the number of hours worked by employees of the company. There would be no officers, directors or stockholders listed on it.

Your research on this corporation is rapidly grinding to a halt for lack of information, isn't it? But let's assume you've gone a step further and subpoenaed the resident agent to get the corporate records relating to this particular corporation. Nevada resident agents are not required to have a copy of the actual stock ledger on file as is required in many states. They are only required to have a statement that provides the name and address of the person who *does* have the actual stock ledger in their possession.

That stock ledger could be in another state, another country, or 10,000 miles away. Nevada law does not require the stock ledger to be in Nevada at any time. If the corporation so desired, it could force you to spend a lot of time, effort, and energy pursuing the information you're looking for. By then, you might be asking yourself if the lawsuit is going to be worth all the hassles. A truly frivolous suit would have long since been cast aside because of the cost and effort involved. Remember, the attorney does not get paid during all of this research and will not get paid unless they win the case.

What about the corporate secretary? They keep records, right? They do, but they are under no legal obligation to reveal any information about the stockholders of their corporation. In fact, a corporate secretary in Nevada is not required, or *allowed* to provide that kind of information to you or even to another shareholder of the company unless that shareholder controls enough voting power to force the issue.

Minority shareholders with less than 15% ownership do not have such power. However, NRS 78.257 provides that any stockholder who owns at least 15% of the issued shares of a corporation has a right to inspect all books and records, but must bear the costs of such an inspection.

If you were an outside creditor (*not* a majority stockholder), do you think you would be getting frustrated with your research yet? Then put yourself in the position of a judgment creditor who has *no* ability to access corporate records or documents. The only way you could get information in that case is if there were some criminal investigation that warrants your access.

Now think about this. The right of judgment creditors to access a corporation's stock ledger was removed by the Nevada Legislature in 1993. If potential creditors attempt to obtain and use corporate records for any interest other than a shareholder's, they can face civil penalties.

Subsection 3 of that statute states that:

> Any stockholder or other person exercising (these rights) who uses or attempts to use information, documents, records or other data obtained from the corporation, for any purpose not related to the stockholder's interest in the corporation as a stockholder, is guilty of a gross misdemeanor.

The penalty for using corporate information for any purpose than to have stockholders defend or demonstrate their interest in the corporation is up to one year in the county jail and up to a $2,000 fine. A non-shareholder in a Nevada Corporation has *no* authority to view the stock ledger. The burden of proof falls on the corporation to prove improper motivation for such a request.

With that kind of protection in place, the only other viable source of ownership information is found on the stock certificate itself. Then the real shocker to creditors comes when they find out that the stock of a Nevada Corporation may have actually been issued as "bearer shares" (more on this later) where there is no actual name tied to a given stock certificate.

This means that stocks may be recorded on the stock ledger as having been written to the "bearer" of the certificate. Shares like these could have first been issued to the trustee of a voting trust, or in the care of an attorney, who can then exercise attorney/client privilege to avoid providing information. In the end, the corporate secretary may have no direct knowledge of who currently possesses the bearer shares. Talk about a dead end! Do you understand the power in this?

Nevada is currently the only state that allows corporations to issue stock to the "bearer," which some people compare to checks written for "cash." Whoever controls the bearer certificates, or has the shares physically in their possession, technically has the power to redeem those shares as the beneficial owner. Since they are negotiable instruments, it may be very difficult to determine how many times bearer stocks have changed hands since they were issued.

The use of bearer shares in Nevada Corporations is a key element in seminars, newspaper advertising, and promotional brochures of Nevada incorporating companies. Bearer shares can be an attractive solution for people who want to own or control assets or business activities, while maintaining a seemingly airtight seal of financial privacy.

While it is true that ownership privacy can be accomplished through bearer shares, there are many issues which are still misunderstood regarding the use of such shares. Let's take a brief look at how this concept has developed, and how Nevada has adapted the concept to fit its own unique style of corporate law.

As you have learned, most states base their corporate law statutes on the Revised Model Business Corporation Act as developed by the Committee on Corporate Laws of the American Bar Association. It should come as no surprise then, that there are significant similarities in the Corporation Codes of most of the states.

The Model Business Act has been refined and modified many times though, and because of the independent nature of state legislatures, they do not always conform to the Model Act. In the process, each state has developed its own features that set it apart from the rest.

In Nevada's case, one key area where it adapted its Corporation Code away from the Model Act was in the information required on stock certificates issued by a corporation. Specifically, the Model Act does not allow or even contemplate the use of shares issued to a bearer.

The Model Act stipulates that a stock certificate is required to contain:

1. The name of the issuing corporation and the state under which it is organized,
2. The name of the person to whom the stock is issued, and
3. The number and class of shares and the designation of the series, if any, that each certificate represents.

The Nevada Revised Statutes, by omission of parts of the language in the Model Act, create an opportunity to issue shares of a Nevada Corporation to "The Bearer." NRS 78.235 (1) reads in part:

> Every stockholder is entitled to have a certificate, signed by officers or agents designated by the corporation for the purpose of certifying the number of shares owned by him in the corporation.

In other words, Nevada law only requires two things:

1. The name of the corporation, and
2. The number of shares represented by the certificate.

As far as I can determine, Nevada is the only state with this abbreviated language in regard to stock certificates. Since the name of the shareholder is not specifically required on the certificate, the use of bearer shares is *not* prohibited in Nevada.

Despite that, officials with Nevada agencies such as the Attorney General's office, the Securities Division and Corporation Division of the Secretary of State's office are reluctant to take an official position one way or the other on bearer shares. The only prohibition on a corporation using bearer shares would seem to be on those corporations attempting to qualify to issue a public offering of stock. This provides a great opportunity for the smaller closely held corporations.

There are two main reasons why corporations would want to issue bearer shares. The first one is bearer shares are unsurpassed as a method of achieving total privacy in corporate ownership. This is because true ownership of the stock is extremely difficult to determine, even under the best of circumstances. The second is bearer shares simplify things considerably as a vehicle to provide for convenient transfer of ownership interests (more on this later).

You already know that there are only two tangible sources of information on ownership of a Nevada Corporation—the stock certificates and the stock ledger. The ledger must contain the names of the stockholders, their residence addresses, and the number of shares owned by each. This list has to be revised annually, and would be a wealth of information for any creditor seeking payment on a judgment. You have also learned that there are penalties for the improper use of this information. That leaves only the stock certificates themselves as a good source for determining true ownership. What happens with bearer shares when civil or criminal liability is involved, since there are no names on the certificates? That's where things get a little dicey.

In the discovery phase of civil litigation, it is possible that a judge might require full disclosure of stock ownership. In a criminal case, the grand jury might make the same requirement (although materials submitted to a grand jury are considered confidential unless presented in support of a specific criminal indictment). So if you are using bearer shares, you are not completely bulletproof after all. Keep in mind however, that the privacy you are looking for is, in regard to civil (not criminal) lawsuits against you. If your intention is to gain secrecy from disclosure of criminal activity, put this book down right now. That is not what I'm about. I'm about protecting those assets which you've worked so hard to accumulate without losing them in a situation which may not be your fault. This is what asset protection is all about and bearer shares can help you to do just that.

What are some of the potential uses of bearer shares? Though I'm not advocating any of these situations, they do come up, and are probably more frequently used in Nevada than anywhere else. Once again, I must stress that I am not advocating nor do I particularly condone the following tactics. I include them for no other reason than to show you the extent of the flexibility offered through Nevada's laws. I find that I am able to learn things much easier if I can look at extreme examples and then focus on things which are more mainstream. It is my belief that if I can learn better this way, perhaps you can as well. Having added that caveat, let's take a look at some of these way out examples.

1. You might want to remain anonymous to close a specific business deal with people who would know who you are otherwise. Personal relationships can sometimes jeopardize or delay profitable business opportunities, but bearer ownership might allow you to close the deal faster and with less concern for the aftermath.

2. If you were contractually obligated *not* to compete in a particular business in Nevada (former employer, et cetera) bearer shares could provide anonymity to go ahead and compete under a pseudonym or with other stockholders.

3. If you were involved in a heavily contested divorce or family support litigation, bearer shares could be a way to avoid some liability. Once a court sets your alimony or support requirements, you might want to establish a Nevada Corporation using bearer shares to avoid additional appeals for support payments based on your increased income.

4. You might want to keep a low profile in your business dealings, for whatever reason. Prominent people, in particular, want to avoid having their names associated with some investments. Bearer shares are an ideal form of ownership in such cases.

Where most of the confusion comes with using bearer shares is in the transfer of ownership. A bearer instrument has to be negotiated differently than instruments made payable to order. If an instrument is made payable to the order of JJ Childers, it is negotiated by delivery with any necessary signature or endorsement attached. If an instrument is made payable to bearer, however, it is negotiated by delivery.

It is not uncommon for people to believe that bearer shares allow them to transfer ownership of a Nevada Corporation in total anonymity, without any potentially adverse effects. That's not entirely true. Three important facets of bearer shares must be considered:

1. Stock certificates are *not* stock. Stockholders may own stock with or without an actual stock *certificate*. The Nevada Attorney General has published a formal opinion on this subject (AGO38). The certificate is defined as a piece of paper that indicates ownership. Because Nevada does not require corporations to issue certificates at all, it would be an error to argue that possession of a certificate equals ownership of the shares.

2. The Nevada Revised Statutes (78.240) specifically state that shares of stock are defined as personal property. All rules, regulations, and applicable taxes that apply to transfers of personal property also apply to transfers of bearer shares. Bearer share certificates can be bought, sold, stolen, borrowed, lost, duplicated, inherited, or willed, just like any other personal property.

3. Nevada case law requires that any transfer of stocks be registered on the corporation's books before such transfer is valid against the corporation. This is done primarily to protect corporate officers in determining ownership of and the right to vote their corporate shares.

Okay, so can bearer shares be used to transfer ownership of a Nevada Corporation with a high degree of privacy? Certainly they can. But new owners have to register their ownership with the corporation before the corporation can grant any ownership rights or payment of dividends. And, by transferring bearer shares, owners can trigger nasty little things like federal gift taxes, estate taxes, capital gains taxes, and other unusual circumstances arising out of the transaction.

Also, the fact that there is so little published or known on the issue of bearer shares can be somewhat confusing if you are unsure of exactly how to issue the shares and how to handle them *after* they are issued. Keep in mind, though, that there are no statutes that disallow bearer share use, and no significant case law, to date, that invalidates them.

Here is one formula for issuing bearer shares. It is by no means the only way it can be accomplished, but this method does seem to cover all the requisite bases:

1. Hire a sharp attorney who completely understands your need for strategic planning. If your attorney can then form your new corporation in Nevada himself, encourage him to do so. If an incorporating company or a resident agency is used, let your attorney make all the necessary arrangements and communications. That way you provide yourself a degree of anonymity from the outset.

2. Have your attorney hire nominee officers and directors who have no personal contact with the shareholders, but receive all instructions *through* the attorney. The testimony of officers and directors relative to their personal knowledge of corporate ownership is thus limited.

3. In the organizational meeting of the corporation, the nominee officers and directors should be instructed to issue stock certificates to "bearer" in increments provided in their detailed instructions from your attorney. In the stock ledger, the transaction is recorded with the stock being issued "in care of" the attorney, and nothing more.

4. Have the stock certificates and stock ledger forwarded to your attorney's office. The certificates should then be held on file there. The stock ledger should also be held in your attorney's office, or it can be conveyed to any location you want. Your attorney provides the corporation's Resident Agent with the name and mailing address of the person who will be holding and maintaining the stock ledger.

5. All instructions from shareholders to corporate officers and directors should be communicated by your attorney. These communications between the shareholders and the attorney represent privileged information, and thus are protected to a degree.

You should be realizing by now that if it's total financial privacy you are after for your corporation, Nevada is the only state to consider. If you understand the laws, and how they allow you to maintain this privacy, and also how to structure your corporate activities properly, you can make it virtually impossible for someone to discover the ownership of your Nevada Corporation.

Another way this privacy is enhanced is that officers and directors of Nevada Corporations are the only people listed in public records of corporations. Thus, they are the only ones exposed to litigation. Every stockholder can be indemnified as well, although that is almost unnecessary, since no one can find you on public records in the first place. It's very hard to sue someone you can't find. It's even harder to collect in that situation.

The relative section of the Nevada Revised Statutes (78.037) reads, in part:

> The Articles of Incorporation may also contain:
>
> 1. A provision eliminating or limiting the personal liability of a director or officer to the corporation or its stockholders for damages for breach of fiduciary duty as a director or officer, but such provision must not eliminate or limit the liability of a director or officer for:
>
> (a) Acts or omissions which involve intentional misconduct, fraud or a knowing violation of law.

Nevada's Corporation Code goes on to allow the indemnification of all officers, directors, employees, stockholders, or agents of a corporation for any actions that they take on behalf of the corporation that they had *reasonable* cause to believe was legal. Indemnification under this statute covers any civil, criminal, or administrative action. These two laws taken together provide almost "bulletproof" protection for officers and directors of Nevada Corporations, provided they act prudently in their duties.

Nevada laws also allow a corporation to make "financial arrangements" to provide a payment method for any possible liability that an officer or director might incur. These "financial arrangements" can be, but are not limited to:

1. Creating a trust fund to pay off the obligation,
2. Establishing some type of self-insurance program,
3. Securing the debt by granting a lien on corporate assets, and
4. Establishing a letter of credit or other surety for payment.

Okay, by now you know that frivolous lawsuits and creditors can't hurt you much in Nevada, that other stockholders can't tie you up in Nevada courts, and that even the state will have a difficult time finding out that you are a corporate owner. So what's left to worry about? The IRS, right? *Wrong!*

This little article is representative of the sentiment people have toward the IRS in the state of Nevada. That sentiment may be the same in every other state, but the difference is, in Nevada, you *can* do something about the IRS. Or, to put it another way, the IRS is severely limited in what *they* can find out about *you*, thanks to Nevada laws.

From the Reno Gazette-Journal, April 29, 1991:

MILLER CLOSES RECORDS TO IRS

"Hands off: Governor says federal agency can't use state computers to find tax cheats.

Carson City Gov. Bob Miller isn't going to let the IRS use state computers to track tax-delinquent Nevadans.

Miller said Tuesday that he refused to open up employment, motor vehicle, and other records to the IRS because there is too great a potential for abuse of peoples right to privacy.

He gave examples of IRS undercover operations into Las Vegas bookmaking and a Reno-area crackdown on reporting casino dealers tip earnings.

'The IRS to date, hasn't treated us the same way it's treated residents of other states,' Miller said.

Miller's announcement during a Las Vegas news conference came a week after the IRS proposal surfaced. Since then, Miller's Carson office has received about 70 phone calls from irate people.

'None of them was in favor of agreeing with the IRS,' said spokesman Mike Campbell.

In Washington D.C., Sen. Harry Reid, D-Nev., was pleased. 'Gov. Miller's decision was the right one,' Reid said, 'It puts the people of the state first, rather than the IRS.'

Reid and Sen. Richard Bryan and Rep. James Bilbray, both D-Nev., still await word on a meeting they've requested this week with the IRS commissioner on IRS activities in Nevada.

Miller's order directed Perry Comeaux, director of the state Department of Taxation, to notify the IRS office in southern Nevada that state records will not be shared.

'I told them we weren't going to do anything to expand any cooperative effort with the Internal Revenue Service at this time,' Comeaux said."

Those are pretty strong words, considering they were directed at the premier tax collecting agency in the world. The kind of information the IRS has asked for and gotten in other states includes such things as unemployment records, welfare and social services records, workman's compensation records, driver's registration, and even motor vehicle registrations. But Nevada has stood its ground by continuing to deny access to the IRS for all kinds of records the state compiles.

In fact, Nevada is the *only* state that does not comply with IRS requests for information. Nevada's governor has routinely ordered the directors of the state Department of Taxation and other agencies to seal state records from the IRS's dogged efforts.

In view of the fact that every other state *except* Nevada has this information sharing relationship with the IRS, it's not surprising that people are dumbfounded when they realize how much information the federal government can compile on them, without their knowledge or consent. For instance, California residents who file either individual or corporate state income tax returns, will have their financial information checked against their federal return without their knowledge. Many states have agreed to allow this because the sharing agreements allow the states, in turn, to have access to IRS records to verify state personal and business tax returns. Is that scary, or what?

There are also a large number of reporting agencies and credit bureaus, like Dun & Bradstreet, that maintain computer links with the various governmental offices across the country. They can buy and sell information on any company contained in the various state databases.

Any information a Secretary of State's office collects is also readily available this way. That includes the officers, directors, and stockholders of a corporation, if the state records hold such information. Even company revenues and net worth can be found out from these sources.

Nevada offers this computer link as well. The difference is that the link can only provide that information which the Secretary of State already collects, and you *know* how limited that is.

An important thing that needs to be mentioned is how all of this privacy from the IRS and others can affect you and your business. For many people, it is as if they are afraid of the IRS and tend to believe that the privacy offered through Nevada surely cannot and will not last. There are two questions which I am asked over and over again at the seminars with regard to the fact that there is no reciprocity agreement between the state of Nevada and the IRS. These two questions are:

1. How do you know that the IRS won't make Nevada sign the agreement?
2. Isn't the IRS going to crack down on Nevada Corporations?

I want to spend a little time addressing these two concerns. First of all, let's take a look at the question of "what if the IRS makes the state of Nevada sign an information sharing agreement?" It really surprises me that I get this question so often because it means that the significance of the small amount of information kept by the state has not been fully grasped. Think about it. If the IRS makes them sign the reciprocity agreement, that would mean that they would have to divulge all of the information that they have. Remember, we are not concerned about this because they don't have any information to share. It is not a problem.

The key issue however, is best addressed by taking a look at the second question: "Isn't the IRS going to crack down on Nevada Corporations?" The main point that you need to understand is that the IRS cracks down on people who do not pay what they owe in taxes, specifically, federal income taxes. Think about the reasons why you need to have a Nevada Corporation rather than any other state's corporation and list them out. Go back through the material if you need to. After looking at your list, ask yourself a question. Does the use of a Nevada Corporation, rather than any other state's corporation, save you even one red cent in *federal* income taxes? *No.* There is nothing about a Nevada Corporation that will reduce your federal income taxes any more than any other state's corporations. With that knowledge in mind, it begs the question, what is there for the IRS to crack down on?

If it doesn't save you any federal income taxes, then why do you need a Nevada Corporation versus any other? The reason you want a *Nevada Corporation* is for the privacy and secrecy it offers you for your asset protection needs. In today's legal environment, this is essential.

When you understand exactly what it is that you need and how a Nevada Corporation can meet that need, the questions with regard to the continuation of Nevada's situation become insignificant.

In addition to protecting your financial privacy with its stringent corporate laws, Nevada also guarantees corporations a significant degree of flexibility in organizing ownership interests to fit the needs of each individual business. This is in direct contrast to most other states, which adhere to the Model Act when outlining what a corporation can and cannot do with such things as stocks and assets.

A Nevada Corporation has the right, for example, to issue different classes of capital stock, and to assign different series within each class. Owners of the different classes or series of stock may then be assigned different rights and/or privileges within the corporation. This provides a great deal of flexibility for you.

Various classes of common and preferred stock are allowed to be issued, each with their own specific rights described in *that* corporation's Articles of Incorporation. Typically, preferred stock is differentiated from common stock by the fact that its owner is first in line to receive a distribution upon the liquidation of the corporation. When a variety of preferred stock classes are represented, they can be ranked in order of preference for such distributions.

Another example would be that a board of directors may, if their Articles of Incorporation so stipulate, divide a class of preferred stock into a series with its own assigned rights and without any approval from the stockholders. This allows a board of directors to issue a series of shares in a special circumstance without the normal costs and delays caused by special meetings of the stockholders to authorize a new class of stock. This can be especially beneficial when dealing with corporations that have a large amount of shareholders.

Nevada Corporation Code also has no requirement that a minimum amount of capital be invested in a corporation. You can start your operation on a shoestring, if necessary. Now, that can be good news or bad news unless you are careful, because if your corporation loans out a disproportionate amount of its funds for whatever reason, the IRS can jump in and reclassify the loans as stock purchases. Of course, the IRS has to find out about it first, then it has to determine by a formula that the corporation is undercapitalized. If you follow the rules in this area, you probably won't have any problems.

What about the sale of assets? That part of the Nevada Corporation Code is pretty much cut and dried. It requires that the shareholders approve the sale of all assets of a corporation. Approval takes a majority vote of shareholders that have voting rights, unless the original Articles of Incorporation require a larger portion of the outstanding shares. In the event of a dissolution of the corporation, all proceeds not required to pay existing debt at time of closure are distributed to shareholders, and their shares are then canceled.

Before we move on to the actual procedures for setting up your corporation, I want to mention one more important aspect of Nevada corporate law. This has to do with *tort* reform.

Webster's defines a tort as "A civil wrong, other than breach of contract, for which the injured party is entitled to compensation." As you have learned, Nevada goes over the top in trying to protect your right to privacy, which in turn, helps eliminate exposure to lawsuits. But what happens if you actually lose a tort case? It is my goal to prepare you for worst case scenarios as well as best.

The goal of tort reform in Nevada has been to reduce the exposure of businesses and their insurers to catastrophic losses. Highlights of Nevada's legislation include provisions which limit exemplary damages and abolish joint and several liabilities (except in certain cases). Let's talk about what this means to you and your business.

Exemplary damages, also known as punitive damages, are those imposed, in essence, to punish someone for doing something wrong. Guilt must have been demonstrated by clear and convincing proof that involved fraud, oppression, and/or expressed or implied malice. Compensatory damages, on the other hand, are those awarded for actual loss or pain and suffering.

Before tort legislation was extensively revised, it wasn't unusual to see Nevada courts award exemplary damages that were from three to five times more than whatever the compensatory damages totaled. A loss like that could often ruin a company by driving it into bankruptcy. This can be the biggest danger involved in lawsuits.

Fortunately, Nevada statute now limits exemplary damages to an amount no greater than $300,000 when compensatory damages are less than $100,000. These limitations do not apply to some cases involving insurer bad faith, the release of toxic substances, or product liability, but will apply in almost all other tort litigation.

In most states, joint and several liability means that if you lose in court, you are not the only one liable for payment. Other members of your corporation can be forced to make restitution as well. When a judgment is entered against several different defendants, they are all equally liable for the *full* amount of the judgment, without regard to their relative fault in whatever caused the damages.

Nevada tort law now requires that a court must assign a percentage of fault to *each* defendant in the case. This can range from zero fault to 100% with the total of the assignments equaling 100%. Defendants found liable are then required to pay a share of the total judgment no greater than their percentage of fault, and the sum of the shares cannot be greater than the whole. That eliminates a huge window of financial exposure for members of Nevada Corporations.

What I'm going to give you now is a kind of quick and easy overview of what it takes to file your corporation. I'll also give you some tips on working with the Nevada Secretary of State's office. This is by no means a detailed schedule of the process, but it will give you some idea of what is involved and how much a filing will cost. We will go much more into detail with all these processes in later chapters. For the time being, just make mental notes of the flow of things so that you will be more comfortable with the concepts involved.

As pointed out before, the first thing you want to do to form your corporation is select a good name for it. The name should be an asset to the operation and it should send a clear message. Most of your advertising and public relations will revolve around the name in one form or another, so you want it to be a good reflection of what it is you are doing. It should tell people what the company does, be consistent with the image you want to convey, and be easy to remember, spell, and pronounce.

You can find out from the Secretary of State's office whether or not the name you want to use is available. It's a good idea to have several variations on the same theme before you contact them, though. That way you will likely be able to use one of the names you've selected.

Nevada's Corporation Code requires that the name of a corporation cannot be "deceptively similar" to the name of another corporation or limited partnership already authorized to conduct business in the state. For example, the similarity of the corporate names "Fred's Fine Foods Exchange, Inc." and "Fred's Fine Foods Company, Inc." would most likely not be enough for the Secretary of State to refuse to file the second corporation. Those names *are* similar, but different enough that both could do business in Nevada.

If your corporate name is determined to be too similar to that of another one, the Secretary of State will only agree to file the new corporation if a written consent to the use of the name by the other company accompanies your filing and Articles of Incorporation. The Secretary of State (the person, not the office) has total discretion in deciding when such similarities exist, and that decision may only be reviewed in a court of law.

What about the name itself? Is there anything specific you need to know before filing for it?

Yes, there is. In Attorney General's Opinion 50, 4-26-1951, it was determined that corporations do not gain the right to exclusive use of geographical words in their corporate names, unless the words have themselves acquired a meaning in the mind of the public associated with the business of the corporation. Thus, Nevaco Trading Corporation would be considered a valid name, even though a Nevada Trading Corporation might already exist, but Mining Corporation and Mining Corporation of Nevada could be considered deceptively similar.

Several different designations may be included in the name you choose in order to indicate that the company is, in fact, a corporation. Such words as "Corporation," "Corp.," "Incorporated," "Inc.," "Limited," and "Ltd." are all acceptable. Such designations are not *required* to be part of the name of your corporation unless without the designation the company name would sound like the name of a natural person. For example, a corporation could not be called "JJ Childers" but could be called "JJ Childers, Inc." Remember, however, I do not advise people to use their own name as the name of the corporation, as it causes you to lose your privacy.

I strongly encourage you to use one of the specified designations in your corporate name. In fairness to people or businesses that conduct their affairs with your corporation, when the proper designation is obvious in the name, then the public is made immediately aware of the limitation on the liability of the individuals who represent your business.

There are several terms that require prior clearance from other Nevada state agencies before they can be used in the name of your corporation. Among these words are:

Accident	Fire	Reinsurance
Appraisers	Investment	Risk
Assurance	Investor	Risk Retention Group
Banco	Liability	Savings
Banking	Life	Surety
Bonding	Loan	Trust

Casualty	Mutual	Underwriter
College	Purchasing Group	University
Engineer	Protection	Variable
Engineering	Realtor	Warranty
Financial	Reassurance	

It doesn't cost you anything to check with the Secretary of State to see if a name is available for use. For a $20 nonrefundable fee, the state will reserve the rights to a specific corporate name if they determine it to be available for your use. The name reservation is good for 90 days, and may be renewed if necessary.

If you are planning to go into business soon, you should either reserve the name you want or go ahead with incorporation under that name as soon as possible. If you are planning to do business in a number of states, the chances are that at least one of the states will have some kind of conflict with the name you have chosen. Only by checking with each state can you be sure that the chosen name is still available for use. Most of the states will now allow you to register the name of your foreign corporations without qualifying it to do business in that state, but you have to remember to ask if that service is available.

If your corporation is going to be a professional corporation, the name you choose must include the last name of at least one of the stockholders, and must be followed by the words "Professional Corporation," "Prof. Corp.," "Chartered," "Limited," or "Ltd." For example, a dentist's office might be incorporated as "Dr. JJ Childers, DDS, Ltd." or something similar.

When your name has been approved for use by the state, you need to make sure that it is not registered as a federal trademark on the Principal Register in Washington D.C. If any similarity exists, a dispute may arise, and you may have to prove that you have a prior right to the use of the name. The Secretary of State's office can help you with that procedure.

After incorporating, your Nevada Corporation must be maintained by paying the $85 annual fee and filing the annual list of officers and directors. If your corporation fails to follow this procedure and is between 60 and 270 days late in filing, it lapses into a "delinquent status."

Delinquent corporations can be brought current any time during this period by paying an additional $15 fee. The Secretary of State is only required to notify the corporation's resident agent, and only in writing, of any delinquency or revocation of a corporate charter. Typically then, the agent contacts the directors, officers, or shareholders to get back into compliance. But a good agent should never let a delinquency occur in the first place. This points out the need for a good resident agent for your corporation.

If, for whatever reason, the corporation has not been brought into compliance within nine months, the corporate charter will be revoked by the state. A corporation that has been revoked may be reinstated any time within five years, by paying all of the fees that would have applied during the period of revocation plus a $50 penalty.

The big problem with delinquency is that once your corporation has been revoked, your corporate name is no longer reserved by the Secretary of State and someone else can incorporate using the same name you were using. And of course, any legal action taken against you during the period of revocation falls outside the protection of your corporate veil. That's *not* a good thing to have happen, especially since the two things required to stay in good standing are so easy to file. There is no reason to go through the entire process of incorporating only to lose your protection this way.

The Secretary of State will issue you a "Certificate of Good Standing" for your corporation when it is current in its filings and fees. This certificate costs $15, and validates that your corporation was in good standing as of the date the certificate was issued. When you qualify your Nevada Corporation to do business in another state, you will be required to provide a Certificate of Good Standing. Banks also require such certification for various reasons, most notably when a corporation is applying for credit or loans.

Like many states, Nevada has adopted the Small Corporate Offering Registration Form, (SCOR Form U-7) which allows a business to develop capital through a public offering of up to $1 million every 12 months. The SCOR program was developed by the North American Securities Administrators Association (NASAA) in cooperation with the Securities and Exchange Commission and the American Bar Association, and contemplates an exemption from federal registration by virtue of Rule 504 of Regulation D of the federal securities code.

This program promotes easy access to public capital at a reduced cost to help new corporations get off the ground. The most popular aspect of the program is the use of a simplified form with a question and answer format that permits an officer of a corporation to fill in the blanks, file it with a state securities administration, and upon approval, use it as a disclosure document in a public offering.

One of the best features of SCOR is a requirement that all shares be sold for a minimum of $5 per share. This avoids the pitfalls of "penny stock" offerings for potential investors, and helps keep the program credible. A SCOR offering is also considerably less expensive than a regular initial private offering (IPO), and your corporation doesn't need expensive underwriters or mounds of paperwork.

SCOR filings may be easier than normal registered stock offerings, but they are no piece of cake either. It can be a daunting task to prepare all the necessary forms and documents, get the state's approval, sell the stock, and then deal with all those additional investors. These offerings can take up to six months to accomplish, so it's not something you want to consider lightly.

SUMMARY

The laws of the state of Nevada have provided a unique opportunity for those wishing to become invisible. In today's legal climate, privacy and confidentiality in your business and personal life have become more than just a desired benefit but an absolute necessity. The invisibility potential offered in Nevada enables people to protect their assets, protect themselves, but most importantly, to protect their families.

V NEVADA CORPORATIONS OUTSIDE NEVADA

> *"The biggest corporation, like the humblest private citizen, must be held to strict compliance with the will of the people."*
>
> THEODORE ROOSEVELT

Now that you have an overview of the advantages of incorporating in the state of Nevada, you need to get a feel for what your Nevada Corporation can do for you *outside* the state. To many businesses, it is the essence of incorporation in Nevada—being able to carry that favorable Nevada "climate" with them wherever they do business.

In that regard, Teddy Roosevelt was right on target with his notion that corporations have to be held in compliance with the law, no matter where they operate. The big question then becomes, "Which laws apply?" In this chapter, we will discuss how laws in various states and even foreign countries apply to your Nevada Corporation's business practices.

The first thing we need to talk about is the concept of incorporating in *international* corporate havens. The Cayman Islands, the Bahamas,

109

Panama, Gibraltar, and a dozen other places have been promoted for viable offshore strategies as a method of protecting assets and eliminating taxes. These places all observe strict secrecy laws when it comes to business information and money transactions, thus creating a favorable tax climate for companies that do business in their jurisdictions.

There can be tremendous advantages realized by using offshore corporations, as long as you don't mind the risks associated with such operations. But it is neither as easy nor inexpensive to accomplish this as some promoters might have you believe. And in most cases, you are not as well protected from liabilities and taxes offshore as you might be in Nevada.

Because of the risks and a myriad of technical problems inherent with operating an offshore corporation, it is probably a good idea to stay away from them *unless* and *until* you become engaged in international trade on a fairly large scale. Without such international trade, the use of an offshore corporation can, to the agencies that monitor such things, constitute a sham and open you up to all kinds of legal problems. If you do not fully understand what it means to set up an entity offshore, and what all is involved, it can cause you a lot of trouble. When it comes down to this type of situation, it's a lot easier to *stay* out of trouble than to *get* out of trouble.

Here are some of the pitfalls of offshore dealings:

1. A foreign corporation that is more than 50% owned by a U.S. citizen, resident, corporation, partnership, estate or trust is called a Controlled Foreign Corporation (CFC). U.S. shareholders of CFCs are taxed on their pro rata share of the corporation's undistributed earnings for that year. That assumes, of course, that the CFC *will* be reporting properly to the IRS and other agencies.

2. Foreign corporations are taxed at a 30% flat rate on any income, without any deduction, that has a U.S. source, and is not "effectively connected" with a U.S. business. This includes rents, interest, dividends, salaries, wages, compensation, premiums, annuities, remuneration, emoluments and other fixed or determinable annual or

periodical gains; gains from lump-sum distributions from qualified employee plans, profits and income, gains on sale or exchange of patents, copyrights, and the like, certain types of gambling winnings, or gains from the disposal of timber, coal, or iron ore.

3. The IRS requires disclosure of any U.S. taxpayer who owns a controlling interest in a foreign corporation, or who can sign on a foreign bank account. Failure to disclose such interest constitutes tax fraud.

Even in the face of such reporting requirements and penalties, people continue to operate offshore corporations in a manner that borders on tax fraud all the time without ever getting caught. The IRS knows who they are and where they are and will eventually catch up to them.

My advice is: don't go betting your freedom and financial future solely on the secrecy laws of the country in which you're incorporated, unless that country is the good old U.S.A. Foreign laws are too often changed, bent, or broken. Foreign officials are too easily bought or intimidated. The bottom line is, if you are *not* a citizen of these little countries, they are not going to go out on a limb to protect you or your business, unless it's in their best interest to do so. The most important thing that you need to understand is that offshore entities are typically not the answer for most people.

So, does this advice mean that you should restrict your business horizons to just one local area? No, on the contrary. Doing business across state lines creates interstate commerce, which is a healthy and positive thing for the whole business community. For corporations, it is the lifeblood of new enterprise.

But, it is also the point at which things become a great deal more complicated for you and your corporate entity. This is especially true for businesses operating out of a tax haven state like Nevada. It is absolutely vital that you and your corporate officers understand certain principles of operating interstate in order to avoid creating more problems than is necessary. Let's take a look at some of those problems and the solutions.

WHAT IS A FOREIGN CORPORATION?

Corporations are "domestic" to the state where they are formed and "foreign" to all other states. "Citizenship" rights for corporations are not immediately transferable from the states where they are formed. For example, if you have an Arizona corporation and try to conduct business in California, your Arizona operation, as a corporate "citizen" of Arizona, becomes foreign to California as soon as your business efforts cross the California state line.

In much the same way as the countries in South America are foreign to this country, corporations are foreign to states other than where they were formed, even though they may conduct business there every day. Citizens of Mexico do not lose their Mexican citizenship just by visiting Texas, but they have to obey the laws of Texas when they visit there. A Texas corporation has to perform similarly when "visiting" in another state to do business.

Now, I don't want you to get confused about what constitutes a foreign corporation. Corporations formed in foreign countries are generally referred to as "offshore" corporations (as you've already learned), while domestic corporations together with foreign corporations, are collectively called "onshore" corporations. Mexican and Canadian corporations, for example, are considered "offshore," even though the United States shares borders and coastlines with them.

Don't make the false assumption that a domestic corporation is any corporation formed in the United States, and that foreign corporations only come from foreign countries. The key point for this discussion is, *foreign corporations* have nothing to do with other countries, and offshore corporations have nothing to do with shores.

Wherever you form your corporation, the state in which you form it has the right to tax the corporation on activity conducted within that state. If your corporation's income comes from business activity or property owned in another state or states, those states can also claim a portion of your corporation's income for tax purposes.

If your corporation is to be subject to taxes in another state, that state must establish sufficient connection or "nexus" with your corporation's business activity. The term nexus is usually defined as the degree of business activity that has to be present before any taxing jurisdiction has a right to impose a tax on the corporation's income.

Typically, corporations establish sufficient nexus whenever they derive income from sources within a state, own or lease property in a state, have employees in a state, or have any kind of capital or property located within a state. The criteria for establishing a nexus are entirely dependent upon a given set of state laws, which specifically define the nexus requirements in that state.

These laws are subject to federal limitations on a state's right to impose income tax on foreign corporations. Such limitations prevent the states from taxing or regulating interstate commerce when the only connection with another state is the solicitation of orders (which is defined by each state) for sales of tangible personal property that are sent outside the state for approval or rejection and, if approved, are filled and shipped by the business from a point outside the state.

Under this law, only the sale of "tangible personal property" is immune from taxation. Rentals, leases, and other dispositions of tangible personal property are not protected from taxation. Nor are sales, leases, rentals, et cetera of real property or intangible property protected. States may or may not tax this kind of unprotected activity, depending upon the individual state's statutes. This highlights the importance of seeking assistance from a good tax professional regarding your state's laws and how you will be treated.

Aside from these minimal federal regulations, states are pretty much free to regulate intrastate commerce any way they see fit. So unless a foreign corporation is engaged solely in interstate or foreign commerce, it must comply with the laws of its host state relating to the conduct of business in that state by foreign corporations, including those related to qualification or registration.

For this reason, many people adopt a specific corporate operating plan to separate their corporate activities from undesirable states. That just makes good sense. Those same people usually go a step further and create nexus in a good corporate haven, like Nevada. They do this by maintaining bank accounts in a desired jurisdiction, setting up a corporate office and telephone, and by obtaining all the appropriate business licenses for that area.

Once all the basic requirements for establishing a business in a state are arranged, it then becomes a matter of action as to whether a business activity is exempted from taxation in that particular state or not. In Nevada, a foreign corporation would not normally be found engaged in intrastate commerce for qualification purposes if it "conducts a single, isolated transaction, which is not done in the course of a number of similar transactions."

That leaves a huge window of opportunity for some businesses, and clearly defines taxation criteria for others, depending upon their business activities. You could, for example, provide your sales representatives in another state with an office *allowance* instead of an actual physical location, thus avoiding the creation of a potential tax nexus. The key is to have options in the way that you conduct your affairs.

CAN I USE A NEVADA CORPORATION IF I LIVE OUTSIDE NEVADA?

Yes, you can use your Nevada Corporation to conduct business across the country or around the world if you choose to do so. Today's teeming global business environment even encourages corporations to conduct business in states or countries other than where they were formed. Truly successful companies are almost forced to, in fact. At the same time, it would be horribly detrimental to your business if you were limited to just one area.

But how does your corporation go about doing that, since most jurisdictions will consider it a foreign corporation? The answer is, your corporation just has to "qualify to do business" in each jurisdiction where it intends to conduct business. Your corporation does not lose one bit of its native corporate protection just because it engages in business activity outside of Nevada. However, the business you conduct in another state has to conform to and operate under the laws of that state.

Qualification in another jurisdiction makes your corporation subject to all the reporting, taxes, and other fees that the state chooses to require of its own corporations. In some states, those requirements are quite extensive.

If you engage in business within a state, whether it's voluntary or not, and you do not go through the state's qualification processes, then you will be considered a kind of "illegal alien" corporation. When you are eventually caught, there will be severe consequences. Make no mistake, with all the computers and information sharing devices used today, you almost certainly *will* get caught sooner or later. Getting caught can then lead to penalties, back taxes and fairly stiff interest charges on money owed.

In addition, should your corporation fail to qualify to do business in another state, that state can find the officers and directors of your corporation *personally* liable for performance on corporate contracts. In some states, you can even be subject to fines or imprisonment, if you knowingly transact business on behalf of an unqualified corporation. States with these kinds of statutes include *Arkansas, California, Colorado, Delaware, Hawaii, Indiana, Kentucky, Louisiana, Maryland, Ohio, Oklahoma, Oregon, Virginia, and Washington.*

In their quest for more and more tax revenue from companies, most of these states (and others) engage in frequent investigations to identify companies that are not properly qualified to conduct business in that state. This can include such drastic measures as sending a team of investigators from building to building to make a list of tenants doing business there. That list is then checked against tax records to insure that all of the tenants are registered to do business and current with their taxes and fees.

Some states use property tax rolls, business directories, licensing information, motor vehicle registrations, and other forms of information exchange programs with sister states or the Internal Revenue Service to identify "alien" corporations. The names and addresses of employees covered by state unemployment and worker's compensation insurance, licensing data, highway use tax records, and even sales tax information can be exchanged in these state-to-state and federal information sharing programs. In short, the prospect for getting caught is just too great to make it worthwhile to even consider *not* qualifying.

So what *does* it take to avoid any problems? Most states will require the following information to qualify as a foreign corporation:

1. The name of the corporation,
2. An original certificate of Good Standing from state of origin,
3. The address of its principal executive office,
4. The address of its principal office within that state,
5. Name and address of its Resident Agent,
6. A Certificate of Acceptance signed by the Resident Agent,
7. All requisite fees,
8. A current list of officers,
9. In some states, either a full or partial list of stockholders, and
10. Certified copies of the Articles of Incorporation, including the most current amendment showing the total authorized number of shares, the par value of each share, and the number of shares not issued.

As long as you have all 10 of those items filed with a state, you shouldn't have too many problems doing business there. However, every state in the union has some version of what are called "long-arm" statutes that make it easier for each state's citizens to sue an out-of-state (foreign) corporation.

You need to be particularly aware of your corporation's out-of-state dealings, even if your business is conducted primarily through interstate commerce *and* you are in full compliance with qualifications where needed. There have been cases where insurance companies have been sued through a long-arm statute because they mistakenly issued *one* policy in a state. The typical long-arm statute provides for suing an out-of-state corporation for any civil wrong committed within the state, or those corporations that make contracts to be performed in whole or in part within the state.

It is also possible for long-arm statutes to be used in some jurisdictions to place judgments against foreign corporations. If your company has no resident agent or is not otherwise qualified to do business in a particular state, you can be sued and have a judgment slapped on you without ever receiving notice of the suit, since there is no place for the state to serve process on your company. Default judgments are not that uncommon in such cases. Obviously, this is something which you must be aware of.

Forty-five states now have "reciprocal tax collection" statutes in place which make foreign corporations liable for state taxes incurred in outside jurisdictions. Nevada is one of the few states that does *not* have this kind of a statute, even though they have allowed such cases to be heard in their jurisdiction.

Where these statutes do exist, a state that determines that a foreign corporation owes a tax liability may go into the courts of that corporation's *home* state to sue and attempt to collect on their claim. The courts in the corporation's home state are required to hear the case even though it involves taxes imposed by another jurisdiction.

Keep in mind, also, that when you qualify your corporation in other states, you will generally lose some of the protection your corporate veil provides for you in Nevada. For instance, a Nevada Corporation is not required to list its stockholders with the Secretary of State, but when you attempt to qualify in another state, your list of stockholders may become public record if that state's laws require such a list.

A key feature in many qualification requirements is how each state defines "transacting business." Most states define that feature in the broadest of terms, and then provide exceptions to their specific rules. It's quite possible that the nature of the business you want to conduct in a given state will automatically require your corporation to be qualified. If so, file the necessary papers and stay in compliance.

It's also possible that by using some creative strategies (more on this later) you will be able to structure your corporation's business so that it doesn't have to be qualified in a state, and is therefore not subject to the taxation and/or reporting requirements *in* that state. However, don't try shooting from the hip on this, people. If you're *not* familiar with the exemptions, go ahead and qualify your corporation anyway. It's just good business to avoid any problems with outside jurisdictions.

That's especially true in California, which has probably the most refined and scrutinized Corporation Code of any jurisdiction in the whole country. California's court systems are loaded with case laws on just about every conceivable corporate situation, including the infamous "transacting business" concept. Many states have copied from these statutes or adopted entire sections for their own use, so let's focus on California's definition as a good working example.

In California, these provisions are found in Chapter 191 of the Corporation Code. Under those statutes, you are defined to be "transacting business" by having entered into "repeated and successive" transactions of business in that state. In the broadest sense then, you have established a corporate nexus in California by doing some kind of business on a repetitive basis, even if it's just selling lemonade on the street corner.

As I said though, there are exemptions which allow a foreign corporation to be considered as *not* transacting business in that state. For example, if you incorporate in Nevada to take advantage of its corporate haven and you transact business regularly in California, here are some of the things you can do within California's borders *without* having to qualify. In other words, this list contains activities that are exempted from establishing a sufficient tax nexus:

1. Your corporation owns or purchases real property in California,
2. Your corporation has a California bank account,

3. A subsidiary of your corporation is conducting business there,
4. Your corporation conducts an isolated transaction in California within a period of six months without repeated transactions of like nature,
5. Your corporation conducts its business in California through use of independent contractors,
6. Your corporation holds board or stockholder meetings in the state,
7. Your corporation is involved in an administrative or legal action in the state,
8. Your corporation is involved in loan-connected activity in the state, but maintains *no* office there, or
9. Your corporation maintains transfer agents or the like in the state for the sale of corporate securities.

By understanding the formalities involved with maintaining a Nevada Corporation in a state outside of Nevada, you are much better situated to operate your business more effectively and safely. The next point you need to understand is the tax treatment of these corporations outside of Nevada.

HOW IS THE CORPORATION TAXED OUTSIDE NEVADA?

One of the best reasons for incorporating in a haven like Nevada is to establish a business structure from the outset that helps reduce or eliminate state corporate taxes. This is the number one strategy promoted by many of the companies that advertise incorporating services in Nevada.

What we are talking about here is a technique known in the business world as "upstreaming." This term is generally applied to businesses that allow their company profits to legally accumulate in jurisdictions where various tax burdens are either reduced or eliminated altogether. This practice is most common in international operations where firms conduct business in a number of countries, each having their own distinct tax laws and regulations. But it is an equally effective strategy for corporations operating domestically as well, if done properly.

The practice of upstreaming income has become a commonly recognized and supported concept by governments all over the world. It is promoted most often under the umbrella of governmental economic development efforts.

Governments know that many corporations will jump at the chance to reduce costs and increase profits by avoiding taxes any way they can. Jurisdictions that aggressively recruit new business routinely provide tax breaks and other kinds of tax incentives. This is especially true for the giant corporations. They implement this technique all the time by structuring their business activity to take advantage of the different taxing entities wherever they find them.

Nevada has become the standard bearer for providing the same kind of favorable taxation of entities in the United States. It has created one of the most aggressive economic development policies of any state in the union to attract new business. The tax structure of the state, in and of itself, provides tremendous incentives for companies to relocate and that is over and above all the other protective concepts built into Nevada Corporation law. When companies come to Nevada, they not only get favorable tax treatment, but lots of other benefits as well. With benefits come jobs and economic growth.

It's no surprise then, that many companies seek to incorporate in Nevada to take advantage of the favorable corporate climate. What is surprising though, is that a lot of these companies actually reside in and conduct their primary business in another state.

So why do they want to establish whole new corporate operations in Nevada if they are already operating successfully elsewhere? In most cases, it's because their business activities *are* so successful in these other states that tax considerations alone are significant enough to make such a strategy worth considering.

Remember the figures you learned earlier about state corporate tax rates? They can be as low as 1%, all the way up to over 12% of profits. That's a lot of money to give up every year just because your business is located on the wrong side of a state line.

But isn't it expensive to move all of your employees and offices and vehicles and such from one state to another, just to save on taxes? Yes, it is. In most cases, in fact, it is prohibitively expensive to *physically* move all of your business operations to another state.

So let's take a different approach to the same problem. Let's look at this the way a successful millionaire business person would look at it. I think you will again see that by following the methods millionaires use, your business can benefit tremendously.

For a moment I want you to assume the role of a moderately successful business owner who operates a small manufacturing company in San Bernardino, California. Now, you already know all about the notorious California regulatory environment, both from the standpoint of manufacturing and taxation. Your company exists as a California corporation, and has been subject to its state corporate tax rates of almost 10% for several years.

You've just returned home from attending one of my Nevada Corporation seminars, where your eyes were opened to a whole new way of thinking about taxation and corporate law. You had already considered incorporating your business in Nevada a year before, but decided that taking that step would have been prohibitively expensive. Why? Because all of your business activity is based in California with a prominent location at a California address.

You employ a lot of people, all of whom are California taxpayers. You've had to collect and pay California personal income taxes for those people, and as a result, cannot possibly be considered exempt from California taxation. In short, you have established every facet required of a corporate nexus in California. That, in your mind, had precluded any further consideration of Nevada's delightful corporate climate for your business operations.

After all, a Nevada Corporation would simply be forced to "qualify to do business" in California, and thus be subject to the same heavy tax burden and same corporate regulations you were already laboring under, right? Besides all of that, you assume that the annual cost of maintaining a Nevada Corporation in California would be just as expensive or more so than a domestic corporation. So, why go the Nevada route?

Let's say the material you brought back from my Nevada Corporation seminar is reviewed by you and your accountant and you both learn some rather interesting things. First and foremost, you learn that California's exemptions for qualifying a foreign corporation might permit *some* aspects of your operations performed by a Nevada Corporation (using the proper methods) to be *exempted* from California taxation.

You also learn that certain kinds of Nevada Corporations can operate in another state without having to qualify as a foreign corporation, simply because of the nature of the business. And, like many people who attend my Nevada Corporation seminars, you learn that the cost of filing a Nevada Corporation is not nearly as expensive as you thought it would be, particularly when compared to the potential tax savings that might result.

The really big revelation though, was that like most business people, you and your accountant had never really thought about converting *parts* of your business into separate entities to save on taxes. All of your corporate operations are more or less lumped under one corporate umbrella, with one set of managers and one bottom line, and that's not something you are particularly anxious to change. Or are you?

"Why change something that's working just fine?" you ask. Or, to put it another way, "If it ain't broke, don't *fix* it!" But that's not how millionaires think, is it? A millionaire would say, "Hey, it's working well, but there's a way to make it work even better, and I've got a strategy to accomplish that."

Let's suppose then, that you and your accountant decide to form not just one, but several Nevada Corporations to implement this new strategy. You could for example, partially finance your manufacturing company's research and development through a private Nevada financing company. The Nevada Corporation could lend money to fund new product development in increments over a number of years. The loan could be secured by a deed of trust on your company's California real estate, and the California company could then make regular interest payments to the Nevada Corporation.

Your financing on this part of the new strategy could be set up any number of ways, but let's suppose that the loan is structured as an interest-only package for 10 years. On paper, your manufacturing company is fortunate to get this kind of "back-end loaded" financing package at all, due to its existing debt load, so it's willing to pay a higher interest rate than a more conventional loan might have required from a traditional lender in California.

The difference in interest rates you will pay is offset by the Nevada Corporation not having to pay state income taxes on the proceeds of the loan. Those proceeds ultimately affect the bottom line for your whole corporate conglomerate.

Are you beginning to get the picture? Are you beginning to see how a millionaire would approach this problem? Before we get back to our hypothetical corporation let's look at two other major advantages you have just gained for yourself by incorporating in Nevada.

The first thing is insulation from lawsuits. You are now beginning to operate as a "secret millionaire." Let's take a look. The more successful your business becomes, the more liability you incur from such things as lawsuits and judgments. However, if your primary business concern is mortgaged or indebted up to its ears, that may not be such a big potential problem for you.

Judgment attorneys are likely to check to see what your California corporation's net worth is before accepting a case against you. If most of your assets there are already pledged for existing debt in Nevada, a smart attorney will look elsewhere for business. That is especially true when they learn how Nevada corporate laws work.

That's because they want to be paid for their services, and paid well. Contingency cases are a gamble under the best of circumstances, since the lawyers only get paid if they win the case or it is settled favorably out of court. Attorneys know that if they are pursuing a corporation with "deep pockets" their odds of getting paid go way up.

If your pockets don't appear to be so deep, sharp attorneys may determine that it's in their own best interest to require their potential client (who wants to sue you) to pay a retainer in advance and hourly fees thereafter. And believe me, nothing goes further to eliminate frivolous lawsuits from the outset than those $200 per hour fees quoted up front.

The people most often targeted by such frivolous lawsuits are medical professionals, contractors, large employers, manufacturers, and attorneys. There are two reasons these people get sued the most. Professional people are automatically perceived to have money or other assets and/or they have lucrative insurance policies. If, on paper, you have neither of these, you just don't qualify as a big enough "fat cat" to target for a contingency fee basis lawsuit.

Let's say for argument's sake that you do, somehow, get involved in a legal dispute resulting from your California business activities. First off, your adversaries will know nothing about your Nevada corporate holdings, which will instantly reduce the likelihood of litigation. Even if the circumstances suggest a fraudulent conveyance of assets or some kind of a sham, and it can be proven that you were somehow connected, the suing attorney will only find out *then* that your Nevada assets exist. Most likely, you would then be sued in Nevada as well as California, and a judge would have to decide how the dispute is handled from there.

Are you worried yet? Probably not, because the primary advantage to incorporating in Nevada is that the reporting and disclosure requirements are so minimal. While the officers and directors are a matter of public record for your Nevada holdings, the shareholders are not. As a result, it can be extremely difficult to discover who the real owners are.

Your legal adversaries might get as far as the corporate resident agents in Nevada. But, when asked for the actual stock ledgers, those agents can report that their sets of books are all kept by different attorneys (with attorney/client privilege, of course), in lock boxes from New Zealand to Newfoundland. Resident agents can be the source of all kinds of useless information in cases like this. And it's all perfectly legal. Nevada corporate law provides you with an almost inviolable personal and financial fortress for your assets.

Okay, now that you've been sued and survived, let's go back to your hypothetical situation and take it a few steps further. The in-house marketing department you have been using to make media buys, produce your promotional materials, and oversee advertising has always been something of a break-even proposition (at best) in your corporation.

What if it can switch to using a Nevada advertising agency to provide all those services? The ad agency might be able to purchase printing and advertising at a significant savings over what the California company had been paying, and in the process, allow you to reduce some overhead (staff) in your in-house marketing group.

That's good news for you, but bad news for the people who are terminated as a result, right? No, on the contrary, nobody loses in this arrangement. Those people who were working in-house could very easily decide to become independent contractors with a particular Nevada advertising agency which just happened to have a contract with their former employer. Those people, then, being independent, can now work out of their homes, since they are no longer salaried employees of your California corporation.

Everybody wins, because instead of being paid a salary, they are paid straight commission, based on what your California company spends each month on its advertising. These people can also develop potential new clients for their ad agency in Nevada, since they are independent contractors.

Who knows? They might even sign up a Nevada Corporation that you could refer to them, which provides financing for some California manufacturing and development companies. If this sounds too complicated, it is in reality not all that difficult to arrange. Remember, with Nevada Corporations, a substantial portion of what you are doing with your business is nobody's business but *yours*!

This is getting interesting, isn't it? You've gone from a simple California corporation to a corporate giant on paper, with ad agencies, finance companies, and independent contractors working for you in two states. It gets even better.

Your California corporation has decided, since Nevada seems to be such a good place to do business, that your purchasing department is going to make a few changes also. Your purchasing managers look for and find a new equipment wholesaler in Nevada that is tailor made to fill all your equipment needs. In fact, this Nevada supplier carries almost every conceivable item the manufacturing branch of your business needs, including computers, desks, bathroom fixtures, office supplies, chemicals, parts, and conveyers. The items cost a bit more because of freight and handling charges, but the ease of purchasing such a wide array of items from a single source more than offsets the higher costs.

Now, you're probably saying this is all too good to be true. Believe me, it's not! This is how real business is done. This is how successful people think. This is how millionaires make and *keep* their millions. But what about taxes in all this? Have we really accomplished the primary aim of cutting or eliminating those nasty state taxes? Let's talk about this more fully.

How can i eliminate state income taxes?

By incorporating in Nevada, there is virtually no outside evidence of any connections in the ownership of all these businesses. Nobody knows who really owns any of these Nevada Corporations. They all have separate officers and directors, separate filings and separate agents. On paper (what little paper there is) these companies may not be connected at all. The only similarity is that each of these Nevada Corporations has become extremely profitable while paying no state corporate taxes at all.

But what about your California operation? It has borrowed money, invested in new equipment, contracted new outside sources for advertising, and now, it is struggling to make monthly payments on all that debt. The Nevada equipment supplier has secured its part of the debt through a series of UCC filings which give it first options to seize all equipment and inventory in the event of some catastrophic financial occurrence in your California corporation.

Oh, and what about the finance company note, which is being paid back over a long period of time? It is secured by a deed of trust on the real estate, remember? And the debt load that note requires is leaving very little profit for the California business. Because the California company is less profitable now, it pays state corporate income taxes that are considerably reduced from what it had been paying in the past. At some point, the company might even pay *no* taxes if its profits continue to erode. That would be a real shame for California, wouldn't it? But *you* will be smiling all the way to the bank.

Make no mistake, people. This kind of corporate strategy is not for the faint of heart. To make it work for you requires quality legal and accounting knowledge. You will learn most of the nuts and bolts in this book, but my advice is to seek professional help before you implement any of the action. Whether it be a qualified attorney, accountant, or company specializing in the area of Nevada Corporations, it is crucial that you get the proper assistance.

Success with this strategy depends on meeting or exempting your Nevada businesses from specific statutory requirements. This, in turn, requires an attorney who is very familiar not only with Nevada law, but the laws of the state you want to operate out of as well.

Note, too, that a Nevada Corporation will help reduce your *state* taxes, but federal taxes must still be paid. Federal taxes apply unless you go a step further by setting up a tax-free jurisdiction outside the United States. That's an area where specialized knowledge is even more important than Nevada law. It's also an area I would advise you to avoid until your business warrants such a move and you are better equipped to handle all the intricacies of an offshore operation.

By that time, you will probably be a millionaire anyway, and know what most millionaires know. You will know how to get assets, and then protect them. You will know how to survive lawsuits and to protect yourself from liability. And you will know how to maintain your financial privacy. Most important, you will know how to use your Nevada Corporation as a tool for accomplishing *all* of the above.

VI SECRET MILLIONAIRE TAX PLANNING

"The marvel of all history is the patience with which men submit to burdens unnecessarily laid upon them by their governments."

WILLIAM BORAH

If you are tired of what Borah called the tax "burdens unnecessarily laid upon" you by government, then it's time to start doing something about it. This chapter will provide you with some good general guidelines of how corporate taxation really works. The next chapter, *Secret Millionaire Tax Magic*, will show you some of the strategies that most millionaires use to establish policies that make their corporate deductions work FOR them to help reduce their tax burdens. You can do the same thing by doing what successful people already know how to do.

Now, this book is by no means a complete reference guide to corporate taxation. That would (and actually does) take a book several dozen times larger than this one to detail the intricacies of tax law. Consult a qualified tax advisor if you need further information or help in structuring your tax strategies. For now, just concentrate on the basics, so that when you get ready to form your Nevada Corporation, you know what you can and can't do in regard to taxation.

HOW IS THE CORPORATION TAXED?

Okay, so what determines your corporate taxation? Corporate taxable income for most corporations is defined as gross income minus any deductions allowed to corporations. There are more tax deductions available to corporations than to any other form of business. At most income levels, corporations have favorable tax treatment over every other tax category (personal, married, et cetera).

Corporate income includes gross profit from sales, all rents and royalties, all interest and dividends, and all gains and losses. Capital contributions, however, are not part of income. Once we understand what is considered income to the corporation, we must delve a bit further into how that income is taxed.

You must understand that corporate taxable income figures can be misleading when compared to individual taxable income. A corporation is allowed to take full deductions for many expenses that provide benefits to individuals involved with the corporation, while those same expenses are not deductible to sole proprietorships or partnerships. Deductions against corporate taxes can include such things as entertainment, life insurance premiums, 401(k) pensions and profit sharing plans, health or disability insurance, travel expenses, and various qualified personal expenses. We will go into those deductions in more detail in the next chapter.

A major advantage for corporations in paying federal taxes is that they may elect to adopt a fiscal year other than the calendar year. That can, and does, allow for some creative tax situations, especially in multiple corporation structures. In some situations, it is even possible to defer taxes for a significant period of time by using different corporations with different fiscal year-ends. This will be covered more fully later in this chapter.

Since corporations are treated separate and apart from their owners, they are also treated as separate taxpayers under federal income tax guidelines. If one corporation owns at least 80%

of the outstanding shares of another corporation, the income and losses of the two corporations may be combined for tax purposes as if they were a single corporation.

You've already learned that in the vast majority of states, *state* corporate income taxes are also collected. Such taxes are almost always applied against income determined to be "sourced" or earned within a particular state. For example, the use of a corporation from Nevada, which does not have a state corporate income tax, will not exempt that corporation from paying state corporate income taxes in California, if California's corporate and franchise tax laws define the income of the Nevada Corporation as having its taxable source *within* California's borders.

Conducting business inside another state can be very profitable on the one hand, but complicated on the other. If you will remember our example from the previous chapter, state taxes can be avoided, but only through using proper strategies that are both ethical and legal. By separating elements of your business that are considered "trade or business" by the appropriate state taxing authority from business that would not be considered "trade or business," you can eliminate much or all of a state's corporate tax burden. But you must do this carefully and within the confines of the law. Otherwise you can open yourself up to penalties, interest, and back taxes.

If that happens, you're in worse shape than when you started. I tell you that not to scare you but to explain the importance of doing things properly. If you ever have a question about your taxes, seek assistance from a qualified tax advisor. I have included a chapter devoted to finding this type of assistance later in the book.

Another important item to understand when discussing corporate taxation is corporate filing requirements as opposed to individuals. Corporations must file annual tax returns, either IRS Form 1120, U.S. Corporation Income Tax Return, or the short form 1120A. The return is due by the 15th day of the third month after the close of their tax year. So if the corporation uses a calendar year, its tax return is due every March 15.

A corporation is entitled to a six-month extension to file its tax return (using IRS Form 7004), until September 15 if you use a calendar year to report. If your corporation owes any corporate tax, it must be paid along with the extension filing to avoid penalty and interest charges. Corporations must also make quarterly estimated tax payments, similar to self-employed individuals, if the corporation will owe taxes.

In the next chapter, we will be outlining some of the phenomenal tax benefits available to corporations. For now, however, I believe that it is important to tackle some of the potential taxation pitfalls of corporations.

WHAT ARE THE POTENTIAL TAXATION PITFALLS OF CORPORATIONS?

Without a doubt, the biggest question I get from people when discussing corporations is: what about double taxation? I sometimes wonder if it is a legal requirement for accountants and financial advisors to try to talk people out of a corporation. I can tell by the way that the question is asked that someone has made the decision that this person does not need a corporation. The reason is primarily because of the scare tactics used regarding the issue of double taxation. Is double taxation an issue? Yes. Should it keep you from incorporating? *No!* To gain a better understanding, let's take a look at that issue.

DOUBLE TAXATION

The single largest problem with using a corporation is in dealing with the possibility of double taxation. What does double taxation mean? Basically, this occurs when the corporation generates income, then pays taxes on the taxable portion of the proceeds at the applicable corporate tax rate. Of course, the corporation can deduct necessary expenses, but if after salaries and expenses have been paid, the company makes a profit, another tax could be triggered. The size of that tax depends on what the corporation intends to do with those profits. If the corporation decides to keep its profits for new product development or some other legitimate reason, it will pay the appropriate corporate income taxes.

The problem of double taxation comes into play when the company declares a dividend for its shareholders. In that instance, the income gets taxed twice. First the income is taxed as corporate profits, then it is taxed again (a second time) as personal income to the shareholders. When this happens, the income from the dividends is subject to a shareholder's respective rate of taxation. What's worse, when a corporation declares a dividend to its stockholders, this amount is not deductible to the corporation as a business expense. Pretty bad deal, huh?

Dividends always mean double taxation. But what exactly are dividends? Before we get any deeper into the area of double taxation, let's discuss dividends in more detail.

WHAT ARE DIVIDENDS?

Dividends are the distribution of a corporation's profits to its shareholders. When corporations are formed for profitable purposes, the IRS expects to see them pay out their profits on a timely basis. The decision to distribute corporate profits is generally at the discretion of a corporation's Board of Directors.

Most corporations establish a formal dividend policy and record a resolution for that in the corporate record books. Regular dividend payments help to establish both the corporation's credit history and its credibility to creditors and the IRS.

It is not essential to enter a resolution to declare a dividend, but it is still a good idea in order to avoid problems later. The corporation must file an informational tax return and provide IRS Form 1099-DIV to each stockholder receiving a dividend over $10 during the year.

Dividends should only be paid when there is a genuine surplus of profits. Any dividends paid when there is no surplus can be declared illegal, particularly if such payments jeopardize the stability of the company. A dividend can be paid when there is no profit in the current year, provided there is a surplus from previous years. If the corporation has accumulated any deficits, those deficits must be erased before dividends can be paid.

When a dividend is declared illegal, the corporate officers responsible for it can be prosecuted for authorizing such payments. Penalties can range from fines to imprisonment, depending on the jurisdiction. If creditors can't be paid because of an illegal dividend, the officers can be held personally liable, and the dividends can be subject to forced repayment from the shareholders.

There are three basic types of dividends. They are:

1. *Cash dividends*: payments of money.
2. *Shares dividends*: distributions of additional shares of stock in that corporation (usually represented by a fractional share of stock already owned by the shareholder).
3. *Property dividends*: also known as "in kind" distributions, these can include distribution of real property, such as real estate, stock in another corporation, or inventory.

Now that you know the kinds of dividends, let's look at this double taxation problem some more. Besides being taxed on dividends at two levels, the other big problem with double taxation comes when you sell a business organized as a C corporation. The taxation works essentially the same way here as it does with dividends, only the tax bite and the number of dollars involved can be a whole lot bigger.

Let's say you set up a corporation and over a period of years you are very successful. Your goal then is to cash in on the business and retire. A major corporation approaches you about buying your business. With their offer, there's a hefty profit built in for you, that is, until your CPA points out that the corporation is going to pay taxes on a huge capital gain. You will have to pay taxes *again* on the same amount if you want to put any of the money in your pocket.

Fifty or sixty percent of the profits on the sale of the company will go just to pay the taxes on the sale. "That's disgusting!" you say. You are right. But that's how the tax laws work.

To illustrate the impact of this double taxation even more graphically, if your corporation earns $10 in taxable income, it will pay around $1.50 in federal corporate taxes, based on the minimum rate. That leaves the corporation with $8.50 after tax. If that $8.50 is then paid in salaries or dividends to you at the 28% rate, you're going to pay another $2.40 in taxes, leaving a paltry $6.10 out of the original $10.

The good news is that getting around double taxation is not difficult. Money paid to a nonactive shareholder as an independent contractor for services performed for the corporation is not considered a dividend. Be aware that there is a trade-off. You need to understand that the person performing these services and the corporation must pay both Social Security and Medicare taxes on the compensation paid to that shareholder. The bottom line here is that you must factor in the tax situations of both shareholders and the corporation in deciding whether to pay salaries or dividends. If you are in this situation, speak with your accountant and/or tax advisor for more information.

Because most profits are paid out as tax-deductible salaries and fringe benefits, most small corporations aren't concerned with corporate tax rates. But there are times when paying out all profits is not the best alternative. An example of this is when a business is planning to expand and needs cash to do so. Profits kept in the business are taxed at the initial tax rate of 15%, which is typically lower than the individual income tax rates of its owners. This can be a major advantage corporations have over all other types of businesses. This is not the case for businesses which are not incorporated.

An important consideration with corporations is that once the corporation reaches the $100,000 profit level, after paying salaries, benefits, and other deductible expenses, retaining earnings produces smaller tax savings. Corporate profits between $100,001 and $335,000 are hit with a tax surcharge of 5%. In essence, this effectively eliminates the benefits of the lower tax rates imposed initially.

When you operate as a corporation, you are now in the big leagues as far as your taxes are concerned. Corporate tax complexities can be absolutely mind-boggling. Now that we have dealt with the overall issue of double taxation, there are three other potential federal taxes that a corporation might be subject to:

1. Personal holding company tax,
2. The accumulated earnings tax, and
3. The corporate alternative minimum tax.

Let's take a look at these potential tax pitfalls one by one.

PERSONAL HOLDING COMPANY TAX

The IRS imposes a special penalty tax on corporations that are deemed to be nothing more than incorporated "pocket-books." This tax code section targets corporations that derive 60% or more of their income purely from investment sources, which are considered passive investment entities. An example of this type of income would be dividends and royalties. This "personal holding company" tax doesn't affect many small businesses which are *active operations*, rather than passive investment entities. For more information, see a tax advisor or if looking into the issue yourself, read IRC 541 and the following sections. Pay particular attention to the distinction between *active* and *passive*.

ACCUMULATED EARNINGS TAX

One great advantage of a corporation over other business entities is the ability to accumulate earnings to fund future growth. The corporation is taxed on these earnings, but the taxes are imposed at lower rates than if they were distributed to shareholders who then put the money back into the corporation. A potential problem arises if a corporation accumulates too much money. In that case, the corporation is subject to an "accumulated earnings" tax of 39.6%. The good side of this is that most small corporations need not worry about this tax as it doesn't take effect until the accumulated earnings of the corporation surpass $250,000 (IRC 531).

CORPORATE ALTERNATIVE MINIMUM TAX

Even if a corporation takes full advantage of all pertinent tax benefits, it still can't avoid taxes altogether. The corporation is subject to paying a minimum amount of tax, called the "corporate alternative minimum tax." The goal of the tax is basically to disallow some tax breaks. This is accomplished by requiring the corporation to pay a minimum amount of income taxes. To learn more about this particular tax arrangement, consult a tax professional. If you would like to study this more fully on your own, see IRC 55-58, Reg. 1.56-.58. Don't worry about this too much. Only a select few small corporations ever find themselves in this situation.

Now, I've pointed out some of the potential taxation pitfalls associated with the taxation of corporations so that you will be aware of these issues. In the next chapter, we will go through some of the amazing benefits offered to corporations. Don't fall into the trap of thinking that you don't need a corporation after hearing the disadvantages. As you will see, the advantages far outweigh any of the negatives.

Before we go on to the next chapter, it is important to take a look at some important procedures involved with corporate taxation, the bookkeeping and record keeping requirements.

WHAT TYPE OF BOOKKEEPING/RECORD KEEPING IS REQUIRED?

Far too often, business people mistakenly believe that if there is money in their business checking account at the end of the month, they must be doing well. Keeping good records is the only way to truly know if your business is making or losing money. An accurate bookkeeping system is also an essential part in preparing your federal and state income tax returns. Believe me, if you go through the year adhering to certain guidelines, things will be much, much easier come tax time, for you and your accountant.

Any tax accountant or tax preparer will tell you that it is essential to keep good records. As a matter of fact, this is so important that it specifically states in the tax code the need to keep "records appropriate to your trade or business" (IRC 6001). While the code doesn't require most records to be kept in any particular form, they do have to be accurate (Reg. 31.6001-1(a)).

Another great reason to keep really good records is to have a way of knowing whether changes need to be made in your operation. Operating without good records can not only be dangerous, but it can be costly as well. Perhaps the most important piece of advice I could possibly give you with regard to taxation is to take record keeping seriously. Record keeping must become part of your everyday business routine. That's probably nothing new to you, but what records are needed?

What kinds of records to keep

There are basically three major categories of business records which need to be kept. It is important to understand a little bit about these three categories. These three are as follows:

1. Income
2. Expenses
3. Capital expenditures

The first two categories are somewhat self-explanatory. The third category however, "capital expenditures", is a bit more ambiguous. So that you'll understand each of the categories better, we'll discuss all three.

Income records

The first category is income. Specifically, this refers to the fact that your business may take in money from various sources, depending on what line of business you are involved with. Your records should account for all gross income and also show the source of each item. An example of this would be for you to label the sources of that income, for instance, "sales" or "services." This is necessary because money you put into your business's bank account may not always be taxable income. A good example of this would be a loan to the business.

Keeping up with income can be done in several ways. Oftentimes, retail stores will use cash registers to produce register tapes or sales printouts. A number of businesses evidence income primarily from bank deposit records. If you do this, be sure to keep copies of all deposit slips listing the deposits into your business bank account, as well as the bank statements showing the deposits. Deposit slips should be kept as a way to indicate the form of the item received, whether it be in the form of cash, checks, or credit card payments. This becomes especially important since this is not always reflected on the bank statements.

Expense records

Chances are, you will have to spend a great deal of time to get your company to the point where it is making a lot of money. Once you finally do get to that point, your partner will want a large portion of it. Who is that partner? Uncle Sam. Sure, he didn't take any of the risks nor did he spend any time getting the business up and going. He still expects his share of the profits though. The good news is that most "ordinary and necessary" business expenses can be deducted against your gross income each year. Additionally, most asset purchases are deductible either over several years or during the year of purchase depending on their cost. There are special rules which outline how this all takes place and it requires special record keeping treatment.

Keeping good records of these expenses is essential. However, recording these expenses is only part of the job. You also need to keep some documentation as proof the expenditures were made. This documentation can take many forms such as receipts, invoices, credit charge slips, canceled checks or lease agreements. An easy and effective way to do this is to put paid bills and invoices into designated folders or envelopes according to expense categories.

Two standard ways to document business expenses are by keeping canceled checks and paid receipts. If you don't have the actual canceled checks or charge slips, the IRS will also accept statements from financial institutions showing check clearing or electronic funds transfers. This covers credit card statements and banks that do not return canceled checks. The financial institution's statement must show the date, name of the payee and amount of expense in order to satisfy an IRS auditor. In the event that the auditor is dissatisfied with the information listed on the statement for some reason, you may have to order copies of the checks from the bank. Although there may be a slight charge for this in many instances, it can be money well spent.

An important thing to keep in mind is that proof of payment in and of itself does not qualify you for a business expense deduction. In the event that you are audited, you will also need to verify that the expense was related to your business. This is fairly self-explanatory for many items, but not for others. Items that you are afraid might not look business-related to the IRS (travel, entertainment), it is a good idea to document those expenses at the time they are incurred. This can be done in a separate journal or on the receipt. The key is to explain the business purpose. Once again, when it comes to records, err on the side of keeping too many rather than keeping too few. The simple rule is, it is better to have it and not need it than to need it and not have it.

CAPITAL EXPENDITURES

For those expenditures which provide a benefit past the year you make the purchase, the item must be categorized as a business "asset." Good examples of this would be a computer, fax machine, copy machine, building, car or office furniture. These business assets must be documented in a separate manner from other expenses. They must also be recorded separately from other business expenses by your record system. It is a good idea to keep a separate file for each individual asset or category of assets acquired by your business. It is also advisable to show the date of purchase and the type of asset purchased. It wouldn't be a bad idea to also write a short explanation of how the asset is used in the business. Remember, the asset has to be related to your business in order to be deductible.

There is a separate procedure implemented for these business assets. The items must be deducted a bit differently than everyday operating expenses. Typically, you won't be able to deduct the entire cost in the year of purchase. For these assets, you will take "depreciation" deductions over a period of years. One important exception to this rule is that for assets up to $19,000, these may be written off in the year of purchase under a special tax code provision, IRC 179. This is a great tax code section which you should be taking full advantage of. If you are not currently doing this, see a tax advisor for ways to implement this. When we cover this at the live seminars, it is always an eye-opener.

Standard records to keep

Speaking of the live seminars, one of the biggest questions which comes up with regard to record keeping is, which records need to be kept? If you have business assets, you must keep records for the IRS showing several different things. First, you will need to show a description of the asset, the date acquired, and how you acquired it. Generally, this information is evidenced by an invoice or receipt. It is important to note the kind of asset acquired. This is because the tax code has different rules for writing off different categories of assets.

Another record which should be kept is the date when you first started using the asset or the date it was placed in service. Typically, this will be as soon as you acquire it, but this is not always the case. It is a good idea to make a note of it and place it in your asset records. An additional item which needs to be kept is your tax basis in the equipment. This generally means the amount you paid for it. However, your tax basis could be larger than what you paid if you spent money on improvements or modifications. An example of this would be added memory to your computer's hard drive. There may also be a reduction to the tax basis. For instance, depreciation deductions may have been taken. Two final records which should be kept are the sales price of the asset when you dispose of it, and you should also document any costs associated in selling the asset.

Be sure to keep good records for your corporation. The primary focus of this book is on asset protection. You may be asking yourself: "Why so much attention to taxes?" The reason is that if you fail to operate as a corporation, you can lose your treatment as a corporation and hence, the benefits which result from that treatment. By maintaining your corporate tax status, you are solidifying your corporate status in general. The result is more asset protection.

The next question we need to answer here is one which comes up quite frequently when discussing taxes. This is a topic which applies to corporations but not to many other types of business entities. A good tax advisor can assist you immensely with this area, but you will need a little background before you get that far. The question deals with accounting year ends. This is a tax issue rather than asset protection. Let's take a look.

SHOULD MY CORPORATION HAVE A CALENDAR OR FISCAL YEAR END?

One of the great benefits of having a corporation is that it is separate and apart from its owners, not just for asset protection, but for tax purposes as well. Specifically, corporations can have a year end which is different from the year end for individuals. For individuals, the tax year is the same as the calendar year. It starts on January 1 and ends on December 31. For the most part, small businesses are generally required to use the calendar year. In most cases, it is because of the pass-through nature of the income for most entities.

Corporations, however, are able to use an alternative tax-reporting period. This is a separate year end called the "fiscal year." This is any one-year period that does not end on December 31. A business notifies the IRS of its accounting period by checking the appropriate box on its tax return form. Once the accounting period is chosen, it usually cannot be changed without written approval from the IRS. This leads to a lack of flexibility but also offers potential benefits in the form of tax deferral.

The majority of small businesses choose to use a calendar year as their tax year end. Some businesses are even required to by the IRS. Sole proprietors, partnerships, limited liability companies, S corporations and personal service corporations are required by the IRS to report on a calendar-year basis, unless they can convince the IRS they qualify for an exception. This is often difficult. To get permission, file Form 8716, *Election to Have a Tax Year Other Than a Required Tax Year.*

SHOULD MY CORPORATION HIRE A BOOKKEEPER?

In keeping the records for your small business, there are really only two good choices. The first choice is to learn to do it yourself. The second is to hire someone who truly knows how to do it. This can be a very difficult decision. If you're anything like me, you think that you can do just about anything if you put your mind to it. While this may be true, it generally makes little sense to spend your time doing something which you could pay someone to do it for, perhaps even much better than you could do it yourself.

Too many times people will make the mistake of trying to do the job themselves and they end up doing it badly. Other times, folks will make the decision to hire someone but they end up hiring the wrong person. Many small businesses can't afford someone to keep records when starting off, but once you are up and running, you should seriously consider obtaining some solid bookkeeping assistance. By hiring someone else to keep your records, this leaves you with time to more effectively utilize your business talents. In the end, this works out to be less expensive.

The most important thing is to be safe. I highly recommend you find and consult with a qualified tax professional. If you decide to keep up with the books yourself, at least have your tax advisor take a look at your system to make sure it is what you need. While this certainly costs a little more initially, I can assure you that you will be pleased when it comes time for filing tax returns. By the way, your tax accountant's fees will also be deductible expenses.

SUMMARY

One of the most important steps you could possibly take in forming your own business is to go through some tax planning. You need to develop an understanding of how your corporation will be taxed and the requirements for keeping the records. Hiring a good bookkeeper can be a crucial part of this overall process. Remember, the time and effort you spend in planning for your taxes can pay off sooner than you realize.

VII SECRET MILLIONAIRE TAX MAGIC

"There is nothing sinister in arranging one's affairs as to keep taxes as low as possible . . . for nobody owes any public duty to pay more than the law demands."

JUDGE LEARNED HAND

The modern income tax law was first introduced in 1913. Back then, only one person out of 271 was affected. The reason for this was that the vast majority of individuals didn't make enough money. Do you think that many of those people would have loved to have a tax problem? That may sound like a stupid question to some of you. Why on earth would anyone want a tax problem? Why? You need to understand that if these people had a tax problem it was because they were making more money. Do you understand that? Do you see why they may have prayed for a tax problem? If I ask the question a little differently, perhaps I'll get a little different answer. Do you suppose these people would have liked to make more money? The answer to that question is almost always yes.

In this country, we must pay taxes on our income. That is the case whether we operate as individuals, sole proprietorships, partnerships, or even as corporations. The key is to learn to handle these taxes in the best way possible. There are certain expenses which we all must pay. The trick is to use before-tax dollars on these items rather than after-tax dollars. Specifically, we need to find a way to deduct these items from our gross income. But what expenses are deductible? Let's get into this topic so that we can start reducing our tax bills.

WHAT IS DEDUCTIBLE TO MY CORPORATION?

I am not the type who feels that it is necessary to memorize all of the tax code sections, but I do believe that there are certain tax code provisions which are essential to your success. Section 162 of the IRC is one of those sections. Basically, it is the cornerstone for determining which business expenses are deductible. The section is so important to your overall success that I wanted to include the initial portion. Section 162 says:

> "Internal Revenue Code section 162 "Trade or business expenses."
>
> (a) In general. There shall be allowed as a deduction all the ordinary and necessary expenses paid or incurred during the taxable year in carrying on any trade or business, including
>
> (1) a reasonable allowance for salaries or other compensation for personal services actually rendered;
>
> (2) traveling expenses (including amounts expended for meals and lodging other than amounts which are lavish or extravagant under the circumstances) while away from home in the pursuit of a trade or business; and
>
> (3) rentals or other payments required to be made as a condition to the continued use or possession, for purposes of the trade or business, of property to which the taxpayer has not taken or is not taking title or in which he has no equity."

Many times, legitimate business expenses are quite obvious. In some cases, such as expenses associated with travelling, the IRS provides specific instructions for determining what is "ordinary and necessary." This is done through published income tax "regulations." These regulations are very important and as such, you should familiarize yourself with them or develop a relationship with a tax advisor who is familiar with them.

Nowhere does the tax code specifically define the terms "ordinary and necessary." Instead, federal courts have tried to determine what Congress intended with this language and have tried to apply it to a particular set of facts. "Ordinary" has been held by courts to mean "normal, common and accepted under the circumstances by the business community." "Necessary" means "appropriate and helpful." By looking at these two together, it appears that "ordinary and necessary" refers to the purpose for which an expense is made. For example, renting office space seems like one of the most ordinary and necessary expenses you could possibly incur in your business. However, it is neither ordinary or necessary if it is not actually used in running your business.

The term "ordinary and necessary" is really quite vague. Given this vagueness, it's not surprising that many businesspeople have tried to push things. Unfortunately, the IRS has pushed back. A compromise is sometimes reached, and sometimes the issue is even thrown into a court's lap. The court's determination then becomes a precedent for future decisions.

One way that people will try to push things a little too far is by paying exorbitant amounts for items so that they can receive an exorbitant tax deduction. The IRS knows that people don't intentionally overpay for anything. For this reason, amounts paid aren't usually questioned. However, auditors do sometimes object to expenditures they deem to be unreasonably large. While the tax code itself contains no limitation on what is considered too large of an expense, courts have ruled that it is inherent in IRC 162. Outrageous amounts fall outside of the "ordinary and necessary" parameters.

The biggest concern of the IRS when auditing business deductions is whether purely personal expenditures are being claimed as business. The IRS keeps a close eye on this since business people regularly try it. The good news is that you can often arrange your affairs legally in a way that lets you derive considerable personal benefit and enjoyment from business expenditures. The most important thing is to understand what you can and cannot do.

One of the best pieces of advice I could possibly give you is to be careful if you deal with relatives. The IRS will probably be suspicious about expenses paid to a family member, or to another business in which your relatives have an ownership interest. In tax code parlance, these are termed "related parties." An IRS auditor may suspect that profits are being taken out of your business for direct or indirect personal benefit under the auspices of business expenses when actually the person is merely trying to avoid taxes.

When studying tax information, it is important to note that tax rules cover not only what expenses can be deducted but also *when* they can be deducted. As discussed earlier, certain expenses are deductible in the year they are incurred, while others must be taken over a number of years.

The first category is called "current" expenses. Current expenses are generally everyday costs of keeping your business going, such as the rent and electricity bills. The tax rules for deducting current expenses are fairly straightforward; you subtract the amounts spent from your business's gross income in the year the expense was incurred.

The second category is "capitalized" expenditures. These expenditures are made to generate revenue in future years. These are "capitalized." What this means is that they become assets of the business. As these assets are used, their cost is attributed to the revenue they help earn. This is allows the business to more clearly account for its true profitability from year to year.

The tricky part is to know what is a current expense and what is a capital expense. Normal repair costs, such as fixing a broken copy machine or a door, can be deducted in the year incurred. The cost of making improvements to a business asset must be capitalized if the enhancement:

1. Adds to its value,
2. Appreciably lengthens the time you can use it, or
3. Adapts it to a different use.

"Improvements" are usually associated with real estate. Costs for items with a "useful life" of one year or longer cannot be deducted in the same way as current expenses. These costs are treated as investments in your business, and must be deducted over a number of years. The deduction is usually called *depreciation*. There are many rules for how different types of assets must be depreciated.

The tax code lays out limits on depreciation deductions. These limits cover how many future years a business must spread its depreciation deductions for asset purchases. It is important to note that all businesses, large and small, are affected by these provisions (IRC 167, 168, and 179).

A valuable tax break creating an exception to the long term write-off rules is found in IRC 179. A small business owner can write off in one year most types of its capital expenditures up to a grand total of $19,000. Businesses should take full advantage of this provision every year. This is what is oftentimes referred to as "asset expensing."

One thing which you must realize is that different items are treated differently. Some common and not-so-common business expenses have special rules that govern how they must be tax deducted. One of the most common refers to the deductibility of automobiles.

AUTOMOBILE EXPENSES

A common corporate perk for many small businesses has always been the use of a company car. In particular, outside sales people have come to expect this as part of their compensation package.

However, more and more companies are allowing employees to drive their own cars because they can eliminate a lot of internal paperwork and have less trouble with the IRS at tax time. The reason is, most employees use their company car for personal use, anyway, as well as their business purposes. Employers then have to keep track of all of the personal use and treat it as taxable income to the employee. That produces additional paperwork and a record keeping nightmare.

To eliminate much of that record keeping and the significant tax liability that results, a corporation can just *give* a car to an employee. That means that you can write off the cost of any car your Nevada Corporation gives to an employee, including yourself. Mileage accumulation is eliminated as a factor for tax reporting purposes as is the difference between business to personal mileage. Any employee personal use is just considered a compensation expense.

Then, by requiring employees to use their own vehicles and reimbursing them for their expenses, your corporation can reduce those annoying paperwork requirements even further. If you are planning to do this, your corporation should adopt a standard procedure requiring employees to submit expense account forms regularly which detail specific mileage usage on behalf of the business, either weekly or monthly.

The IRS treats such reimbursements as a wash. The corporation does not show the reimbursement as taxable income to its employees and employees are not required to keep or provide records of expenses on their tax returns. Any employee who requires additional reimbursement can attempt to deduct them on Form 2106, "Employee Business Expenses," and that money is treated as a miscellaneous itemized expense.

You may choose to set up a reimbursement plan for your corporation that is not based on the standard, so many cents-per-mile method. You could, for example, pay a flat rate to your employees that you have determined over time is a fair compensation for using their own vehicles for company business (including your own, of course). Or, you could combine a flat rate, say $250 a month, with a reduced per-mile rate. These plans require more record keeping on your part, but they also reduce the risk of having problems with the IRS down the road.

Now, since the use of a company owned car is considered a taxable fringe benefit, the value of the personal use is subject to federal income and state unemployment taxes. This requires your corporation to put a dollar amount on the value of the personal usage. There are a couple of ways to go about this.

You can consult the lease tables in IRS Publication 535 to learn the lease value of any vehicle. If your employees only use their cars part of the year, you can use the daily value listed in Publication 535, or a value can be prorated for any portion of the year. Using records submitted by the employee, you must then determine the percentage of time the employee drives the car on personal business.

Next, calculate the personal value of the car by multiplying the percentage of personal use by the annual lease value of the car. On a vehicle driven 10,000 miles per year, which an employee shows he uses 15% of the time on personal business, then 1,500 miles become personal miles. Assuming that a vehicle has an annual lease value of $3,600, 20% of that, or $720, is taxable income to the employee that drives it.

An employee can then be reimbursed for either the actual cost of gasoline or a standard 5.5¢ per mile. So, if the employee has been reimbursed $550 (10,000 miles x .055) for gas for the year, he would have to include that in his gross income, which he could offset with an itemized deduction for gas expenses.

The other method that your company can use is the standard mileage rate of $.28 per mile to figure the value of personal use on the vehicle. In the previous example, that 1,500 personal miles would be reported as $420 of taxable income.

It is advisable to seek the assistance of a qualified tax professional in determining exactly what type of method you should implement.

Your corporation will have several choices on how you withhold taxes on the taxable income an employee draws due to the use of a company car. You can either withhold using the flat 20% rate or adopt the normal withholding method for supplemental wages. Either way is fine, provided you are consistent.

Another option is to not withhold anything. But you must notify your employees before January 21 of a given tax year (or within 30 days of providing the car) so they have a chance to change their W-4 forms. You want them to be able to hold back additional withholding from their paychecks to cover any additional taxes. Your company will also be responsible for Social Security and unemployment taxes on the value of a company car for some employees in the higher income brackets.

One of the big tax savings for you and your corporation is the ability to purchase a new luxury car each year at a relatively small cost. For purposes of this example, let's say the vehicle you buy costs $40,000. The tax law considers the additional compensation that you have received to be equivalent to the interest you would have had to pay to your corporation on the loan for the car.

In other words, you are paying the interest on the loan with the extra compensation you are receiving. So, tax consequences become a wash. Although the compensation is still taxable, you get an offsetting deduction because the interest that you should be paying is deductible as long as the note doesn't exceed $100,000. Your corporation can also pay you 75% of the maximum allowed first year depreciation on the business use portion of the vehicle. That amounts to $1,995 in this example, which is tax free to you and deductible by your corporation.

Next year, you can then sell that $40,000 vehicle for, say, $34,000, and use the proceeds plus an additional $6,000 out of pocket to pay off the loan to your corporation. What then? Repeat the process, of course. This strategy can allow you to drive a new $40,000 car every year at a net cost to you of around $4,000 per year ($6,000 out of pocket minus the depreciation).

EDUCATION EXPENSES

One question which always comes up in the seminars is whether education expenses are deductible. The rule of thumb is that you can deduct education expenses if they are related to your current business, trade or occupation. For these expenses to be deductible, the tax code requires that an education expense must be either:

1. To maintain or improve skills required in your (present) employment, or
2. Required by your employer or as a legal requirement of your job or profession.

Let me add one caveat here. Education expenses that qualify you for a new job or business are not deductible under the tax code. This tax rule has been interpreted rather narrowly by the IRS and courts. For this reason, it is advisable to consult a tax advisor before you deduct these expenses.

TRAVEL EXPENSES

Travel expenses are those incurred by employees while traveling away from home, including their meals and lodging. The IRS makes a clear distinction between "travel" expenses and "transportation" expenses. Transportation expenses include only the actual costs of travel which are incurred in the conduct of business while the employee is *not* away from home. Meals and lodging are *not* included in such expenses.

For example, if you lived in Dallas, but were assigned to work in Denver, you couldn't deduct any of the expenses for traveling, meals or lodging in Denver since that is your *tax* home of record. Going home to Dallas over a weekend, in this case, would not be considered "for business purposes" by the IRS.

"Home" is clearly defined for travel purposes by the IRS as a taxpayer's place of business, employment station, or post of duty, no matter where the taxpayer actually lives. Corporate "travel" and "transportation" expenses are both deductible, but they must be separated for IRS reporting purposes.

So, what are deductible travel expenses? The following are considered to be normal and necessary travel deductions:

1. Any "common carrier" fares (air, bus, rail, boat, taxi, et cetera)
2. Baggage charges
3. Meals and lodging (either en route to or at the destination)
4. Rental or maintenance of an automobile
5. Reasonable cleaning and laundry expenses
6. Telephone, telegraph, computer, or fax expenses
7. Cost of transporting sample cases or display materials
8. Cost of display or conference rooms

9. Cost of maintaining and operating an airplane
10. Cost of secretarial help
11. Tips paid incident to any of the above expenses (within reason)
12. Other miscellaneous expenses related to travel

Full deductibility is allowed by the IRS for all travel expenses incurred while looking after income-producing property, including travel to consult with investment advisors and brokers. In most cases, stockholders are not allowed to deduct the cost of travel expenses to attend stockholder meetings of companies in which they own shares.

Travel costs incurred traveling out of the United States to establish new foreign markets for existing products may be deducted as long as such expenses are reasonable and necessary. Lavish and extravagant expenditures are not deductible. (Note what does *not* qualify under foreign travel below.)

Travel and transportation expenses incurred while looking for employment in the same line of work are fully deductible. However, any payments made by a prospective employer as inducement to accept their employment is considered income and must be reported.

There are several kinds of travel expenses that do *not* qualify as IRS deductible expenses. For example, if you travel away from home but do not stay overnight, the IRS has ruled that you cannot deduct meals and lodging. This ruling has even been upheld by the Supreme Court. So "per diem" payments you receive in such situations must be reported as income.

If you travel with your spouse, most costs for the spouse are not deductible unless you can establish that your spouse's presence served a bona fide business purpose. Deductions have been allowed by the IRS in situations where a taxpayer could prove that a spouse's presence was considered important for the company's public image.

If you are traveling in the U.S., and your trip consists of both business and personal pursuits, the IRS has ruled that you cannot deduct the costs associated with the trip unless there is *clear evidence* that the primary nature of the trip is related directly to your trade or business. In many cases, expenses incurred at your destination which are properly associated with your trade or business are deductible, even though the travel to and from the destination are not. In other words, if you travel to a resort to close a business deal, but spend a day on the slopes skiing afterward, the travel *to* and *from* the resort may not be deductible, but the expenses incurred while actually doing business *can* be. Every situation is different in the eyes of the IRS. Keep that in mind.

Now, if you travel outside the U.S. for primarily business purposes, but there are some nonbusiness activities done in the process, the cost of travel from home to the place of business and back *may* not be deductible by an individual. The cost may have to be allocated between business and nonbusiness activities, unless any *one* of the following tests is relevant:

1. Travel outside the United States is for a week or less,
2. Employee is not related to an employer and are not managing executives,
3. Employee had little control over making trip arrangements,
4. Less than 25% of the time outside the U.S. is spent on personal activity, or
5. Vacation time was not a consideration in scheduling the trip.

Costs for travel related to educational purposes are not normally deductible either, unless such travel is necessary to engage in activities that are designed to promote deductible education. For example, a Russian language teacher is not allowed to deduct the expense of going to Moscow on vacation simply to improve his or her knowledge of Russian culture and language. But if the same teacher were to conduct an educational tour for high school students through the Russian countryside, those expenses might be considered deductible since the teacher incurred them while educating students, which is a language teacher's primary trade.

In order to deduct registration fees or travel and transportation costs associated with attending conventions, seminars, or trade shows, you *must* be prepared to prove to the IRS that such income-producing purposes are directly related to your trade or business. Typically, the expenses incurred in connection with financial planning or investment seminars and meetings are not allowable deductions.

For travel expenses incurred while identifying a new domestic location for an established business, or for expenses incurred while trying to go into a new business, no deductible expense is allowed. Such travel expenses must, instead, be capitalized into the cost of the new property.

To get around this problem, you may want to take a personal deduction for all of your costs. Then set up a new corporation for the specific purpose of identifying a new location and follow the rules for treating its stock as Section 1244 stock. Then purchase the stock from the corporation in the amount you expect the search is going to cost. Have the corporation take on the expenses for the search, then if you don't find a good location, you can liquidate the corporation and take your losses as an ordinary deduction instead of a capital loss.

For deductible travel expenses, taxpayers must provide evidence of the following elements to support their deductions:

1. The separate amount of each expenditure,
2. Dates of departure and return home for each trip,
3. The travel destination for each portion of each trip, and
4. Reason for the travel, or the expected business benefit derived.

LEGAL AND OTHER PROFESSIONAL FEES

From time to time you will need to seek the assistance of professionals. Professional fees for attorneys, tax professionals, or other consultants generally can be deducted in the year incurred. For instance, fees for forming the business are immediately deductible. On the other hand, when professional fees clearly relate to benefits which will be received in future years, they must be deducted over the life of the benefit. Some fees fall into a gray area. For these types of fees, you can choose between deducting them all in the first year or spreading them over future years. This is a decision which you should make with the assistance of your tax advisor.

Speaking of your tax advisor, I have some good news for you. Tax assistance is fully deductible. Many times, business people want tax advice covering both their business and individual taxes. Oftentimes, these are interwoven. For instance, you might ask your tax advisor how to minimize taxes on all of your income from all sources. Her fee qualifies as a business tax deduction in proportion to the *business* advice given. The remaining portion can also be deducted, but as a personal itemized deduction on Schedule A of your personal return. This is another expense which should be run by your tax accountant.

ENTERTAINMENT EXPENSES

One of the biggest arguments in corporate expense meetings is invariably, "Who can be entertained by the business and be considered as a legitimate write off?" You might be surprised to learn that the IRS has *no* specific list of the kind of people who can or cannot be entertained. IRC regulations indicate that it almost always depends on the circumstances of a particular situation. Typically, any customer, supplier, employee of a client, agent, partner, or professional advisor can be entertained, whether they are established or prospective.

Entertainment costs for these people must be ordinary and necessary for carrying on the trade or business, and are not deductible unless business is discussed before, during, or after a meal, or the meal is "directly related" to, or "associated with," the conduct of business.

The deduction is limited to 50% of the actual cost, as long as such cost is not determined to be lavish or extravagant. The only exceptions to the 50% rule are expenses that fall in the following categories:

1. Employer paid recreation for a company picnic, holiday party, et cetera,
2. Minor fringe benefits including such things as holiday gifts, et cetera,
3. Any amount treated as compensation to the recipients, whether they are employees or not,
4. Promotional samples and materials made available to the public,

5. Tickets to charitable sporting events, to the extent such expenses meets three conditions:
    A. The event's primary purpose is to benefit a qualified nonprofit organization,
    B. The entire net proceeds go to the charity, and
    C. The event uses volunteers to perform the event's work. IRC rules cover the entire cost of the event, including parking and meals, and are often used to deduct the cost of such things as charity golf tournaments and other sports outings.

You need to be careful with five above, as deductions taken at what the tax code describes as "entertainment facilities" are usually disallowed. Places like ski lodges, hunting lodges, yachts, swimming pools, beach houses, hotel suites, or other housing located in recreational areas are red flags on most IRS reports. Even dues paid to social and athletic clubs are no longer determined to be "ordinary and necessary" expenses to the extent that the club is used as a source of valuable business contacts.

The giving of business "gifts" is another gray area for most corporations. What can you write off, and what can't you? The IRS code has simplified this question considerably. Expenses for ordinary and necessary business gifts are deductible to the extent they do not exceed $25 in a year to any one person. The $25 limitation does not apply to items that cost less than $4 and have the giver's name permanently imprinted, all obvious promotional materials, or any item awarded to an employee because of length of service, productivity, or safety achievements (that do not cost more than $400).

For deductible entertainment expenses, in addition to the above information, taxpayers must provide evidence of the following elements to support their deduction:

1. Name, address, or location of the place of entertainment,
2. The type of entertainment if that is not apparent by the name,
3. Purpose for expense, or the expected benefit derived for business, and

4. Occupation, title, name, and other designation to establish the business relationship of the persons entertained to the taxpayer.

To make sure you don't encounter problems with the IRS with these deductibles, employees should keep a detailed expense diary on a timely basis that clearly delineates all of the above information. This should be itemized carefully and kept as current as possible. It is also very important to keep all receipts on file for at least three years from the date of filing an income tax return on which any such deductions were claimed.

REIMBURSEMENTS

An "accountable plan" is a reporting method that qualifies under rules on what the IRS will accept as a reimbursement arrangement for business expenses incurred by employees. The difference between a properly documented accountable plan and a "non-accountable plan" can mean significant tax savings to you and your employees.

If your plan is accountable, your corporation does not report its reimbursements to employees as income. The reimbursements and the employees expenses are considered trade-outs by the IRS, and thus do not have to be included in anyone's income.

Under a non-accountable plan, though, reimbursements must be included as part of the income that employees report on their W-2s. Such reimbursements (since they are considered income) must also have income taxes, unemployment taxes, and Social Security taxes withheld on them. That means more work for your corporation's accounting department.

Employees then have to deduct all business expenses on their tax returns as miscellaneous itemized deductions. These expenses are only deductible to the extent that they exceed 2% of adjusted gross income. This usually results in a situation where the additional income exceeds the deductions and the employee ends up owing additional taxes. If you happen to be both a shareholder of the corporation and an employee, this means you get taxed *twice* on the same income. The corporation incurs additional employment taxes, and you incur additional personal income taxes.

The IRS requires that such reimbursements meet three requirements:

1. Reimbursements must have a direct business connection,
2. Expenses must be properly substantiated, and
3. Excess reimbursements must be returned to the corporation.

Item (1). Deductible reimbursements must be directly related to expenses incurred by an employee while conducting business for the employer. Such reimbursements can be paid in advance to prevent employees from having to use their own personal money for anticipated expenses, or can be paid in regular increments (per diem, et cetera) to employees who have regular entertainment or travel expenses.

It is *not* a good policy to provide advances to employees for expenses when they aren't expected to incur such expenses right away. The IRS has ruled in such cases that the money should be counted as income to the employee at the time it was paid. It is also a really good idea to repay all reimbursements to employees with separate checks that identify the payment as such. You always want to keep wage payments and records as separate and distinct as possible from reimbursable expense payments.

Item (2). The IRS regulations are quite specific about what is and is not deducible, and virtually every reimbursement item must be substantiated by a specific type of record. Personal recollection, or rule-of-thumb ("That's how we've always done it,") policies are not considered adequate reporting methods.

Almost every expense that would normally be incurred in the course of business (yes, that makes for a lot of rules) has special substantiation rules included in the tax code. The rules require that employees provide their employer with proof of the expense, including a time, place, and business purpose. When an employee has expenses that are not covered under IRS rules, the corporation is expected to get information that enables it to identify the nature of each expense and conclude that such expenses are substantiated before reporting them one way or another.

Item (3). Accountable plans require employees to return any and all amounts that exceed the substantiated expenses. Corporations should never pay money in advance more than 30 days before an anticipated expense is incurred. Employees should provide substantiation no longer than 60 days afterward and then provide any returns of excess payment within at least 120 days. Employers should provide employees with a detailed expense account report once per calendar quarter to allow them to substantiate or return any excess expense amounts.

Medical expenses

A major consideration for corporations these days is medical care for employees and other associated medical expenses. The IRC is quite explicit on what can be deducted in this area. For most situations, 100% of all of the following medical expenses can be deducted:

1. Accident and health insurance
2. Acupuncture
3. Adoption
4. Air conditioner (for allergy relief or other medical condition)
5. Alcoholism treatment
6. Ambulance costs
7. Birth control pills
8. Blind person's attendant (to accompany student, et cetera)
9. Braille books and magazines, seeing-eye dogs, or any special education and/or educational aids for the blind
10. Capital expenditures (or home modifications for handicapped individuals, primary purpose medical care)
11. Car or van equipped to accommodate wheelchair passengers, including handicapped controls
12. Childbirth preparation classes for expectant parents
13. Chiropractors

14. Christian Science treatment
15. Clarinet and lessons (to alleviate severe teeth malocclusion)
16. Computer data bank, storage and retrieval of medical records
17. Contact lenses
18. Contraceptives
19. Cosmetic surgery
20. Crutches
21. Deaf person's hearing aids (hearing aid animals, lip reading expenses, note taker for deaf student, computer modifications, et cetera)
22. Dental fees
23. Dentures
24. Doctor's fees
25. Domestic aid
26. Drug addiction recovery
27. Drugs and prescriptions
28. Dyslexia language training
29. Electrolysis
30. Elevator to alleviate cardiac condition
31. Eye examination and prescription glasses
32. Hair transplants
33. Halfway houses (drug, alcohol rehabilitation, et cetera)
34. Health club dues prescribed by physician for medical condition
35. Health Maintenance Organization (HMO)
36. Hospital care
37. Hospital services (outpatient)
38. Indian medicine man (Native Americans)
39. Insulin
40. Iron lungs
41. Laboratory fees
42. Lead paint removal
43. Legal expenses (authorization for treatment, et cetera)
44. Lifetime medical care
45. Limbs (artificial)
46. Mattresses (prescribed to alleviate arthritis, et cetera)
47. Nursing homes

48. Nursing services
49. Obstetrical expenses
50. Operations
51. Orthopedic shoes
52. Osteopaths
53. Oxygen equipment
54. Patterning exercises for handicapped children
55. Prosthesis
56. Psychiatric care
57. Psychologists
58. Psychotherapists
59. Reclining chairs for cardiac patients
60. Remedial reading schools (special education or handicapped)
61. Sexual dysfunction
62. Sterilization operations
63. Swimming pool (for treatment of polio or arthritis, et cetera)
64. Taxicab to doctor's office
65. Telephones, equipped for deaf persons
66. Televisions (close captioned decoders, et cetera)
67. Transplants
68. Vasectomies
69. Vitamins
70. Wheel chairs
71. Wigs (for alleviation of physical or mental discomfort)
72. X-rays

The following is a short list of other assorted expenses allowed to corporations. Within IRS guidelines, most corporations are allowed to deduct 100% of the following expenses:

1. Advertising expenses
2. Auto expenses
3. Awards
4. Cleaning expenses
5. Depreciation and Section 179 expenses
6. Convention expenses
7. Delivery expenses
8. Dues and publication expenses

9. Foreign conventions
10. Gas and oil expenses
11. Insurance expenses
12. Legal and professional expenses
13. License fees
14. Mailer expenses
15. Meals on premises expenses
16. Office expenses
17. Pension expenses
18. Per diem meals, including incidental expenses
19. Per diem lodging, including incidental expenses
20. Postage and freight expenses
21. Trade shows and conference expenses
22. Tax expenses (including payroll, property, sales, et cetera)
23. Utilities (phone, electric, gas, water, garbage, et cetera)

SUMMARY

Depending upon your actual corporate operations, there may be ways to significantly reduce your tax bill. Every company is different, and every situation is viewed differently by the IRS. Consult with a qualified tax attorney or accountant to make sure you are in compliance before assuming something is deductible. It is much better to *not* include something as a deductible that you have doubts about, than to hope the IRS agrees with you. *Hope* is *not* a method! Millionaires don't make money by hoping things will happen. They follow a preplanned strategy to *make* things happen. And that is what I want each of you to start doing today.

VIII A Million Ways to Incorporate

"What we must learn to do, we learn by doing."

ARISTOTLE

Don't worry, there really aren't that many ways of incorporating. But I got your attention with the title, didn't I? And titles are what we are going to explore in this chapter; specifically, the titles for stocks and the various kinds of corporations that use them.

In addition, you are going to learn what kinds of corporations are advantageous for specific business pursuits and how the stock for those corporate structures is issued and used. You will also get an overview of the types of stocks and what their functions are in the corporate world.

WHAT IS STOCK?

This may seem quite simple to many people, but we need to pay it a bit of attention. To establish any corporation, it is usually necessary to capitalize the business start up through the issue of some kind of stock. Each state has rules governing what types of assets may be used to capitalize a corporation in that state. These rules range from the most restrictive definition, such as requiring corporations to issue stock *only* in exchange for cash or some other physical assets, all the way up to include even intangible assets.

Some states do not allow the issuance of shares for intangible assets because they are difficult to accurately value for stock trade purposes. The corporation laws of the state in which you want to incorporate should be studied to see what considerations are allowed.

For example, under Nevada law, a corporation may issue shares in consideration of *any* tangible or intangible asset. Such assets may include, but are not limited to: cash, services, property, promissory notes, contracts to perform services, or any other security. Not every state has such a broad range of considerations for the issuance of stock.

The nature of intangible assets is hard to determine in most cases, so the value of intangible assets is often difficult to pin down. Who decides what intangible assets are worth for stock trades? Typically the board of directors are the ones who decide, and in Nevada, their decision is final. The Nevada law allowing stock to be issued for intangible assets is a major advantage for business start ups and creates considerable flexibility in establishing and managing a new corporation there.

This is particularly true of corporations that start up with a large amount of "sweat equity." Investors who have sacrificed time and energy to get the corporation rolling can be issued stock for the value of their work efforts alone. The value of the work and its stock equivalent will be determined by the board. This might seem like an unusual way to capitalize a corporation, but it's quite effective with Nevada Corporations, and just as binding as other kinds of capitalization. This method is rather simple and offers limited downside.

I had a student in Houston who was very interested in getting their corporation up and going but they were a little short on funds. They had looked around for a business entity which would enable them to get up and running without a large amount of capital but which would also help them to acquire the asset protection which they needed for their business and for their family. The student related his problem to me and stated that he had been told that he could not have a corporation unless he had a minimum amount of capital to place inside this entity. During the seminar we went over the benefits offered by the state of Nevada and he was able to accomplish all of his objectives. The only way that he was able to do this was by acquiring the knowledge of how to do it. That is the key for those interested in accomplishing different things and getting different results.

Those start up corporations that want to develop banking relationships for lines of credit are better off issuing stock for cash or saleable assets only. Banks won't lend money against "sweat equity." It is helpful, though, to have the flexibility of issuing stock for other considerations if a situation warrants it.

WHAT ARE SHAREHOLDERS?

A corporation that is organized from the outset for profitable purposes *must* have shareholders. They are the people who own the stock in the corporation. Without properly documented shareholders, it is possible that a corporation's existence could be set aside under some legal scrutiny.

In Nevada, like some other states, corporate laws do *not* require that stock be issued to stockholders within any specified period of time. Theoretically, stock could remain unissued forever. But, stock represents ownership. Typically, to own a piece of a corporation, there must be some form of exchange of assets. When an exchange of assets takes place, you have in essence *created* a stockholder.

Some people have attempted to avoid liability and/or direct connection to their corporations because stock was never actually issued to them. That tactic won't hold water! If you planned from the outset for an exchange of assets to be a long term loan, or whatever, you are still connected to the corporation. Even if no stock exists, it is probable under a given set of circumstances that a court could rule your loan represented a capital exchange and thus, *de facto* stock ownership was established.

Unless and until an exchange of assets takes place, the corporation itself has no assets or owners. With no assets or owners, it cannot act and becomes a useless entity. If a corporation begins operating without shareholders, a court may rule that the corporation was not acting like a corporate entity at all. The court could then hold personally liable any individuals who directed corporate activity.

The bottom line is, just because corporate law in a state does not *require* that stock be issued, that does not mean you should operate without it for any length of time. Stock issuance is a corporate formality that, if handled properly, will offer almost the same liability protection to stockholders that they would have if they did not own stock in the first place.

The only reason good enough to *not* issue stock is if you want to keep a particular corporate shell on the shelf, so to speak, for whatever reason. If the corporation is not actually *doing* anything, it's unlikely it will get you in trouble.

WHAT ARE PUBLIC OFFERINGS?

Public issuance of stock is a whole different kind of exposure for a corporation and its investors. There is a vast web of state and federal laws that regulate public stock sales and distribution. Corporations must be VERY careful in planning and executing a public sale of stock in order to guarantee the validity of the sale and avoid any of the myriad of legal complications that can arise with public sales. I highly recommend that you find a professional advisor well versed in public offerings if you are contemplating the sale of corporate securities to the public.

To give you some idea of what you are up against with public offerings, let's take an overview of the federal statutes regulating securities transactions. They are the Securities Act of 1933 and the Securities Exchange Act of 1934. These acts were written to ensure that there would always be a fair disclosure of information to potential investors of public stock companies and to help prevent fraudulent securities transactions.

The Securities Act of 1933 requires that any person or issuing corporation who attempts any sale of a security should file a registration statement that discloses a broad range of information about the security, the company, and the seller. The act also lists several exemptions from the registration requirement.

For example, there are exemptions for most, but not all, sales of securities that are made by parties other than the original "issuer," which is generally the company which created the security. There are some other exemptions that remove the registration requirement from some security sales made by the "issuer" as well. The main exemptions are:

1. **INTRASTATE OFFERINGS**

   If a corporation is incorporated and is conducting business solely in one state, and sells its securities only to residents of that state, it is exempt from registration. This rule has seen some interesting implications develop out of it since a violation can occur if a nonresident is offered a security, or if a resident purchases a security and subsequently sells the security to a nonresident.

2. **SMALL OFFERINGS**

   This exemption concerns the dollar value of offerings rather than the actual number of investors. Sales of less than $5 million worth of securities are not required to register.

3. **PRIVATE PLACEMENTS**

   Private placements are defined as a sale or solicitation to not more than 35 people. General promotional efforts or advertising of the solicitation to potential investors are prohibited.

The 1934 Act has somewhat broader disclosure and registration requirements than the earlier act. It also contains provisions designed to reduce the risk of market manipulation, insider trading, and other kinds of fraud.

Companies that are either listed on a national securities exchange, or that have more than 500 shareholders and more than $3 million in assets (this usually applies to stock that trades Over The Counter, or OTC) *must* be registered. The upgraded requirements include registration statements for all classes of securities offered for sale and Securities and Exchange Commission (SEC) approved updates through annual reports.

These federal securities laws apply consistently to all American corporations and in all states. However, each state has its own securities laws that not only can differ dramatically from the federal mandates in their intent, but may also indirectly contradict the federal restrictions in some aspects.

Some states, for example, regulate the sale of corporate stock to any individual outside the original group of incorporators. This allows the state to follow up and keep track of all transactions that may be taxable events under state income tax laws.

Another type of state regulations are known as "blue sky laws" in which states prohibit fraud in public offerings by requiring complete disclosure of the offering through state registration. If a corporation intends to sell stock publicly outside of its home state, the offering must qualify for exemption or comply with *all* of the various blue sky laws in the states where the offering is to be made. To acquire more information on these laws, you should consult an attorney familiar with the law of corporations.

In Nevada, corporations are allowed to sell stock to as many as 25 stockholders per year without needing any additional authorization from the state to hold a public offering. Above 25, a corporation must then meet the Secretary of State's requirements for an intrastate offering that will allow additional sale of stock, as long as the sale takes place *within* the boundaries of the state. This requires filing a formal prospectus for the stock offering with the Securities Division of the Secretary of State's office.

What about the individual sale of stock to others? While a company can be regulated in selling stock, the restrictions on individuals can vary widely from state to state. In some states, original stockholders must hold their stock for a specified minimum length of time.

In Nevada, however, the law defines shares of stock as *personal property*. That means individuals can theoretically sell shares on their own with *no* regulation at any time they want. It is conceivable that a corporation in Nevada could issue all of its stock to five people, who could then sell their shares as personal property to as many people as they wanted. If, for example, the stock was originally issued at $10 per share, the stockholders could sell them for $20 a share to other investors. The corporation has thus sold *all* of its stock, but the transfers from the original five holders might result in thousands of individual stockholders.

WHAT KINDS OF STOCKS ARE THERE?

Stockholders buy stocks to share in the benefits and risks of a corporate entity. The terms "stock" and "shares" are used synonymously in most cases and represent the primary elements of ownership that stockholders purchase. At the most basic level, a share of stock represents the right to receive a distribution of surplus profits from the corporation, and the right to a part of the funds left over after all the debt of the corporation has been paid in the event of a dissolution of the corporation.

Ownership of stock is physically represented by stock certificates. Stock certificates are written acknowledgments from a corporation that the holder has an interest in that corporation's property and assets. You can almost think of a stock certificate like a bank draft. When someone writes you a check, you have something of monetary value that represents the value of money, but no actual money. When you cash the check, the draft is converted into money.

Stock certificates function much the same way, except that the value of a check is always fixed (a $50 check is always going to be worth $50) while the value of a stock certificate can vary. A stock certificate, like a check, can be exchanged for value, which makes it a negotiable instrument. However, stock certificates are *not* actual stock, but are merely papers indicative of ownership of the amount of stock stated on them. In most states (Nevada included) stockholders own their stock, whether they have their certificates in hand or not. The exception to this is if the corporation issues the stock to "bearer," which will be discussed later in this chapter.

There are fourteen common varieties of stock. Here is a list:

1. *Capital stock* refers to the total amount of money and property authorized to be paid into the corporation. The total capital stock is set for each corporation in its Articles of Incorporation. To arrive at the total capital stock, multiply the number of shares authorized in the Articles of Incorporation by the par value of each share. The result will be a dollar amount that represents the total capital stock of the corporation. This figure always remains the same unless the Articles of Incorporation are amended in this regard, and has no direct bearing on the actual value of the corporation's assets.

2. *Authorized stock* is what the Articles of Incorporation state for the number of individual shares that the corporation is authorized to issue. The total authorized stock includes all shares, issued or not.

3. *Common stock* is for corporations that prefer to issue only one class of stock. Common stock is sold to raise sufficient capital for the growth of the corporation. Common stockholders all share identical rights and responsibilities, and have rights to annual dividends (which are not guaranteed) in an amount equal to the prorated percentage of their ownership of shares. Common stock is often divided into separate classes, the most common division being between "voting" and "nonvoting" shares. Since the natural assumption is that all stock is voting, any nonvoting shares should clearly indicate the fact on the stock certificate to avoid confusion. When common stock is divided into voting and nonvoting shares, the classes of common stock are usually called "Class A Voting Common Capital Stock," and "Class B Non-Voting Common Capital Stock."

4. *Preferred stock* is a class of stock given a preferred status in distribution of dividends. Preferred stockholders receive dividends before any holders of common stock. Some corporate Bylaws guarantee that preferred stockholders will receive a specific annual return on their shares. For example, if there is 3% preferred stock issued, that 3% dividend must be paid before anything is paid on common stock. This often creates the end result that a dividend distribution to preferred stockholders will wipe out all of the available dividend distribution, leaving nothing for common stockholders.

   Preferred stock can be further categorized as either "cumulative" or "noncumulative." Cumulative stock means that in a year in which preferred stockholders receive *no* guaranteed dividend because of poor earnings, or whatever, the guaranteed dividend is then added to the next year's dividend, and so on until the accumulated dividends are paid. Noncumulative preferred stocks simply lose their dividends.

5. *"Participating" preferred stock* entitles the holder to all the rights of the preferred stockholder, but also participates with the common stock in any earnings above the percentage agreed upon for preferred stockholders.

6. *Deferred stock* is any class of stock to which dividend payments are deferred until *after* dividend payments have been made to other, more senior classes of stock. By this definition, common stock is deferred when preferred stock is issued. Nevada corporate law allows for the creation of an unlimited number of stock classes. This makes it possible to create an array of stock classes, all of which are deferred until all prior classes are paid.

7. *Treasury stock* refers to shares issued to individuals, and subsequently reacquired by the corporation for whatever reason. When it does no harm to the creditors of the corporation, the stock may be repurchased and held in the corporate treasury, where it can remain indefinitely. The stock can then be retired or reissued again at some point. It is important to note, however, that shares of treasury stock do not give the company its own voting rights.

8. *Redeemable stock* is used when a corporation retains the option to purchase stock back from its stockholders. Depending upon the specific Bylaws used, a corporation may either have the right to exercise its option any time, or may be limited to exercising its option in only certain circumstances. Usually, the stock is redeemed at par value, unless otherwise specified.

9. *Assessable stock* is used when a corporation wants to retain the right to assess, or "bill" its stockholders if it needs cash resources beyond the available capital stock. Capital stock is made assessable when the Articles of Incorporation provide that "the capital stock of the corporation shall be subject to assessment." Most stock, however, is nonassessable, meaning that the corporation cannot request additional cash from the stockholders without issuing additional stock.

10. *Restricted stock* is used when a corporation wants to restrict the transfer of its shares by specifying a desired restriction in either the Articles of Incorporation or the Bylaws. Restricted stock certificates must contain a legend that either states the restriction or refers the holder to the provisions in the Articles or Bylaws that contain them. A common restriction used is giving either the corporation or a specified class of stockholder the first rights of refusal (first right to buy) on stock when it is transferred.

11. *No-par value stock* is stock that has no specific par value assigned to it in the Articles of Incorporation. Although no-par value stock is not specifically covered in Nevada's Corporation Code, a 1956 Attorney General's opinion says that, "corporations may organize, provide for, and issue no-par stock for varying considerations." The value of no-par stock depends entirely upon what the market will bear, and on the actual value of the corporation. The board of directors has the authority to determine a set value for any no-par value shares. This is done by resolution.

12. *Bearer stock* is that stock which is issued to the "bearer," and those who physically possess such certificates are technically the owners of the stock. Only the name of the original bearer has to be recorded in the books of the corporation, so it is possible that certificates have been transferred many times since they were originally issued. That makes them very difficult to track.

    In theory, holders of bearer shares would eventually surface, and provide the corporate secretary with the record of transfers that prove they have the right to the stock. However, until that happens it may not be possible to prove who owns what stock at any given moment. Until holders of such certificates register their ownership with the corporation, they do not have any voting rights or rights to dividends declared during their period of ownership.

13. *Convertible stock* is stock that may be converted to another class of stock at the option of the corporation. The most common use of convertible stock involves preferred stock that may be converted to common stock.

14. *"Watered" stock* is stock that has been issued gratuitously, or by some agreement under which the holder paid less than its established par value. This type of stock issuance is binding upon the corporation and any of the stockholders that agree to the transaction. Dissenting stockholders have the right to sue for cancellation of such stock.

Now that you are familiar with the various types of stock, the next topic which you need to develop an understanding in is the different types of corporations.

WHAT KINDS OF CORPORATIONS ARE THERE?

Now that you know all about stocks, let's take a look at the corporations that use these stocks. The first thing you need to know here is that corporations can be classified in a variety of ways. The five main ones are:

1. By tax treatment (C vs. S corporations),
2. By form (stock or non stock),

3. By interest served (public, private, or quasi-public),
4. By purpose (profit vs. nonprofit), and
5. By membership (aggregate vs. sole, et cetera).

WHAT IS AN S CORPORATION?

A question asked quite regularly at my seminars and in my dealings with individuals regarding corporations is whether it is a C or S corporation which I recommend. The type of corporation that I deal with is a C corporation. There are several reasons for this as I will point out. Before I do that however, I need to address what it means to be an S corporation.

The Subchapter S corporation is a sort of hybrid corporate structure that offers the protection of limited liability for its corporate shareholders but is not a taxable entity at all (except for certain types of capital gains). Income for S corporations, whether distributed or not, is transferred directly to the stockholders who then pay taxes on their corporate income at the appropriate *personal* income tax rate.

In essence, this ends up treating S stockholders as if they were partners. There is a much wider range of corporate deductions applied against the income of individual S stockholders. The biggest advantage of this kind of incorporation is that any potential for double taxation is eliminated at the outset.

That's *not* the case for C corporations. The double taxation that we've talked about before can have a huge financial impact on regular C corporations and their shareholders. However, a number of methods have been attempted to help circumvent the double tax problem. The simplest of these is to just not declare any dividends at all. Without dividends, there can be no double tax. Most C shareholders, though, would sooner have the double taxation than to lose those dividends. A lot of this will depend on the nature of the shareholders of your corporation.

Because C corporations were attempting to circumvent double taxation by not distributing profits, Congress passed Section 531 et seq. of the IRC, which penalizes a corporation that accumulates profits "for the purpose of avoiding the income tax with respect to its shareholders." Under that portion of the law, a corporation may only accumulate profits which are reasonably necessary for business. The law provides for an amount that may be accumulated without regard to the needs of the business, which is currently set at $250,000. Just as soon as this law went into effect, companies started trying to avoid paying the accumulation penalty while still attempting to avoid their taxable distributions to shareholders.

Some closely held corporations have even attempted to distribute their corporate profits in the form of nontaxable fringe benefits. Things like meals, health insurance, life insurance, disability insurance, company cars, gasoline, parking, and all kinds of business entertainment were paid for by the companies in lieu of their profit distributions. In response, Congress turned right around and reduced or eliminated many of these opportunities to some degree. But as you learned in the chapter on taxation, there are still a large number of items which can be deducted.

Another major tax problem with C corporations is that the tax benefits of net business losses do not, generally, pass through to the shareholders. Shareholders don't usually like to see net operating losses anyway, but when it happens they would like to be able to take the deduction against income they earn in other areas. This is especially true if a corporation has "paper" losses that spring from loopholes in such things as depreciation schedules and so forth.

All of these perceived problems with C corporations and the impact they created for closely held corporations led to the development of the Subchapter S concept. For maintaining limited personal liability, the S corporation allows shareholders as much insulation as possible. At the same time, income or losses pass untaxed through the corporation.

Perhaps the best way to illustrate the way this works is to go through a typical scenario. For example, if Childer's Corporation were a C corporation and had a taxable income of $30,000, it would pay $4,500 in federal corporate income taxes at the current corporate tax rate. Assume the remaining $25,500 is distributed to its one shareholder, JJ Childers. In addition to JJ's salary, the dividend brings his total (net) taxable income for the year to

$50,500. Since he files jointly, his personal income tax for the year would be $9,200. Thus, the total liability for the year for both JJ and his corporation would be $13,700 ($4,500 + $9,200). This does not include other amounts taken out for Social Security, et cetera.

But let's suppose Childer's Corporation had elected S status. First, there would be no $4,500 federal corporate tax. JJ's taxable income would be $55,500, ($30,000 passed through from the corporation). Now his total tax bill is only $10,500. The S corporation status just saved JJ Childers the tidy little sum of $3,200. For many people, this sounds like the ideal situation and is advised by many professionals.

S corporations also have no corporate tax on the sale of corporate assets, or upon the liquidation of the company. Corporate losses, with some restrictions, pass through to the shareholders as well. This means that a shareholder can offset income derived from other sources with S corporate losses. Additionally, S corporations are not subject to any accumulated earnings penalties, or the personal holding company tax, which automatically results in the highest possible corporate tax rate if a corporation qualifies.

That's the good news. The bad news is that while an S corporation is much simpler to operate from a tax perspective, there can be some real drawbacks to using them. For one thing, stockholders in an S corporation are subject to tax on the income of the corporation whether they receive a distribution of profits or not. If the corporation has to retain some of the income, shareholders must pay their taxes out of pocket.

Another problem is that no more than 35 stockholders can participate in an S corporation, but a husband and wife are counted as one stockholder. Generally stockholders are considered as "natural persons," but certain specified types of trusts and estates may also own stock in an S entity. However, nonresident aliens, corporations, and partnerships are not eligible to hold S stock.

Technically, S corporations can have only one class of stock, although that one class of stock can include both voting and nonvoting shares. IRS regulations allow for S corporations to issue stock options, which permit individuals to retain a distant interest in the corporation without endangering the S corporation election.

One of the major drawbacks of the S entity is that there is little privacy in S corporations. Shareholders must be reported to the IRS to determine the proper Federal Income Tax obligation of the individual shareholders. This disclosure includes how much stock everyone owns, when it was acquired, and Social Security numbers for all those involved. Thus, corporate anonymity goes right out the window. So much for your status as a "secret millionaire."

Because taxes are paid by individual stockholders, most S corporations are limited to a calendar year election rather than fiscal year arrangements. There are, however, a few exceptions to this rule.

An S corporation can make a Section 444 election, which generally allows for a tax year ending September 30, October 31, or November 30, but estimated tax payments must be made that would undermine any advantage a shareholder might gain by having an offsetting fiscal year. Also, the application form for S election provides for requesting a fiscal year, but the typical IRS approval rate for fiscal year applications is quite low. The IRS charges a $200 fee to submit Form 1128, which is the application for a change of tax year.

S corporations have to have a viable business reason or some kind of natural business year for any chance at fiscal year approval from the IRS. To prove cause for something other than a calendar year, at least 25% of the corporation's gross receipts must be received in the last two months of the selected tax year for the last three years. That allows for seasonal operations to pay their taxes without an undue tax burden placed on them by a calendar year ending.

Tax law changes in the administrative requirements may also have some negative effects on S corporations who have already successfully qualified for fiscal year treatment. Because they are not subject to normal calendar year deadlines, these corporations have to make tax-like deposits each May 15. The rate is one percentage point above the prior year's highest personal-income tax rate. Worse still, those deposits earn *no* interest.

You can convert a C corporation into an S corporation by filing IRS form 2553, which must be signed by each stockholder. This form has to be mailed to the Internal Revenue Service within 75 days of starting business. Existing corporations can elect S status within 75 days of the start of any corporate tax year.

Turning an existing C corporation that holds assets into an S corporation can cause some associated tax consequences, especially in two specific cases:

1. If a corporate asset has a fair market value at the time of the S election which is greater than the tax basis, and the asset is sold within 10 years of S election, the IRS will tax the "built-in" gain at the maximum corporate tax rate for the year the sale occurs.
2. If a corporation's passive income (interest, dividends, royalties, annuities, gains, et cetera) exceeds 25% of gross receipts, it is taxed at the top corporate rate.

However, since the tax obligations flow through an S corporation to the shareholders, it is important to remember that the shareholders are taxed on their portion of corporate income, whether or not the income is distributed to the shareholders. If income is *not* distributed, then the shareholder's basis is adjusted to reflect undistributed income (which will have the same tax impact as if the income had been distributed to the shareholder, but immediately reinvested in additional shares).

The IRS uses a per-share, per-day formula to determine the income tax obligation of each shareholder in such situations. If the stock ownership remains the same throughout the tax year, the calculation is easy. Just divide each tax item by the percentage of outstanding shares issued to each stockholder.

Now, if the ownership changes, things get a little more complicated. First, divide each tax item by the number of days in the year (365, except leap years) to find its daily value. Then multiply the daily value by the percentage of outstanding shares issued to each stockholder. Finally, multiply this figure by the number of days each stockholder owned the stock.

C corporations can avoid accumulated earnings penalties by electing S corporation status and making a timely dividend distribution to the stockholders. This is true for the life of the S corporation election, and applies to the preceding tax year as well, if handled properly. The S corporation can also eliminate the personal holding company penalties, which are equivalent to the top individual tax rate, and problems with unreasonable compensation.

Another drawback for S entities is that there are a number of significant differences between fringe benefits allowed to S corporations as compared to C corporations. For example, C corporations can deduct the entire cost of health insurance premiums and group-term life insurance (within limits) without resulting in taxable income to shareholders or employees. S corporation shareholders have to report all paid premiums as taxable income if they own more than 2% of the stock. This can make a substantial difference.

Also, S corporation employees may deduct only 25% of the cost of medical insurance as adjustments to their income. Additional amounts may be deductible if itemized, but only to the extent they exceed 7.5% of the shareholder's adjusted gross income.

Unless and until an S election is terminated, a corporation can keep the S status as long as it likes. There are several ways to cancel S status. The simplest way is to have more than 50% of the ownership vote to terminate the election. This is called an elective termination.

An S entity's termination can be forced by corporate activity that is not allowed under S status. This can include having more shareholders than is allowed by law, creating additional classes of stock, creating too much passive income for three consecutive years, or any other action that violates S status.

One caution here! Once your S status is lost, intentionally or otherwise, your corporation cannot elect it again for five years unless the majority of ownership changes hands. Accidental terminations can be corrected if the IRS allows you to use special waiver provisions *and* you agree to pay any necessary tax adjustments.

Be aware, also, that S corporation status is not recognized in every state. In some states, the S corporation is subject to the same tax basis as regular C corporations. If an S corporation operates in more than one state, the tax laws of each affected state must be checked to see whether state law recognizes S corporations, whether any special state or city elections are required, and whether all of the shareholders of the corporation need to be residents of a particular state.

In cases of multi-state operations, problems may arise in regard to the apportionment of income among the various states for tax purposes. Some state laws stipulate that nonresidents must be subject to state income taxes on income from an S corporation operating in that state. Other states require nonresident shareholders to file written consents or agreements to pay income tax on their shares of the S corporation's taxable income. In all of these cases, *know* the state law and follow it accordingly. Or, avoid the whole issue of state laws by doing what smart people and millionaires do—incorporate in Nevada and maintain all of your business activities within the state.

S CORPORATIONS SHOULD BE USED FOR

1. BUSINESSES WITH HIGH START-UP LOSSES,
2. BUSINESSES WITH NO INTENT TO ISSUE MULTIPLE CLASSES OF STOCK,
3. BUSINESSES WITH NO INTENT TO GO "PUBLIC,"
4. BUSINESSES THAT MIGHT BE SUBJECT TO THE ALTERNATIVE MINIMUM TAX,
5. BUSINESSES SUBJECT TO TAX ON EXCESSIVE ACCUMULATED EARNINGS,
6. BUSINESSES WHOSE SHAREHOLDERS UNDER A C CORPORATION STATUS MIGHT BE SUBJECT TO CHARGES OF EXCESSIVE COMPENSATION BY THE IRS, AND
7. BUSINESSES WITH NO DESIRE TO PROTECT THEIR IDENTITY FOR ASSET PROTECTION PURPOSES.

S CORPORATIONS SHOULD NOT BE USED FOR

1. BUSINESSES THAT WOULD VIOLATE ANY S ELIGIBILITY REQUIREMENTS (MORE THAN 35 SHAREHOLDERS, INELIGIBLE SHAREHOLDERS, ET CETERA),
2. BUSINESSES REQUIRING TAX DEDUCTIONS FOR SIGNIFICANT SHAREHOLDER OR EMPLOYEE FRINGE BENEFITS SUCH AS:
   A. ACCIDENT AND/OR HEALTH INSURANCE PLANS,
   B. LARGE DEATH BENEFITS FOR AN EMPLOYEE'S ESTATE,
   C. UP TO $50,000 OF GROUP-TERM LIFE INSURANCE ON AN EMPLOYEE,
   D. MEALS OR LODGING FURNISHED FOR EMPLOYER CONVENIENCE.
3. BUSINESSES WITH SUBSTANTIAL EARNINGS AND PROFITS THAT MUST PAY A DIVIDEND TO SHAREHOLDERS WITHIN THREE YEARS OF ELECTION OR ELECTION WILL BE TERMINATED,
4. BUSINESSES WITH MORE THAN 25% OF GROSS RECEIPTS RESULTING FROM PASSIVE INVESTMENT INCOME SUCH AS RENTS, ROYALTIES, INTEREST AND DIVIDENDS, AND
5. BUSINESSES INTERESTED IN KEEPING THEIR INFORMATION PRIVATE FOR ASSET PROTECTION PURPOSES.

WHAT IS A PERSONAL SERVICE CORPORATION?

Some small service type business owners who incorporate as C corporations are not allowed to take advantage of the benefits that apply to other corporations. The tax laws classify the work of these service-oriented businesses in such a way that they can lose all the tax advantages associated with incorporating. This classification is known as the Personal Service Corporation or PSC.

Personal Service Corporations must use a calendar year much like the S corporation. The limitation on accumulated earnings for PSCs is $150,000, which is $100,000 less than the amount available to a regular C corporation. PSCs, like individual taxpayers, cannot offset normal business income with passive losses.

The tax rate for Personal Service Corporations is the flat corporate rate of 35%, instead of the graduated rate that starts at 15%. This rate applies to all income, beginning with the first dollar. When profits are distributed to shareholders in a PSC, they will be taxed again at the shareholder's personal rate, thereby incurring double taxation.

Section 448 of the IRC defines PSCs that are subject to the flat tax rate. The first criteria is that at least 95% of the employee's time is spent working in one of several specified fields. Actors, musicians, doctors, nurses, dentists, veterinarians, and consultants paid for their advice and counsel (as opposed to commissions) are included in this group. The second criteria is that at least 95% of the value of the stock is held, either directly or indirectly, by employees who provide the services, or retired employees, or their estates or their heirs within two years of getting their inheritance. Under these criteria, many small corporations qualify. If you fall into this category, you should certainly consider Nevada as a home state. At least there, you can avoid the additional burden of state income tax.

WHAT IS A HOLDING COMPANY?

Any corporation that owns or "holds" control of other corporations, (subsidiaries) is called a holding corporation. Internal Revenue Service codes define "control" of a subsidiary as consisting of at least 80% ownership of its stock. At that point, corporations are able to combine their income and expenses for filing a consolidated tax return or they can put together a consolidated financial statement to apply for financing. That makes them, in essence, a single entity.

More often than not, a holding company is the primary business entity, and by virtue of its business activities, can decide to separately incorporate individual aspects of its business. The assumption that holding corporations are only involved in the passive business of owning other companies is not always correct. The California corporation example in a previous chapter was a good example of a holding company growing out of the main operation in order to take advantage of multiple corporation tax benefits.

The IRS also designates any corporation with over 60% *passive* income, whose stock is owned (more than 50%) by not more than five people at any time during the last half of the tax year as a *personal* holding company. In determining stock ownership requirements, the IRS considers stock owned by a corporation, partnership or estate to be owned proportionately by its shareholders, partners, or beneficiaries.

Personal holding company income is taxed at the personal income tax rate instead of the fixed corporate rates, as long as it is being distributed. If it is not distributed, a surtax of 39.6% of undistributed earnings is levied. Personal holding company income includes the following:

1. Taxable income from estates and trusts,
2. Dividends, interest, royalties, and annuities,
3. Royalties from mineral, oil, gas and copyrights,
4. Payments under personal service contracts, or
5. Rent adjusted for the right to use corporate property.

WHAT IS A NONPROFIT CORPORATION?

The IRS recognizes a nonprofit corporation as any corporation that is organized for a public or charitable purpose and is thus tax exempt under Section 501(c)(3) of the Internal Revenue Code. Nonprofit corporations do not issue shares, nor do they have ownership. A nonprofit corporation must have at least five directors or trustees, and upon dissolution must either distribute its assets to the state or federal government, or another entity recognized as exempt under IRS code.

For private use purposes, nonprofit corporations have severe limitations. Most corporations that are formed for profit are allowed to engage in any lawful business activity. Nonprofit corporations are required to state a *specific* purpose that benefits either the public at large, a specific segment of the community, or some membership-based group.

However, it is not unheard of for someone to set up a nonprofit corporation for charitable purposes with the intent to realize favorable tax treatment and benefits from it. It is quite possible for a nonprofit corporation to hire family members or friends to run the company and draw a salary. There is nothing to prohibit a nonprofit corporation from paying salaries to its employees.

In order to claim nonprofit tax-exempt status, the nonprofit corporation must be formed for religious, charitable, scientific, educational, or literary purposes. Only with such tax-exempt status is a corporation eligible to receive tax deductible contributions from donors.

Contributions to nonprofit corporations are exempt from federal estate taxation as well. Lots of wealthy people make contributions in their estate plans for qualified nonprofit corporations. Estate plan contributions are actively pursued by many nonprofits as part of their campaign for public funds.

Even though nonprofit corporations are limited to specific activities and are tax-exempt, such entities are still allowed to make money *unrelated* to their avowed nonprofit purposes. Such unrelated income is subject to taxation as unrelated business income under most state and federal corporate tax laws.

Nonprofit corporations enjoy a few major advantages over regular corporations. Such advantages are often essential to the success of the nonprofit organization. Some of those advantages are:

1. Postal rates are lower on third class bulk mailings,
2. Advertising rates are almost always cut for nonprofits,
3. Enhanced eligibility for many state and federal grants,
4. Free radio and TV public service announcements, and
5. Employees are eligible for federal, state and local employment programs where salaries are paid out of government funds (job training).

It is essential that nonprofit corporations meet all IRS rules, restrictions and limitations in order to maintain their tax-exempt status. To maintain eligibility, nonprofit corporations must:

1. Be organized and operated for religious, charitable, educational, scientific, or literary purposes,
2. Not distribute profits or gains to directors, officers or members,

3. Not substantially engage in grass roots legislative or political activities except as permitted under federal tax rules,
4. Not participate in political campaigns for or against candidates for public office, or
5. Distribute assets remaining upon dissolution to another qualified tax-exempt entity, group, or governmental agency.

WHAT IS A CLOSE CORPORATION?

A few states allow for the formation of corporations that are specifically designated as "close corporations." A close corporation is designed for small groups of investors who function, for all intents and purposes, as a partnership.

At the same time, they retain corporate liability protection and corporate income tax deductions and rates. Close corporations essentially "close" the company to all outside intervention or investment through severe restrictions on ownership, operations and information.

By definition, a close corporation can have no more than 30 stockholders, and is generally prohibited from making public stock offerings. Close corporations must be identified as such on all corporate records and when entering into contracts. In other words, the company must include "a close corporation" stipulation (or something similar) in or after its name on all documents and records.

Investors in close corporations sometimes have different rights from stockholders in other types of corporations. Usually this takes the form of allowing stockholders better access to all corporate records that may not be as readily accessible to stockholders in some other types of corporations. Additionally, there are limitations placed on the transfer of shares of a close corporation that would likely not exist elsewhere.

For instance, a close corporation is commonly used to ensure that all business activities remain in a particular family. The stock would have some kind of restriction placed on it that provides for a transfer of shares *only* between family members. Being able to accomplish this depends largely upon corporate law in the state of origin, so make sure you know how this part of the law works in your state.

Shareholders of a close corporation may, in some states, vote to eliminate their board of directors (but not officers), and make all management decisions themselves. In Nevada, stockholders are allowed to "treat the corporation as if it were a partnership or to arrange relations among the stockholders or between the stockholders and the corporation in a way that would be appropriate only among partners."

If shareholders eliminate their board of directors, they may appoint one person among them the right to sign documents as the designated director of the corporation. Such "pseudo directors" are relieved of all personal liability that could be assigned to them because of not observing the usual corporate formalities.

In close corporations with a board of directors, the board's powers can be severely limited by shareholder agreement. This generally relieves directors of any liability but automatically transfers that liability to the shareholders who have the voting rights to regulate the board of directors.

The concepts involved in operating a close corporation can vary significantly from state to state. As always, make sure you check your state's corporate laws before opting to set up a close corporation.

SUMMARY

The incorporation process is an essential area for you to develop an understanding in. You must do what it takes to become familiar with this essential information. As always, knowledge of this area will enable you to accomplish much more than you would accomplish without it.

IX THE SECRET MILLIONAIRE'S MILLION DOLLAR STRATEGIES

"The personal right to acquire property gives to the property, when acquired, a right to protection, as a social right."

JAMES MADISON

Our fourth President, James Madison, certainly knew what he was talking about when it comes to property. Since his day, the people of the United States have come to acquire more property than almost any other free people on the planet. With that property has come the burden of ownership and the added responsibility of passing property on to our heirs.

A whole industry of legal manipulations has grown up around this issue of property, with well over a million court cases being the result. How to get it, how to keep it, how to take it away from others, and how to pass it on to our children—all of these are major considerations for property owners. That is what you are going to learn in this chapter. You are going to study the effects of incorporating to help improve your right to asset protection, estate planning, tax reduction and liability limitation using the Nevada Corporation.

HOW CAN I USE A CORPORATION FOR ASSET PROTECTION?

Do the goals and objectives of asset protection cause you concern? Surprisingly enough, that's *not* the case with most folks. Many people feel that there is just no need for them to implement any protective measures because they have done nothing wrong and do not plan on doing anything wrong in their lives. Today, you need not do anything wrong to be taken to the cleaners in a lawsuit. All you have to do is *own* something.

Out of all the reasons there are for incorporating, asset protection stands out above the others. With asset protection, you are implementing limited liability or protection for your personal assets and property in the event they are sought by creditors.

In today's society, everyone is faced with the potential threat of a devastating lawsuit. Now more than ever, you must have a plan to protect your assets. The corporation can help you immensely with this task. A corporation organized in the right place and operated in the right way can help you even more. This chapter will introduce you to key strategies to help you meet your objectives.

In this wildly litigious society, then, asset protection can be a great comfort. All you have to do is read the newspapers or watch television to see the nature of the legal nightmares that face property owners. The people of this country are more conversant in the concept of litigation than they have ever been in our history. It seems the solution to everyone's problem these days is to find someone to sue, and it doesn't matter who, as long as they have *assets* to seize.

One major lawsuit in this kind of environment can completely wipe you out, if you are not properly protected. However, there are ways to make sure you *are* protected. You can avoid many of the risks of property ownership by implementing asset protection measures if you are willing to do what it takes.

To accomplish that, all you need to do is take a proactive stance in organizing your affairs. Today you hear of courtroom judgment amounts which completely and absolutely defy all logic. What you must realize more than anything else is this—it *can* happen to *you*!

Protecting your assets is completely legal, provided it's done right. Having stated that, I have to add a brief caveat, and coming from an attorney, that's probably not too surprising for you. In structuring your overall affairs in a way which protects your assets, you *must* abide by the law. You cannot engage in illegal acts such as concealing assets, issuing false information, or committing perjury.

The good news is that you can develop a solid and effective asset protection plan which is in full compliance with all the rules, regulations, and laws *without* doing anything wrong. The Nevada Corporation is the central element in that plan.

As you have already learned, when you create a corporation, you create a legal entity, effectively, a legal person. It is as if you have created a clone of yourself. This new entity is now responsible for its own acts. The importance of this is that you are not individually responsible for the acts of this separate legal entity, *unless* you act fraudulently or criminally. In this event you can be subject to personal liability for your actions and all the repercussions that result. To prevent this, let's take a look at what constitutes fraudulent acts, so that you can make sure what you and your corporation are planning to do is not illegal.

When corporations lose a big lawsuit, there's always a desire to attempt to transfer some or all of the corporate assets to help keep them protected from creditors. Judgment creditors are just too smart to let most assets "slip through the cracks." They have the courts on their side, armed with more technology now than ever before.

The law refers to this kind of illegal transfer of assets as a "fraudulent conveyance," and it will almost always get you into hot water with the courts. The term is used to describe any attempt to improperly transfer assets to avoid lawsuits or the judgment awards that result. You must understand that *"a conveyance for the purpose of avoiding collection of damages in a pending action for a tort is fraudulent."* If you are concerned about whether or not a particular transfer that you are contemplating is fraudulent, consult with an attorney familiar with the law of fraudulent conveyance. My suggestion for finding such an attorney is to contact one specializing in bankruptcy law.

Fraudulent conveyance is based on the principal that creditors have a right of remedy against a debtor. If the court determines that a creditor's right to collect a viable debt is infringed due to transfer or conveyance of assets by the debtor, the debtor's entire transaction can be set aside.

Unfortunately, I can't give you a complete, proper and always applicable definition of fraudulent conveyance. The reason for that is because it changes with each judge's interpretation, and is more often than not based on specific circumstances. The courts rely on certain facts like the length of time that separates a transfer of assets from an action that results in liability. That time can vary widely in different situations. There is no hard and fast rule.

However, the Uniform Fraudulent Conveyance Act (UFCA) is in effect in most states, and the Uniform Fraudulent Transfers Act (UFTA) is used in the remaining states. These two laws are virtually identical in the way they define two categories of fraudulent transfers. They are:

1. *Fraud in-law*: also known as constructive fraud, this occurs when there is a gift or sale of a debtor's property for less than the fair market value. This must be done in the face of a known liability, which renders the debtor insolvent or unable to pay the creditor. Fraud-in-law can only exist when all the above elements exist. There is no need to prove that the debtor had *intended* to defraud the creditor.
2. *Fraud-in-fact*: also know as actual fraud, this occurs when creditors prove that a debtor intended to hinder, delay, or defraud them.

Transfers found to be fraudulent allow the court to force a retransfer of the assets to the creditors. Parties which receive the fraudulent transfer, and are deemed to be an innocent third party (unaware of the fraudulent intent) can place a lien against the transferred assets up to the amount that was paid for them in order to recoup their money.

Creditors have to act within a specific time frame to properly challenge a transfer done under fraudulent conveyance statutes. In most states, the statute of limitations is four years after the transfer is made or the debt is incurred, or one year after it could have reasonably been discovered, whichever occurs last.

In a federal bankruptcy case, the bankruptcy trustee usually has two years from the first meeting of creditors to begin a fraudulent transfer claim. The major exception to this is if the bankruptcy trustee chooses to bring fraudulent transfer charges under state law instead. Believe me, you *do not* want a federal bankruptcy trustee to file such charges.

How do you avoid this? Simple. Put a strategy in place before you have a problem. Planning in advance gives your strategy a much better chance of being upheld by a court.

The primary concept here is, that for any transfer of your corporate assets to be protected, it needs to be supported by legitimate business reasons. Transfers must be made prior to any event or situation that results in a lawsuit. Once an event has actually occurred, such transactions can be subject to intense scrutiny. If a transfer of assets takes place *after* you have been served with a lawsuit, it will be virtually impossible to justify the transaction as legitimate in the eyes of the law.

You have already learned that Nevada corporate law provides some of the best liability protection there is for corporate officers and directors. But knowledgeable directors should also insist upon indemnification by their corporation for any lawsuit brought against them resulting from their corporate duties. To make this indemnification stronger still, the company should obtain director liability insurance.

When corporations purchase this kind of insurance for their directors instead of having the individual directors purchase their own policies, defending claims becomes far less complicated, writing off of the cost of premiums becomes less problematic, and the policies are usually far less expensive than individual policies would be.

Look for the following features in your director's insurance package:

1. What coverage does the policy provide? A good policy should have a minimum of a million dollars in coverage per occurrence. Larger corporations involved in high risk activity, such as public transportation or hazardous waste, will need a lot more.

2. What actions are excluded from coverage? Does the policy exclude claims based on fraud, dishonesty, libel, slander, securities violations, insider trading, or other such activities? These exclusions can often be negotiated back into your coverage at a higher premium.

3. What kinds of deductibles are there? Many policies use a "split deductible" approach to claims, where the policy only provides, say, 90% coverage and you pay the rest. On large judgments, though, even 10% can be a hefty amount of money. Some policies also have a flat deductible of $5,000 per director.

4. Will the company notify the directors if coverage is canceled?

5. Will supplemental insurance be provided that covers deductible lapses in coverage or exclusions?

The best way to avoid lawsuits, of course, is to keep your name off the corporate records in the first place. In Nevada, only the officers and directors are listed on any public records. That means if you can find someone else to act as a director, then your name doesn't have to appear on anything. This provides an added layer of privacy.

Nevada incorporating companies and/or resident agents can often provide "nominee" officers and directors for corporations that they are in the process of forming. Fees for this can range from a few hundred dollars a year up to a couple of thousand. If you're considering using such services, be sure you read the contracts because there are usually some additional costs for certain activities, such as excessive use of time.

To take things a step further in this strategy, and especially if confidentiality is a major priority for you, have your attorney hire the nominee officers on your behalf. The nominee officers and directors never need to know who you are, and if they take all their instructions from your attorney, that gives you additional protection because of the attorney-client privilege.

For professional people like physicians, dentists, architects, lawyers, and accountants, it is often a real struggle to find the right mix of tax breaks, liability protection, and corporate practicality under one corporate umbrella. As a result, many professionals use a professional corporation, which provides a high degree of liability protection, as well as tax benefits specifically geared toward building a good pension plan. Unfortunately, even in well organized professional corporations, professional people can still be held personally liable, regardless of their corporate status.

The solution to this problem is a strategy that was designed especially for a medical practice. This is how it works:

1. The professional sets up a professional corporation through which the professional service is performed.
2. A second, regular business corporation is formed for the purpose of managing the practice, and which will also own the client base.
3. The stock of the business corporation is issued to the professional's spouse as his or her separate property. (An option would be to issue the stock to an irrevocable trust as described earlier.)
4. The business corporation hires the professional corporation, by contract, to provide the professional service in return for a set annual fee. *If you do this, be sure to have a contract drafted which outlines the specific terms of the agreement.*
5. The client, or patient, pays the business corporation, which handles the billing, for all services rendered.

This strategy ensures liability protection by separating the risk associated with the professional service's efforts from the real assets of the business. If the professional is hit with a judgment in court, the business corporation could then exercise a provision in the contract between the two companies that allows it to, in essence, *fire* the professional corporation and replace it with another professional service provider. And the real asset, the professional person's skill, can then be transferred to a new entity with relatively little trouble. Then the process is repeated. In the event that you decide to implement this strategy, you should seek the assistance of a qualified attorney specializing in this area.

HOW CAN I USE A CORPORATION FOR ESTATE PLANNING?

At first, many people find it strange to be talking about a corporation as a way to take care of estate planning concerns. Some people consider estate planning to be the act of preparing for death, but it is *not*. It is the act of preparing for *life* for your assets after you are gone. It is the act of taking the worry out of your passing for those you care the most about—your children, your spouse, and even your corporate partners.

One of the easiest and best ways to provide an estate plan for yourself and other important people in your life is to incorporate. A corporation can protect assets that would otherwise be difficult or impossible to liquidate under normal estate planning techniques.

A commercial operation, for example, could not easily be split up among two children and a spouse, but the *profits* from such an operation could be, provided those profits are funneled through a corporate entity. The corporation also provides a shield against taxes and other sources of disruption that could destroy a viable business, in the event of your death.

The corporation's single biggest benefit to your estate planning strategies is its unlimited life span. Unlike people, corporations don't die of natural causes. Shareholder deaths do not, in and of themselves, cause the corporation to suffer. At the same time, the corporation can absorb much of the shock of a major stockholder's death, provided that stockholder has put estate planning techniques in the forefront of corporate planning.

Here is another little "what-if" scenario for you to contemplate. I think it will demonstrate rather dramatically how estate planning can be a real blessing to you and your heirs.

Let's suppose that you decide to open a business and you wisely choose the Nevada Corporation as the structure. You issue Class A Voting stock and Class B Non Voting stock at the outset. Your total capital to start is $10,000, and of that amount, $1,000 is capitalized in exchange for Class A Voting stock and $9,000 is a loan to the corporation.

Now, you issue yourself some Class A stock, representing only 5% of the company. You then issue your spouse an equal 5% of Class A stock. You also issue 45% of the corporate stock to both of your children. However, they are issued Class B Non Voting stock instead of Class A.

That is a total of 100% of the corporate stock that has been issued, but you and your spouse still control the whole thing by virtue of issuing the two classes of stock. Even when your children get old enough to be responsible for their shares, they have no voting rights, so the corporation stays under your complete control.

Okay, so the corporation's business booms for the next 10 years and all of a sudden is worth $2 million. Unfortunately for you, a massive heart attack intervenes. This leaves your wife and children to cope with a myriad of legal problems, tax problems, creditor problems and liability problems, right? *No*, actually it doesn't. The corporation does business the day *after* you die just like it always has. Much of the weight of your death falls on the corporation instead of your family. But, having the solid foundation of Nevada corporate law, your corporation hardly even wavers.

Instead of your estate containing a business worth $2 million, which would leave the family with a massive federal estate tax bill of over half a *million* dollars, your estate only contains 5% of the $2 million business, or a paltry $100,000. Since the $100,000 value of your part of the business is well under the $625,000 lifetime exemption, your family will have no estate taxes to pay upon your death. You just saved your spouse and children from losing almost 25% of the worth of *their* company.

Do you feel good about what you accomplished for your family? Well, since you're a fictional fatality of the scenario, you probably won't know the difference. But your family certainly will. Now, let's take a look at some more million dollar strategies for estate planning.

This next strategy uses the corporation and a limited partnership to transfer assets of enduring value to your heirs.

1. You have to form a corporation with No Par Stock, preferably in a corporate haven, such as Nevada. This corporation will exist solely as a "shell" having no assets, liabilities or value.

2. Once your corporation is set up, have the Board of Directors pass a resolution that sets a par value for corporate shares at a nominal amount, such as a penny per share.

3. Now you want to sell shares to your heirs at the price determined in the corporate resolution. Since they are purchasing the shares, the corporation is not being "gifted" to anyone, and there is no taxable event.

4. Next, you want to form a limited partnership for the purpose of owning the shares of the corporation. Give the partnership an extended life span, such as 50 years. The limited partnership agreement should provide for a termination of the partnership upon the death of the general partner. You become a 1% general partner and have the exclusive right to vote the shares of the corporation. The limited partners are your heirs.

5. Now, your heirs (the stockholders of the corporation) transfer their shares into the limited partnership in exchange for an ownership interest in the partnership. The general partner (you) owns 1%, you also own an additional 1% as a limited partner, and your heirs become 98% limited partners.

6. It's time to sell your personal assets to the corporation for the lowest fair market value that you can defend. (*It would be a good idea to consult a tax advisor for this.*) Take back a demand promissory note with a long maturity period. The note should bear interest at a reasonable market rate, and can provide that in the event of your death, the corporation will forgive any debt still owed.

7. Your corporation pays the interest as it becomes due under the note, providing you with some taxable interest income, but not a lot.

8. The end result is, if you die, your heirs will already own any assets you intended to leave them.

This strategy can mean a great deal to both you and your family if properly implemented.

This next strategy will help minimize estate taxes on appreciating assets or on profits generated through a corporation by transferring capital gains taxes to an irrevocable trust.

1. First, you must form another Nevada corporate shell having no assets, liabilities, or value, just as before. You and your spouse can be the shareholders or you can go it alone. This corporation's purpose is to own appreciating assets, or to be the beneficial party in a profitable business dealing.

2. Step two is to form an irrevocable trust, using an independent trustee, naming your heirs as the beneficiaries.

3. Now, you need to transfer the corporate shares into the trust under the $10,000 federal annual exclusion from estate and gift tax. Since the corporation is essentially worthless, this transfer triggers no taxable events, assuming you've made no other transfers that approach the $10,000 exclusion limitation. The trust now owns the corporation, and the Trustee controls the shares for the benefit of your heirs.

4. All appreciating assets you own should now be sold to the corporation for the lowest *defensible* fair market value, in exchange for a demand note bearing interest (similar to the limited partnership strategy). *Once again, it is advisable to consult with a qualified tax advisor to determine the appropriate amount.*

5. For a new business opportunity, the corporation is now able to entertain that business activity, since any value the enterprise builds will take place outside of your estate. Gains that occur will then be passed on to the trust automatically. This is a strategy which can enable you to significantly minimize the estate taxes involved in your estate.

In a closely held corporation, the death of a major shareholder can cause some real problems unless you have a strategy in place to deal with this well in advance. These problems not only affect the estate of the shareholder, but can have serious ramifications as to whether the corporation can continue to operate or not. Here are a few of the problems a closely held corporation would face:

1. Creditors of the corporation can immediately pressure the company for early repayment of any loans, or impose additional restrictions or requirements on the company's operations until such loans are repaid.
2. Employees of the corporation may wonder if the corporation will be liquidated due to dissension between remaining shareholders, or a lack of cash when creditor demands are placed on it.
3. Beneficiaries of the deceased shareholder may need money, which could induce the executor to make some kind of hasty distribution. That could put the deceased shareholder's executor in the position of having personal liability for unpaid taxes.
4. The deceased shareholder's estate will have the burden of proof in establishing the value of corporate shares. The IRS typically establishes as high a figure as possible for such stock, which the executor then has to dispute with fairly concrete proof. That is not always possible.

One way around these problems is to have your corporation establish some sort of a buy-out agreement to protect against the loss of any key shareholders. The most popular form of a buy-out agreement is called a "buy-sell agreement" in which other stockholders agree to purchase, at a predetermined price, all of the shares of any party who dies.

After the death of a shareholder, remaining shares would be sold to the other shareholders who were parties under the buy-sell agreement. The value of the shares for estate tax purposes would set the price at the time of the transfer, because that price represents an actual sale at arm's length between two shareholders who couldn't know at the time they signed the agreement whether they would end up being purchasers or sellers of the stock.

In most cases, the IRS will honor the value of the deceased owner's shares under a viable buy-sell agreement if you follow these guidelines:

1. A valid buy-sell agreement must restrict stock transfers while the shareholder is alive. The corporation and/or the shareholders must have the right of first refusal on the transfer of shares, at the price specified in the agreement.

2. State a valid business reason for the buy-sell agreement. The IRS won't let you get away with buy-sell agreements that are designed solely to pass on corporate shares at less than full market value. However, the IRS does usually recognize that maintaining family control and ownership over a corporation is a valid business purpose for a buy-sell agreement.

3. An *option* to buy or sell the stock is not sufficient for a valid buy-sell agreement. The deceased's estate must have an obligation to sell the shares at a specified price and, either the corporation or the shareholders must be obligated to purchase the shares.

4. The buy-sell agreement *must not* allow the number of shareholders to drop to a level where a personal holding company would result. This can happen if there is passive income involved or there are undistributed earnings present.

5. Last but not least, you *must* be reasonable. If you use a realistic method to set the value of shares, such as basing it on the earnings, or appraised value, et cetera, the IRS will agree with the value you set. Using a fixed price can create problems because the IRS knows that the real value of any corporation is likely to change over time.

What happens with a buy-sell agreement if no one has the funds to buy the outstanding shares when the time comes? The best way to eliminate that problem is to have each shareholder take out a life insurance policy on the other shareholders for this specific purpose. The policies could be assigned to a trustee to ensure that the proceeds will *only* be used to purchase shares from the estate. The insurance premiums won't be tax deductible, but any legal expense you incur to set up the plan and draft the agreement may be.

HOW CAN I USE A CORPORATION FOR TAX REDUCTION?

Now that you have your assets and estate protected by the Nevada Corporation, the next strategy you need to learn is how to reduce those nasty taxes on it. Again, the strategies you are about to learn are perfectly legal as long as you follow the law. Remember, too, that we are talking about tax "avoidance" and *not* tax "evasion." Avoidance will reduce the amount of taxes you pay; evasion will reduce the amount of freedom you have.

The toughest part of reaping financial benefits from a corporation these days is to take as much money out of the company as it can afford to pay you, while giving up the least amount of taxes to the government in the process. Owning your own business gives you the right to the money your corporation earns, but at the same time, the government has a right to take away some of your profits. Knowing how to legally avoid as much of that taxation as possible is a key strategy in building a viable plan. However, you have to be very careful how you go about putting that money in your pocket, otherwise you can seriously jeopardize the protection your corporate veil provides.

You've already learned that a Subchapter S corporation can go a long way toward reducing the negative tax consequences of double taxation to which other kinds of corporations are subjected. What do you *do* about this double taxation? How do you *keep* the money without violating the law? The ideal solution would be to have your Nevada Corporation spend the excess earnings in ways that will benefit you and your employees, and still avoid having double taxation apply to it.

Here are some of the most effective methods for taking cash or benefits out of your company and still avoiding the problem of double taxation:

1. Salaries
2. Bonuses
3. Commissions
4. Loans

5. Leases
6. Employee benefit plans
7. Independent contractor fees for services
8. Fringe benefits and expense accounts

HOW DO SALARIES HELP THE CORPORATION AVOID TAXES?

Setting salaries for owners or employees can be crucial in your efforts to avoid double taxation. Ideally, if you're threatened with double taxation you'll want to take out as much money in the form of salary as possible. That will likely make your personal income tax rate higher than you would like, but remember that salaries are deductible expenses for the corporation. However much money you receive in the form of salary, the corporation does not pay taxes on that amount and double taxation is at least reduced if not cut out altogether.

Once again, though, the IRS will have something to say about how you pay yourself. They will want to determine your importance to the business. If your role is determined to be "hands-on," (meeting with clients, coordinating activities, setting company goals and directions) then you can prove you have a personal impact on the entire operation of the business and are thus crucial to the company. But, if your work is "hands-off," and can be accomplished by someone else, your role might be considered less vital by the IRS and thus not worth the kind of salary you are paying yourself.

Whatever the case, the IRS will take a long, hard look at high salaries because if they can prove that the high salaries are there solely to avoid declaring dividends, they can make you pay more taxes. This is called a "Reasonableness Test," although it might be more appropriately called an "unreasonable test." The test applies a series of IRS standards to your compensation packages to determine if there are any disguised dividends built in anywhere.

Discretion plays a huge part in this testing process and is almost totally up to the IRS in most cases. So you need to pay particular attention to the following facets of the test to see just how they may apply to your situation.

The first thing the IRS looks at to justify your salary is the role you play in managing and directing your corporation's business. Many businesses are specialized or more complex than others, which may warrant significantly higher salaries across the board. In other words, the question becomes, "What would you be paid if you performed the same kind of specialized duties for some other business in the marketplace?"

If you can prove that you would be paid something similar to what you are currently making by another company, then you will likely have no trouble with the IRS over your salary. The best evidence here would be if you can show that you have received an offer to run a similar company at a similar salary.

You can also find out what other people are being paid by consulting the statistics that state agencies provide on unemployment claims. Libraries, newspapers, classified ads, and industrial trade associations can also provide information to back up your claim. If that type of information is hard to come by for your type of work, then expert testimony is also accepted by the IRS.

The next test is how much time do you actually put in at your job? The IRS usually determines that executives who receive full time pay for part time work are receiving "disguised" dividends. Most of you real entrepreneurs who work 16 hour days won't have to worry about working too little, though. As long as you keep accurate records of your work days, you shouldn't have any trouble proving that you work full time.

The next test is, how does your background, experience and education relate to your work? The more specialized your training and experience, the higher you can justify your salary. Keep on file all of the educational credits, seminars, degrees, certificates, and achievements that relate to your work. Many of these things will be considered significant when or if the IRS evaluates your salary.

Next, the IRS will look at your corporation's history and present financial situation. They will want to determine if your compensation package, including any recent raises in pay, is appropriate for the size and kind of business you are doing.

Further, your salary will be looked at historically to see if it is in line with the company's past growth and profits. If these two determinations seem appropriate, the IRS should accept your salary and raises as justified.

In some cases, the IRS will want to know how much you earned in other jobs. Previous employment records are a good indicator of how much the corporation should have expected to pay you to secure your services. You can build a valid basis for your salary by showing a record of promotions and salary increases, even if they are from unrelated companies.

The IRS will always take into consideration the prevailing economic conditions when testing salary levels. Compensation is analyzed with the economic conditions in your particular industry in mind as well as the country as a whole. How the IRS compares your salary will depend to a large degree on whether the national economy and comparable corporations are enjoying prosperity or just struggling to survive.

How your salary fluctuates compared to other employees in your company when overall income is down is another major consideration for the IRS. If your company can afford to pay you a high salary when company income is reduced, you may have to explain the decision not to cut your own pay if you have had to cut salaries for others. This is easiest when you can show that employees who own no stock have continued to be paid by the company and have taken no pay cuts.

In some companies, salaries for managers are a function of a percentage of sales instead of a fixed amount. Computing executive salaries from sales is perfectly acceptable to the IRS as long as the company does not raise that percentage in the middle of a year of high earnings. It is much less of a problem if you keep the percentage constant year around, allowing salaries to consistently rise or fall with sales.

The last things the IRS looks at are your company's dividend and bonus histories. By using close scrutiny of dividend and bonus practices over an extended period of time, the IRS often uncovers bonuses disguised as dividends. In particular, very low dividends paid to stockholders in years of very high bonuses are almost indefensible to the IRS.

Okay, now you know what the IRS tests are for salaries, but be careful here. Even if salaries look reasonable on the surface, certain practices can still raise red flags for illegal tax strategies. You need to structure your corporation so that the following situations will *not* present a problem:

1. Salaries alone are not the whole picture. The IRS is interested in your total compensation package. This includes all kinds of "perks" like pensions, profit sharing plans, insurance, and any company programs in which you participate. Company cars, boats, airplanes and other corporate "toys" are a factor, as are paid vacations and some forms of leisure travel. These all add to the value of your compensation package.

2. Stockholder salaries should never increase any faster than other high-level employees in the company. If stockholder salaries increase 20% during a period when other employees received raises of only 10%, then you can bet the IRS will be looking for some disguised dividends.

3. Never use all of the company's earnings to pay salaries. If the combined salaries of shareholders leaves the company with minimal net earnings, the IRS may determine that the salaries represent disguised dividends. Net earnings should fluctuate right along with company income.

4. Shareholder salaries should never reflect a percentage of ownership. When salaries are proportionate to the amount of stock the officers hold, the IRS will almost certainly deem it as evidence that part of the salary is actually unpaid dividends.

5. By hiring family members to work for your company, you can keep income in the family at a lower tax rate than if it were earned by them as shareholders directly. As long as the work is actually being performed by family members, and their salaries are reasonable, the compensation is deductible. The IRS calls this technique "income splitting."

6. By hiring a spouse, the owner of a closely held corporation can create an opportunity to take advantage of valuable tax deductions. Sometimes a spouse is not paid a salary because the business sees no advantage to adding

another person to the payroll. Then the couple files a joint tax return and half the family income is taxed to each of them, no matter who earns it.

Actually, hiring a spouse for your corporate operations can add some other, equally viable tax-sheltering strategies to your million dollar plan. For example, as an employee, your spouse can participate in such corporate benefits as:

1. *Profit sharing*—your corporation can get a full deduction for all contributions paid into a legitimate pension and profit-sharing plan for you and your spouse every year. These contributions are *not* taxable income to your spouse until he or she cashes in on the fund. At that point, these funds will receive a much more favorable tax treatment from the IRS as retirement income.

2. *Life insurance*—you can purchase life insurance for your employees, including your spouse, and then deduct the cost of the premiums. Any premiums covering the first $50,000 of insurance are not considered income to you or your spouse.

3. *Company travel*—if your spouse is an employee it is easier to show a legitimate purpose for travel in the employment of the company. While it is often difficult to deduct travel expenses incurred by your spouse, if they are on business trips or conventions, their expenses most likely are deductible.

In some situations, it may even be worthwhile to consider hiring your children for a corporate position and paying them a reasonable wage for the work they perform. Beyond the tax-sheltered benefits we have already outlined, employed children can use the full standard deduction to shield their income from taxes on the first $3,900 of earned income.

Your company can pay the children money that might otherwise be paid to you or your spouse in salary or dividends at a higher tax bracket and thus shift it into your children's lower bracket. The tax on children's wages starts in the 15% range and stays there for a wide range of incomes.

Everything has to be done completely on the "up and up" when your children work for you. If their wages are not reasonable, or no work is actually performed, the IRS may determine that the children owe back taxes on their earnings and the corporation could lose its deduction.

Remember, no matter how much your children are paid, you still get to claim them as dependents on your income tax return. However, the children cannot claim a personal exemption on their *own* returns if they are claimed as dependents by you.

The IRS rules say that a child is still your dependent as long as you provide more than half of their support and they either: a) have not reached the age of 19 or b) are between 18 and 24 *and* are full time students during any five calendar months of the year.

The only way to lose this deduction is if your children spend enough on their own support that at least half of it becomes self-provided. To avoid this problem, have your children put at least half of their earnings into a savings account so that you can always meet the criteria for providing at least half their support.

The only big drawback to this strategy (besides potentially having to fire your own kids) is that Social Security, unemployment taxes, and other state taxes still have to be paid for all employees, regardless of their age. These taxes can eat up a significant percentage of the tax savings you would gain by hiring them in the first place. Even this is not a major problem if they actually do fill the jobs that would otherwise go to another person, upon whom you would have such taxes anyway.

As long as we are talking about children, let's look at a very interesting strategy for providing them with a hefty little college fund, all *tax free* through your Nevada Corporation. Here's how it might work.

Let's say you are using a traditional investment plan to sock away $10,000 of taxable income every year for your children's college savings account. Your children are under 14 years of age, so the taxes on this money would look something like this: after the $500 standard deduction, the next $500 would be taxed at 15% ($75) and the rest at *your* personal tax rate, say, 33% (another $2,970). That's a total tax bite of $3,045.

Now, if you hire your children and *pay* them $10,000 over the course of a year for odd jobs at the company, they are only going to pay a little over $1,000 in taxes on the remainder of their earned income after the standard deduction. The tax savings for you, then, for every year you do this, would amount to over $2,000. By the time they are 19, you will have saved $10,000 for their college tuition, all of it tax free.

If you are an owner of a Personal Service Corporation (PSC) you should also take the opportunity to put another worker on the payroll because PSCs pay the flat tax rate of 34%. The more compensation your corporation pays out to family members, the less of its income can be taxed at that astronomical rate.

To avoid any unnecessary IRS scrutiny, you have to be somewhat careful the way you hand out bonuses in your corporation. The criteria for "disguised dividends" can easily be applied to a bonus paid out to yourself or a family member, particularly if there is no obvious reason to warrant such a bonus. If, for example, you were to win a Nobel prize for something you discovered in your work, that would be fairly good grounds for paying yourself a bonus.

Bonuses, then, must be considered a part of your compensation program, especially when it comes to passing that "Reasonableness Test" we've talked about. Most courts have held that a sole shareholder has no right to pay himself a bonus as an incentive to do his best in managing his own company. That is more or less expected of a reasonable person.

Support any bonus program with established criteria, and you will circumvent many problems in this area. Normally, you can give yourself a bonus without attracting IRS attention, provided you tie the bonus to some established, logical, and especially targeted events. As with salary increases, bonuses awarded late in the year are often suspicious. But, if the criteria for payment of a bonus are established earlier in the year, and are based on sensible results like sales quotas or long term company improvements, you shouldn't have any trouble.

You already know that there is an important distinction between capitalizing a corporation with equity and with debt. A debt holder has no opportunity for growth through the money lent to a corporation, but is in a more secure position than shareholders when it comes to getting that initial investment back. A debt holder gets paid back the money loaned the corporation before any shareholders receive a return of their capital.

In closely held corporations, particularly, debt holders are often shareholders who lend money to their corporation over and above whatever their initial capital investment consisted of. There can be some really favorable tax consequences for a shareholder to do this because while dividends are not tax deductible, interest payments *are* deductible, with some limitations.

There should be a board resolution authorizing the corporation to borrow money from a shareholder and a promissory note issued evidencing the debt. The note should include a fair market interest rate on the loan, as well as all of the terms of payment. Those terms *must* be followed closely in order to avoid more IRS scrutiny.

For example, let's say your Nevada Corporation had been capitalized with $100,000 of paid in capital. If the corporation reports a gross income of $70,000 and deductible expenses of $55,000, the $15,000 excess income is then taxable. Any distribution of the profits to the shareholders will result in the double "whammy" of a second tax on their proceeds. But let's suppose, instead of capitalizing the corporation with $100,000, you and your shareholders decided to invest $25,000 in capital stock and provide a loan of $75,000 at 12% interest. What happens to the tax picture then?

Your corporation still shows a gross income of $70,000, but now, deductible expenses have gone up because of the interest on the note. With $9,000 in deductible interest, total expenses now are $64,000. Taxable income has dropped to $6,000 in this scenario instead of the $15,000 you would have had to report before. You and your shareholders still receive as much money (or more) than if the original profits had been distributed through dividends.

The difference is, the loan interest is deductible and no longer subject to double taxation. Unfortunately, the IRS again has discretion in allowing such loan strategies to work. They can declare some or all of the deductions associated with this kind of debt as "constructive dividends" and make you pay additional tax (or penalties) accordingly.

When you lend money to your own corporation, the IRS will be most interested in looking at the ratio of debt to equity that would be reasonable under the existing circumstances of your corporation. This is often referred to as a "thin incorporation" determination. They will be looking closely to see if the debt you've incurred is actually just another form of equity, which makes the interest payments camouflaged dividends.

In situations like this, the IRS will determine loans by a shareholder to be valid, if:

1. A formal written loan document exists that states the details of the loan, including the due date, unconditional promise to pay, terms and interest rate,
2. The corporation has established a valid reason for making the loan and has board minutes to back it up,
3. There is a limit to the loan, and it does not provide unlimited access to corporate funding,
4. The debt is subordinated to other indebtedness of the corporation, and does not have preference,
5. The ratio of the corporation's debt to equity is within established IRS criteria, and/or
6. The debt is convertible into stock.

Another popular strategy for taking cash out of a corporation is by using leasing. Shareholders who have assets that can legitimately be leased to their corporation enjoy a whole range of options to make money this way. Shareholders can use a partnership or another corporation as the primary leasing company, thereby partially shielding themselves from IRS scrutiny. If a shareholder, as an individual, leases buildings, vehicles, equipment, or whatever to the company, tax liabilities and a host of other problems will often result.

There are really three general categories of things that can be effectively leased this way. They are:

1. Employees
2. Buildings or Real Estate
3. Equipment

Employee leasing is one of the fastest growing trends in corporate business practices. Every big city has companies devoted solely to temporary employees. These companies are generally responsible for all of the human resource management problems inherent with employees, instead of their client companies. They handle interviewing, testing, training, hiring, firing, payroll (including payroll taxes), equal opportunity problems and benefits. Leasing companies charge a fee for all these services, but it is usually based on the total payroll for which they are responsible. On a per-employee basis, it can work out to be a real bargain for some companies.

To take advantage of this opportunity, your primary corporate entity would agree to lease all of its employees from another company, at a cost that is slightly higher than the original payroll, but is still fully deductible. The leasing corporation (your *other* Nevada Corporation, ideally) then deducts the total salaries of the employees, along with training costs and other miscellaneous deductions. The end result is that you should be able to take a little more than twice the deduction for salaries than you had the other way, and, you gain a *lot* more flexibility in your human resource management area.

Okay, what about leasing buildings or real estate? A 1981 Tax Court decision established a method whereby an owner can set up a special tax shelter opportunity by tying the lease of a commercial property directly to the gross sales of the company. This kind of percentage lease has become very popular in commercial real estate ever since. Here's how that original situation came about.

When a food distribution company couldn't find financing for a badly needed warehouse, the corporation's shareholders, a married couple, bought land and built a warehouse to lease back to their company for 20 years. The company paid all of the property taxes and maintenance costs during that term.

According to the lease, the company was to pay to the couple an annual rent of $60,000, plus 1% of the company's annual gross sales over $4 million. At the time, the company's gross sales were only $2.3 million, so the couple drew the minimum $60,000 rent. Within eight years, the company's sales reached nearly $10 million and the couple received a total rent payment of $118,000.

The IRS attempted to disallow the company's rent deduction over the fixed amount on the basis that it represented a disguised dividend to the shareholders. However, the Tax Court disagreed, ruling that the couple had a legitimate business purpose in entering into the lease agreement, and were entitled to use the same technique with their own company as they would with any other business tenant. When the lease was drawn up, the court said the provisions were fair, thus the lease arrangement was upheld.

In order for you to use this strategy with no "hitches" you *must* keep all transactions at arm's length, then prove you have a legitimate business purpose, and make sure the terms are reasonable. Getting a certified real estate appraiser to help you with an estimate of fair rental value for the property is always a good idea, too.

Equipment leasing is another way to put money back into your pocket that the IRS wants to take away. Almost any equipment your corporation needs can be leased from somebody, and some of it probably already is. That somebody might as well be yourself, or another corporation set up for that purpose.

To accomplish this, capitalize an S corporation to purchase the equipment, then lease it back to your main corporate operations. The monthly lease payments are deducible to the main operation, and their original cost and depreciation are deductible to your S corporation, which should offset any profits. By using the S corporation, you eliminate the double-taxation problem associated with other forms of taking money out of a corporation.

Most owners of small, closely held corporations believe that they have no choice but to live with the heavy burden of "self employment" taxes. Many such owners don't even realize the magnitude of their obligations until it is too late to effectively deal with the problem. However, consulting with a qualified expert to help you set up your Nevada Corporation *before* you file can go a long way toward eliminating any big tax surprises.

That's because Nevada Corporation law provides for some terrific solutions to help people reduce their taxes. For example, one of the simplest strategies is to have a Nevada S corporation pay you a salary which is comparable to the average salary of someone in the work force holding a position similar to yours. The salary you set for yourself should be the lowest amount that you can defend as reasonable to the IRS. Keep in mind that any salary you earn will, of course, be subject to the usual FICA and Medicare taxes.

Once your corporation deducts all its corporate expenses, it can then pay out the remaining net earnings as dividends. Those go to you, as a shareholder. Those dividends will *not* be subject to FICA or Medicare, which helps eliminate at least part of the self-employment tax trap.

When you operate as a C corporation, any losses you suffer when you sell your stock are usually treated as capital losses. They are deductible only against capital gains and up to $3,000 a year in ordinary income. However, if you would like an ordinary loss deduction for your corporate stock, the solution is to treat your stock as "Section 1244 stock."

This means that such stock must have been issued to you by the corporation in exchange for cash but not in exchange for stock or securities in order to qualify for Section 1244 treatment. Also, your corporation must have received more than half of its gross receipts from sources other than rents, royalties, interest, dividends, annuities, and sales or exchanges of securities during the five most recent tax years. And, the corporation cannot have received more than $1,000,000 as a contribution to capital or paid in surplus.

This deduction can be taken for any class of stock, including nonvoting, restricted, and preferred shares. Losses in excess of the $50,000 individual limit ($100,000 on joint returns) are treated as capital losses. Thus, there are no major disadvantages or downsides to using 1244 stock treatment.

IRS Code Section 351 allows shareholders who contribute noncash assets for their shares to make the transfer without any effect on capital gains or losses. The tax basis of the assets becomes the tax basis of the shares. This type of treatment is only available if the contribution results in the shareholder owning at least 80% of the control of the corporation. This can prove to be a highly effective tax strategy.

One of the best tax strategies available now is the incentive for you to invest in small corporations. Individuals who purchase "small business stock" issued after August 10, 1993, and hold the shares for at least five years can escape tax on *half* their profit when they sell their shares later. The effect of this tax break has been almost unbelievable. Since long term capital gains have a tax rate cap of 28%, small business stock that qualifies for this break is actually taxed at the effective rate of only 14%.

Small business stock that qualifies for this treatment is referred to as "1202 stock" after the section in the IRC that describes its use. Even more important, that same part of the code says that shareholders who can take advantage of this kind of tax break can be C corporations, S corporations, individuals, partnerships, limited liability companies or mutual funds.

All right, now that we have all of your assets protected, your estate is up and running, including all kinds of protection and benefits, and your corporation is booming, what else could you ask for? How about a little tax free *cash*?

Before the Tax Reform Act was passed, many companies provided interest free (and tax free) demand loans to their key executives as fringe benefits. Corporate executives who received interest free loans from their companies were treated as having received "phantom" taxable compensation equal to the value of what the company would have charged on the loan. Executives could then deduct the "phantom" interest expense for the same amount. The end result was that the extra compensation and the deduction canceled each other out and executives paid *no* tax on the interest free loans.

The Tax Reform Act changed all that. Now, such deductions are subject to rules that eliminate many of the possibilities for tax free loans. The no-tax benefit can still be achieved using some creative strategies on interest-free loans. But you must be careful how the loans are structured.

For example, let's look at a $100,000 loan from your corporation at no interest. The IRS assumes an interest rate equal to the Applicable Federal Rate (AFR) for low or no-interest loans over $10,000. This is a rate based on the average market yield on U.S. obligations. If the AFR is 7% and you borrow $100,000 at no interest from your company, the *imputed* interest is $7,000. The IRS declares this as additional income to you and taxes it accordingly. You can't avoid the AFR by just charging yourself a token, low-interest rate, either. The IRS will again impute as additional income the difference between the rate your corporation charges you and the AFR.

However, interest on a home mortgage can still be deducted, so what if the corporation were to give you an interest-free loan secured by your home? The "phantom compensation" and "phantom interest" could be a wash for IRS purposes. You can also borrow from your corporation up to the $10,000 limit, tax free, without paying interest or worrying about taxes. This is the one exception to the taxing rules and should be used sparingly.

Any loan your corporation allows over the $10,000 limit *must* be structured "at arm's length" to keep the IRS from declaring the loan a taxable corporate dividend. To prove that a loan is an actual transaction that must be repaid, make certain you put all the terms of the deal in writing, including a regular repayment schedule. Also, be *sure* you record the date and amount of the loan on the corporation's books. The corporate minutes should also reflect full compliance with the loan, including a vote, if necessary, for approval.

Another way to reduce taxes on your corporation is to take full advantage of all Federal tax deductions that allow you to donate excess or inactive inventory to schools or charities. Regular C corporations can deduct the *cost* of the inventory donated, *plus* half the difference between the cost and fair market value. The total deduction can be up to twice the original cost of the inventory.

Most schools will be more than happy to accept outdated equipment, business forms, or miscellaneous office supplies for use in the classroom. However, any donations over $250 should be supported by a written acknowledgment. And be *sure* you check out a charity before making any major contributions. Find out if the charity is on the IRS list of organizations approved to receive tax-deductible contributions. You don't want to give away inventory, and then find out the contribution has been disallowed.

One of the best ways to reduce your tax bill is by learning what types of expenses are deductible. While I have included many of the items which may be deductible to your business, this is by no means an all-inclusive list. Build your relationships with tax professionals, attorneys, and other small business owners so that you can continually learn how to get better deductions all the time.

SUMMARY

Now you have them: asset protection, estate planning, tax reduction and liability protection—the big four of corporate planning. These are all million dollar strategies that will help you to become successful in your business. With all of these organized under a Nevada Corporation, you will have one of the strongest, least penetrable, and most viable business entities in the world. You will truly be using the millionaire's secrets to gaining wealth and security. You will be well on your way to becoming a "secret millionaire."

X THE SECRET MILLIONAIRE'S PENSION SECRETS

"A consecutive series of great actions is never the result of chance and luck; it is always the product of planning and genius."

NAPOLEON BONAPARTE

Planning and genius—those were Napoleon's two greatest attributes. He knew how to plan for the future and how to put his plans into action when the time came. He used strategies that are still being studied today. That's what I want you to learn in this chapter—how to implement the strategies we've been talking about.

You have already learned the planning part in the preceding chapters. Now you are going to learn how to employ specific strategies through the use of a corporation to build a solid retirement or pension plan for you and your family. I like to call it "The Millionaire's Pension Plan," because even though millionaires don't *need* a pension, they plan for it anyway. Many of them use the Nevada Corporation as the pinnacle of their pension program. By doing so, tremendous benefits can be obtained.

Benefit plans for you and the employees of your Nevada Corporation will not put cash in your pocket necessarily, but such plans have the indirect benefit of eliminating the need for you to pay out of pocket for the same kinds of benefits. If you plan your benefits strategies properly, and the plan qualifies, the corporation can deduct the contributions or expenses immediately, as they are paid out, rather than later.

A good benefit plan should include:

1. Medical reimbursement plans,
2. Dental and optical reimbursement plans,
3. IRA's, Keoghs, or other retirement plans,
4. Group life and accident insurance,
5. Stock option plans, and
6. Employee Stock Ownership Plans (ESOPs)

The benefit of setting up medical, dental and optical reimbursement plans for you and your employees is simply a must, as soon as your corporation can afford it. The psychological benefit of being protected from catastrophic illness alone makes the expense worthwhile. And as you may or may not know, medical expenses for an individual are only deductible to the extent that their total cost exceeds 7.5% of *adjusted* gross income. That means many high-wage earners don't qualify for a deduction for such expenses. The more money you make, the harder it becomes to deduct any medical expenses at all.

Your corporation will be much better able to keep good employees for the long term by reimbursing them for their families' medical expenses through a good medical plan. Such a plan will save you and your employees thousands of dollars and considerably more than that in peace of mind on the job.

This is a tax-free benefit for the corporation from the very *first* dollar spent, provided the plan is nondiscriminatory in favor of key people. Reimbursements are generally *not* included in the income of employees, as long as the reimbursements are not more than the cost of the care, and are not attributed to amounts taken by the employees as medical expense deductions in a prior year. Keep good records on these reimbursements, and you won't have too many problems with the IRS on this part of your million dollar pension plan.

Now, let's talk about pension and retirement plans specifically. First, let me clear up a common misconception about these plans. Much of the literature that promotes pension funds uses the phrase "tax free" when describing a particular plan. Technically, that is quite incorrect. They should more properly be referred to as "tax deferred."

That's because the income taxes on your initial contributions and the interest and dividend earnings they generate over time are not taxed until the cash is actually withdrawn from the fund. However, your corporation is allowed to take the deductions for contributions to a pension plan when they are paid into the plan.

Any amounts withdrawn are then taxed at the appropriate rate upon the retirement of an employee. Withdrawals are supposed to take place when you are in a lower tax bracket as compared to your years of active employment. That's not always true, but that's how it's supposed to work. Ideally, the taxes you eventually pay are less than you would have paid when the income was made.

The benefits of compounding retirement funds without major tax consequences are enormous. The fund grows faster and earns higher interest than comparable investments that are heavily taxed each year. It is even possible that the value of tax-deferred contributions and interest could amount to 500% more than if you paid taxes immediately on the contributions and interest.

The biggest problem with pension plans is the expense and time required to properly administer them. More often than not, government reporting is required, extensive bookkeeping and supervision of the plan are necessary, and there is a lot of paperwork involved. Large companies usually hire an actuary whose sole job is to oversee their pension and retirement programs.

Establishing your pension can be well worth any potential hassles involved, especially if you do it correctly. Only the most wide-eyed optimist believes that our Social Security system will provide enough money for your retirement. It is completely unrealistic to think that Social Security benefits will become more generous in the future. As the ratio of workers to retirees shrinks, the trend is to effectively reduce Social Security by taxing many benefit recipients who have additional income. This means you should create your own retirement plan to close the gap. This chapter is designed to familiarize you with the various types of plans available.

Fortunately, our tax laws help business owners of any size save for a secure retirement. Any kind of business, whether corporation, partnership, sole proprietorship or limited liability company, can set up a retirement plan complete with tax breaks. Without a retirement plan, you are missing out on one of the greatest tax benefits of being in business. But if retirement plans are so great, why is it that only a third of all small businesses have retirement plans?

The biggest problem associated with pensions is that the tax rules on contributions and withdrawals from retirement plans are very complicated. The big companies, however, set up the plans and make it easy for their employees to participate. This chapter presents a broad outline of retirement plan options available to all business entities. You will need more, so find an expert in helping business owners cope with retirement planning and administration. Stock brokerages, banks and insurance companies offer retirement plan advice, mostly as a means to sell their investment products. You need to take the time to understand the retirement plan basic components, and use these resources to establish a good plan.

WHAT IS A TAX-ADVANTAGED RETIREMENT PLAN?

A tax-advantaged retirement plan is one which qualifies for favorable tax treatment under the IRS requirements. If your business's plan qualifies, there are four main tax consequences associated:

1. Your contributions as an owner or employee are tax-deductible from current income up to a certain dollar amount. This has the effect of reducing your present income taxes. Contributions to tax-advantaged retirement plans are based on *earned* income. This means that an investor in a business who isn't active in it can't deduct their contributions to a retirement plan.

2. Income generated by investments in your retirement plan accumulates without being taxed until it is withdrawn.
3. The IRS generally imposes penalties for taking money out of a plan before retirement, but there are some exceptions allowed under the tax code.
4. Depending on how much income you have after you retire, withdrawals from your plan usually will be taxed at a lower rate than would apply to the same income taxed when you were working.

The benefits offered by pension plans essentially establish a deal that is hard to refuse. First of all, you get the opportunity to put aside money tax-free. Additionally, as long as you don't touch the money, it will grow tax-free as well. The keys are to start early and take full advantage of all that the law allows.

WHY A CORPORATE PLAN?

Corporate retirement plans have traditionally offered significant advantages over those available to all other business entities. While the gap between the various plans has become much more narrow in recent years, it is important to understand that a wider range of options are available for corporate plans. This is one of the key reasons why a corporate plan should be implemented. An example of these additional options is that larger contribution limits are available for corporate plans than for small businesses. Additionally, you can borrow from a corporate savings plan, which you can't do from other plans, at least without paying a significant tax penalty. One thing you need to keep in mind as you are reading this section is that if your business is incorporated, then you are treated for tax purposes as one of its employees. Whenever you see the word "employee," this includes you.

Another thing which you must understand is that if your plan is tax-advantaged, it will be governed by a set of federal laws called ERISA. This leads us to our next question which must be answered before we go any further.

WHAT IS ERISA?

The Employee's Retirement Security Act (ERISA) is a complex set of federal laws governing tax-advantaged retirement plans for employees of businesses. ERISA has been around since 1974 and has been revised by Congress numerous times. The ERISA laws are enforced by the Department of Labor and the IRS. Whenever you see the term "qualified plan," it means that it is an employee benefit plan governed by these ERISA rules.

One important function of the ERISA rules is to prohibit corporate plans from discriminating among employees. This means that plans can't favor business owners and officers of a corporation over other employees in granting tax-advantaged benefits. These prohibitions often make ERISA plans too expensive for typical small businesses. A common dilemma is often that a business can't afford to cover all of its employees in its plans, but wants the benefits for the owners.

The law grants some flexibility to owners. A corporation can place specific vesting requirements so that employees can be kept out of a corporate retirement plan until they have stuck around long enough to be valuable to the business. This is a common practice among many smaller businesses with corporate retirement plans. Which type of plan is best for you and your business? To answer that question, we need to know the alternatives.

WHAT ARE THE DIFFERENT TYPES OF CORPORATE RETIREMENT PLANS?

There are several different types of retirement savings plans. Depending on the type of plan you choose, contributions can be made by the business, the employee or both. The tax advantages of having an ERISA plan are:

1. Contributions to an employee's retirement plan are usually tax-deductible expenses to the business, thus reducing its taxable income.
2. Contributions to a retirement plan are made with before-tax dollars rather than after-tax dollars. This reduces taxable income.

Money in retirement plans earns income without being taxed as long as it remains in the plan. Withdrawals from a corporate plan can begin as early as age 55, but can be delayed until up until you reach age $70^1/_2$. These withdrawals are taxed at the participant's then current tax bracket, which is likely to be lower than when she was working.

Participants in corporate retirement plans don't have to stay with the company until retirement age to get their benefits. Whether they leave voluntarily or not, they have a "vested" right to whatever they contributed to the plan the date they leave. They might not be entitled to money contributed by their employer, however, unless they have worked a minimum number of years, often around four or five. And of course, they will have to reach retirement age before the right to collect the benefits kicks in.

Corporate retirement plans are divided into two types. These two types are called defined-contribution and defined-benefit plans. Let's look at each one in more detail.

DEFINED CONTRIBUTION PLANS

The defined contribution plan is the most popular type of corporate retirement plan, because it is usually funded by the employee rather than the business. Here, part of an employee's pay is deducted and put into an investment account.

In most defined contribution plans, the employer decides the contribution percentage for everyone. The corporation contributes a lump sum to the plan, which allocates to each employee's account based on his or her compensation. Plan contributions can be allocated disproportionately to slightly favor owners over employees.

As with most retirement plans, the account balance in a defined contribution plan upon retirement will depend on how much has been contributed and how well the fund's investments have performed. No fixed lump sum or monthly payments are promised to a plan participant, as is the case with a defined benefit plan.

DEFINED BENEFIT PLAN

The traditional corporate retirement plan is called a defined-benefit plan. This type of plan promises a specific monthly benefit for the life of the participant upon retirement. With a defined benefit plan, each participant knows how much he or she will get every month. In general, the longer an employee is with the company, the larger the monthly benefit.

Deciding on what type of plan is best for you and your business is a very important matter. I highly recommend speaking with a pension specialist if you are contemplating establishing a corporate retirement plan.

HOW DO I WITHDRAW MONEY OUT OF MY RETIREMENT PLAN?

One question I seem to always be asked is how someone can pull money out of their retirement plan. Too many times, people are looking for me to be able to teach them some miraculous way to take money out of their plan and never pay taxes. Unfortunately, that's not going to happen.

Money taken out of any retirement plan becomes taxable income. There are a few exceptions to this such as loans, which are possible only from certain types of plans. Withdrawals are taxed at your personal income tax bracket in the year you take out the money. Hopefully, when you retire, your income tax bracket will be lower than when you were working, which could mean a drop from as much as 39.6% to as low as 15%. This will really depend on your overall financial situation at the time. If you don't meet all of the rules at the time you pull money out of your retirement account, you will be subject not only to income tax on the withdrawals but to a special penalty tax as well.

Be careful not to get the idea that the withdrawal rules are any easier than the rest of the overly complicated tax laws on retirement plans. That is certainly not the case. There are different rules for just about every type of plan when it comes to the issue of withdrawals. If you are currently participating in a retirement plan, it will certainly pay to check with a tax or pension specialist before taking any money out of a retirement plan.

CORPORATE PLAN WITHDRAWALS

Distribution rules for corporate plans are more liberal than with other plans. For example, in a corporate plan you can start taking out money without penalty as early as age 55. Before that age, the 10% premature penalty tax kicks in. Like all other retirement savings plans, you must start withdrawing funds by age $70^1/_2$. There is an exception to this rule for those who continue to work past age $70^1/_2$. In this instance, you can put off withdrawals as long as you don't own more than 5% of the stock of the corporation. A minimum amount must be withdrawn each year after attaining $70^1/_2$, based on your life expectancy under IRS tables. For further assistance, speak with a qualified pension specialist.

Defined contribution plans include the following:

1. 401(k) plans
2. Employee Stock Ownership Plans (ESOPs)
3. Stock bonus plans
4. Simplified Employee Pensions (SEPs)
5. Money purchase pension plans
6. Profit sharing plans
7. Target benefit plans
8. Thrift of savings plans
9. Savings Incentive Match Plans for Employees (SIMPLE)

SUMMARY

Corporate pension plans can be a great tool in preparing for your retirement. Not only are the contributions tax deductible, but the dollars inside the plan enjoy tax deferred income growth. Through the miracle of compounding, you could find yourself with several million dollars in a relatively short time. Another great thing about pensions is their protection from both lawsuits and bankruptcy. A pension plan can be an integral part of your overall plan. As always, if you plan on implementing this plan, seek assistance. It will save you far more than it ever costs.

XI THE SECRET MILLIONAIRE'S CORPORATE METHODS

"Method is good in all things. Order governs the world."

JONATHAN SWIFT

Even as early as the 1700s, learned men like Jonathan Swift realized that using good methods in business was the key to their financial futures. Today, there is no finer method to secure *your* financial goals than the use of a Nevada Corporation. Properly set up, correctly managed, and efficiently maintained, the Nevada Corporation can provide for all of your business needs, wants, wishes and desires. But you *must* know how to handle all of the various aspects of the corporate structure correctly in order to ensure that the law is always on your side.

In this chapter, you will learn the three Ps of proper corporate operations. They are *people*, *procedures* and *paperwork*. We will take you from the initial stages of set up, all the way through daily operations, meetings, minutes and a million other things your corporation must do in order to maintain its viability in this litigious world we live in.

Study this information carefully. Make it a part of your million dollar plan. Once you do, you will have taken a giant step toward a happy and secure financial future.

WHAT PEOPLE ARE REQUIRED TO INCORPORATE?

The first thing a corporation needs is someone to fill specific positions that are necessary in order for the corporation to act like a corporation. This person (or persons) acting in their defined roles allows the corporation to retain its separate identity and function as a corporate entity. Without the requisite number of people, a corporation cannot exist.

The organizer of your corporation can be an investor, an attorney, a prospective shareholder or director of the corporation, or a consultant or advisor. There is no requirement that a corporation be formed by you, personally, or even by your attorney. There are firms in Nevada that specialize in forming Nevada entities and providing the necessary resident agent services (more on this in a minute). These companies will help you draft your Articles of Incorporation, and get all the other filings in order, but you have no obligation or liability to them once the corporation is formed.

Various states have laws that stipulate how many people are required, and what their functions are. There is also a mechanism established whereby these individuals are identified to the public. Typically, states require a corporation to file an "annual report" that names all corporate officers and directors, and even shareholders in some cases. The annual report usually contains information regarding the value of corporate assets, as well. Some states may require this information to be included in the annual state tax return as an alternative to the annual report method.

Nevada, on the other hand, has perhaps the simplest, easiest and least invasive disclosure requirements of any state in the country. A one page form requires the disclosure of the President, Secretary, Treasurer, and at least one Director of the corporation. Since Nevada allows for one person corporations, the name of the same individual can be used to file each position. No other information is required on the form.

A Nevada Corporation is not required to file a list of officers and directors any more often than on an annual basis, even if there are several changes of officers during the year. Corporations are not required to keep any officer or director for the entire year. Officers can be removed from office and replaced at any time.

Corporate officers could, theoretically, serve 364 days a year without ever being listed with the State of Nevada. On the last day of the year, whichever officers you would like to have appear on public records can be reappointed for the purpose of the filing, and then serve a single day term. It is quite possible, then, for officers and directors to serve without ever having their names listed on state records.

All officers of your corporation must be elected by a board of directors, and are then assigned responsibilities in the written corporate Bylaws to conduct the regular daily business of the corporation. In Nevada, you must elect a president, secretary, treasurer and resident agent. You have the option to elect one or more vice presidents and any other officers or assistants that you desire. Thus, your corporation could elect to have an assistant-secretary, or assistant-treasurer that is authorized to sign all documents and conduct all business that the original officer would ordinarily be assigned.

Under the law, secretaries or other officers of a private corporation have only the authority specifically delegated to them by the Bylaws and/or board of directors of their corporation. They cannot be held personally liable for debts of the corporation, except potentially by the IRS for payroll taxes or other specific tax obligations.

Here is a list of the officers and their functions:

CORPORATE PRESIDENT

The president's primary duty is to oversee the actions of all the other officers. The president reports to the board of directors and is responsible for carrying out the board's orders.

CORPORATE SECRETARY

The secretary maintains all corporate records and formalities. The secretary's duties include executing and recording the minutes of meetings and resolutions, maintaining the corporate stock ledger and overseeing the issuance and transfer of corporate shares. In many corporations, it is the responsibility of the corporate secretary to ensure that the corporation abides by all internal rules and Bylaws, including the timely distribution of any notices and waivers, and that proper parliamentary procedure is followed in all corporate meetings. The secretary acts as the voting inspector during stockholders meetings, and announces voting results.

CORPORATE TREASURER

The treasurer is responsible for maintaining all financial records and transactions. The treasurer will present a "Treasurer's Report" at all regular meetings, and will oversee stocks, bank accounts, investments and liabilities of the corporation. The treasurer will see to it that the board of directors has whatever financial information they need to make informed decisions about the corporation's financial future.

CORPORATE VICE PRESIDENT

One or more vice presidents may be provided for by the corporate Bylaws or through a resolution of the board of directors. Vice presidents may be assigned any duty the corporation sees fit to assign.

Those are all of the positions that are mandatory to file for your corporation to be viable. You must elect at least one director for your Nevada Corporation, but the Articles of Incorporation should stipulate either a fixed number of directors, or a minimum and maximum number. You may also elect one or more vice presidents, assistant secretaries, and/or any other officers that the board of directors finds necessary. The board may remove any of these officers at any time. Officers elected to a Nevada Corporation must be a natural person (not another business entity) of at least 18 years of age and need not be a resident of Nevada or the United States.

Overall corporate management and control are vested in the *board of directors* by the corporation's stockholders, and are limited by the Articles of Incorporation and the Nevada Corporation Code. Directors that do not meet the standards of care and loyalty in carrying out their duties can be held personally liable to the corporation or its stockholders.

Directors must stay informed regarding all decisions they are asked to make for the corporation. Any decision by a board of directors should be defensible by one or more of the following considerations:

1. The interests of the corporation and its stockholders,
2. The economy within which the corporation is operating,
3. The interests of the corporate community and of society, and
4. The interests of employees, suppliers, creditors and customers.

Directors may *not* use their offices to generate personal profits through the corporation or to produce any other personal advantage due to their decisions. At all times, directors must act prudently in their role, and have reason to believe that their actions are fully lawful, in order to be indemnified from personal liability for their actions.

If stockholders choose not to hold a director personally liable for an action, a court may or may not let such a decision stand, depending upon the legal precedents involved. When a court allows stockholders to *not* hold directors liable for their actions, it is often referred to as the "business judgment" rule.

Sometimes a board of directors can deadlock in such cases if they are unable to make a decision on a particularly important matter, and where no shareholder has enough votes to change the membership of the board. You should have your Bylaws refer any such deadlocked issues directly to the stockholders. If they can't break a deadlock of the board with a vote, then the situation can be referred to a court to decide the issue.

Nevada Corporation Code also allows for committees to be formed within a board of directors. As long as your Bylaws or Articles of Incorporation provide for such, a committee of the board of directors may be formed to exercise the powers of the board in the management of the business and affairs of the corporation. Committees must include at least one director, and unless your Articles of Incorporation state otherwise, the board may appoint persons other than directors to serve on their committees.

The *stockholders* are the actual owners of the corporation, and ultimately have the power to regulate and control whatever the corporation does. Stockholder power rests in the hands of the directors, who are elected by the stockholders and then delegated all the power necessary to carry on the business. Typically, each share of voting stock is allowed one vote.

An investor who controls the majority of the issued voting stock ultimately maintains control over the corporation. The method by which a shareholder exercises this control is through the ability to elect directors. When there is only one investor, the process is quite simple. When there are a lot of shareholders, things can get considerably more complicated.

Since different classes of stock (voting, nonvoting, et cetera) can exist, it is possible for a stockholder to have only a minority interest in the corporation, but gain a majority of the voting rights of the shareholders. When this occurs, special planning is needed to ensure that minority shareholders have sufficient voting rights to give them a level of participation that the Nevada Corporation Code guarantees them, without having to give them an inappropriate amount of control.

Several methods are available to allocate voting power between different groups of investors. These can produce permanent allocations of control, or only temporary allocations for special circumstances. The methods of allocating power among shareholders by issuing different classes of stock are almost endless. For instance, you could have a majority stockholder who owns all of the shares of one class of stock, which authorizes him to elect all of the directors except one. Minority stockholders, then, might own all of the shares of another class of stock, which may equal or exceed the total investment of that majority stockholder, but only allow them to elect one director. Their power would be roughly equal, creating a sort of "checks and balances" arrangement.

Another important person to be appointed for your corporation will be the *"resident (or registered) agent."* Every Nevada Corporation is required to maintain an agent with a registered office within the boundaries of the state. A resident agent may be either a corporation or a natural person, and is required to have an actual street address, not just a post office box or mail drop. And, even though a resident agent is appointed by the corporation, the agent must file an acceptance of that appointment with the Secretary of State's office before it is officially considered the resident agent of that corporation.

The primary purpose for a resident agent is that it requires corporations to maintain a form of physical presence in the state. That, in turn, ensures that any legal service process or notice of litigation can be served on the corporation. Resident agents act for you, and their actions have a binding influence on your corporation.

There's nothing really difficult about that, as long as your agent knows what to do. For example, your Nevada Corporation is required to maintain certain records at the office of the resident agent. These records must include:

1. A copy of the Articles of Incorporation, complete with any amendments, as certified by the Secretary of State,
2. A copy of the Bylaws, certified by an officer of the corporation,

3. The original stock ledger, or a duplicate stock ledger or a statement that provides the name and address of the actual custodian of the stock ledger.

Selecting a good resident agent is essential when you first go to set up your Nevada Corporation. Your resident agent should have established business hours, be easy to find and have a strong familiarity with the procedures of receiving legal service of process. Above all, agents should be highly reputable in the business community.

Several years ago, one of the largest resident agents in Nevada filed for protection under Federal Bankruptcy statutes, leaving hundreds of corporations in the dark as to their legal status while the agent's office was ransacked by bankruptcy trustees. Another Nevada resident agent closed his doors and just walked away from hundreds of clients. These corporations were left with no recourse, having lost their agents.

The point is, your corporation is responsible for anything the resident agent does, or doesn't do, in the name of the corporation. That includes handling legal process, which can lead to some real problems if not handled on a timely basis. I could give you a hundred examples of companies that have had default judgments filed against them because they were not notified by their resident agent on time. If the agent fails to perform, the responsibility for the service of process is still the corporation's problem. To avoid any surprises in this area, know your resident agent, and stay in touch with them frequently.

WHAT PROCEDURES ARE REQUIRED TO INCORPORATE?

Success with your corporate strategies will depend to a great degree on the corporation's ability to demonstrate that it has a valid, viable business purpose, and that it operates like a normal business. With a valid business purpose, your corporation should function just like any other business competing within your industry. If that continues through the life of the corporation, and all procedures are followed, then the chances of your corporate "veil" failing in Nevada are minimal.

Nevada corporate law sets the standards on this difficult and often misunderstood concept. The issue of "piercing the corporate veil" is one of the most often cited reasons that people incorporate in Nevada. That and the advantage of being able to form one person corporations gives you more flexibility than in any other state. The simple fact: it is *very* difficult to pierce the corporate veil in Nevada, especially in one-person corporate structures.

Typically, there are five basic issues that can be used as grounds to pierce a corporate veil. In some jurisdictions, the presence of one of these issues is not normally, in and of itself, sufficient to open up any personal liability problems. But that is no guarantee that it won't be either. The point here is, by doing things correctly, you won't raise any red flags for someone to drag you into court.

The first issue is *undercapitalization*. Corporations that are not prepared to cover any potential damage which could arise out of the normal course of business are undercapitalized. If your corporation causes damage to someone and does not have enough cash or assets to deal with the liability, then you are putting the assets of the corporation at risk of lawsuit. While this has not proven to be a strong enough reason for piercing the corporation veil in every state, it is a significant enough problem that you need to be aware of the potential, regardless of where you incorporate.

The simplest way to avoid this problem is to buy enough insurance to cover the types of risk that are most common to your particular business. That way, if something goes awry, there's no need for the court to start looking at your corporate veil, since you have enough assets to cover any damages.

The second issue is the *commingling of funds*. This is one of the simplest problems to avoid. All you have to do is never, never, never pay personal expenses from your corporate checking account, and don't pay corporate bills from your personal checking account or with cash out of your pocket. If money is tight for whatever reason, there are proper and legal ways to deal with any necessary transferring of funds.

For example, you can execute a loan or purchase additional stock without jeopardizing your corporate veil. As always, any such transactions should be fully authorized by a vote if necessary, and noted in the corporate minutes.

The third issue is *failing to follow minimum corporate procedures*. Nobody should ever have trouble with this issue, but they do, for some reason. All it takes to avoid this problem is to make sure all corporate formalities are adhered to on a regular basis. The best way to defend the actions of your officers and directors is through detailed corporate records that prove someone was properly authorized by the corporation to do whatever it is they have done to cause a problem. By keeping corporate minutes current, up to date, accurate and timely (including any extraordinary activity in particular) you will go a long way toward protecting your corporate decision-making process and your veil.

Here are some things you should make certain are well documented:

1. Any changes in your corporate Bylaws,
2. Any changes in the location of the principal corporate office,
3. Any loans made to directors, stockholders, or officers;
4. Any accumulation of excessive earnings,
5. Any changes in executive compensation packages,
6. Any actions involving changes in retirement or pension plans,
7. Any actions resulting in step transactions, or
8. Any actions resulting in the sale of major corporate assets.

The fourth issue is *failure to have authorization*. If the activities of your corporation are consistently carried out by a particular person and the corporate records do not authorize that person to carry out those duties, you may be opening a window of liability. The corporate veil covering that person may well be nonexistent due to the liability for personal injuries or damages caused by unauthorized business activity.

If, on the other hand, that person is fully authorized as an employee or officer of the corporation to handle his/her portion of the corporation's daily activities, there should be no problem, even if something is done wrong. The principle concept here is, if someone is properly authorized by the directors to carry out a task(s), they keep the corporate veil in place while performing that task(s).

The fifth major issue used to pierce the corporate veil is the *misuse of corporate formalities*. This is probably the most commonly abused issue of them all. You must remember at all times that you are acting as a corporation. You and the employees of your corporation should never, never, never sign anything unless you are authorized to do so. In particular, an authorized officer of the corporation should sign all *formal* documents. This includes contracts, purchase orders, delivery receipts, agreements, leases, loans, and so forth. Never sign "for" someone either, even if it means holding up operations for an hour.

So how does anyone know that you've signed on behalf of your corporation and not personally? If you just sign your name, you are representing *you*, not the corporation. However, if you sign your name and include your corporate title, you are representing the corporation. If you forget and sign something without that corporate title, you can be held personally responsible for the cost of the contract or whatever.

You should also make sure that clients, customers, suppliers, and agents know that when they deal with you, they are automatically dealing with the corporation. The best way to handle this is to include a corporate designation in the name of your company, and use it on everything you put in print, such as invoices, checks, bills, purchase orders, and the like (including your computer correspondence or e-mail). If your business uses the name "XYZ, Inc." in every transaction, there can be little room to question that the company is actually incorporated.

If the courts are able to "pierce the corporate veil" using any or all of the five issues you've just studied, they can assign personal liability to individuals for actions that the corporation has taken. It is quite common for lawyers to name individuals associated with a corporation, including the officers, directors and employees, as defendants in any litigation against that corporation, even if they don't have any direct responsibility for the action upon which the suit is based.

This is done to force the court to make a determination as to whether the corporate veil can be breached, in which case the individuals can then be held personally responsible. If any individuals are held personally liable, it can cost them a lot of money and the corporation a lot of hassle. In almost every case where this happens, the most common problem was uncommon carelessness by the owners.

In many such liability cases, the "alter ego doctrine," is what the court applies when it rules that stockholders have used their corporation in a manner that leaves no distinction between the corporation and themselves. In order for this alter ego theory to be applied, the following requirements must generally be met:

1. The corporation is influenced and/or governed by an individual.
2. There is a unity of interest and ownership between the individual and the corporation that makes them virtually indistinguishable.
3. The presence of the corporation in a given situation would sanction fraud or injustice, even if fraud is not necessarily proven.

The single best defense against this kind of ruling is the corporate record book. Most attorneys and incorporating companies will provide you with a corporate "kit" that includes sample forms to be used for resolutions, minutes and so forth. These generic forms will help you get started, but their limited scope and number almost never provide enough variety to be effective in all situations that require their use.

As you begin to operate your corporation and hold meetings, you will come to understand the use of corporate records much better. Then you should be able to modify any generic forms to fit your particular situation or consult with an attorney to get some help. You can also go out and buy a complete set of sample corporate records that deal with a host of situations, then adapt them to your uses.

One way to avoid a lot of the problems associated with the corporate veil and record keeping is to hire the services of a professional Resident Agent company. These companies offer a "contract office service" or "corporate headquarters service" for a monthly fee. The variety of services offered depends on the provider, but typically they include assistance with obtaining state and local business licenses, assistance with obtaining Nevada bank accounts, use of office and/or conference facilities, a physical location (not a mail drop), mail forwarding, telephone answering and the normal resident agent presence.

The services provided are more or less an insurance policy for your corporation if you are not physically located in Nevada already. An agency arrangement is sufficient proof of your corporation's bona fide existence and should dissuade any frivolous lawsuits based on corporate veil issues.

Such agencies are also quite useful in establishing the facts of your corporation's domicile and base of business operations when a corporation is used as part of a strategy to avoid state corporate income taxes. They can be critical in the corporation's ability to prove the existence of interstate commerce instead of intrastate commerce.

In Nevada, there is no definitive test to determine whether or not a corporation is legitimately conducting business or not. However, it's a good idea for you to consider all of the following if you plan to incorporate in Nevada:

1. Your company should have an actual business address. This is because it has been held that if a corporation does not have a real office, it is likely to be a shell operation or a holding company, and not a legitimate business establishment. The existence of the office should be documented for tax purposes with canceled corporate checks in payment of rent and utilities.
2. Your company should have a telephone listing in the corporate name, at the office address. This should be supported by canceled corporate checks for payment as well.
3. Your company should have all of the appropriate licenses to engage in business activity as required by local jurisdictions.

4. Your company should handle all of its financial transactions through corporate bank accounts set up in the local area.
5. Your company contracts, agreements, transactions, purchases, sales, et cetera should be signed and/or consummated at the corporate office.
6. Your company should have full time employees available at the office during regular business hours to conduct business.

If you plan to physically operate in Nevada, then the option of a contract office is not worth considering. However, the contract office concept meets many of the preceding criteria to different degrees. The question then is: are they worth considering for your business? Clearly, the answer is: it depends on your situation.

In order for contract agent services to be worth your consideration, one of the following situations should apply:

1. You want to draw all attention regarding the corporation away from you for whatever reason.
2. Your corporation is used for asset protection purposes, and needs to appear completely unconnected to you or your personal affairs.
3. Your corporation actually needs the service, and it represents an affordable alternative to outfitting an entire office.
4. You need to project a more stable, professional appearance than you might otherwise be able to display because of limited funding, et cetera.
5. Your corporate strategy relies upon not having to qualify to do business as a foreign corporation in another state.
6. Your corporation's activity is regulated or licensed, and as such must have an office located in the local jurisdiction.
7. Your corporation needs to file for bankruptcy, and you don't want to have to file in your home district.

If any of these situations exist for you, then you might want to consider using an agency service to provide a viable Nevada office. There is no question that having the appearance of a legitimate office can greatly enhance your corporate image. Unfortunately, if your corporation has to defend itself in court, a contract agency service may not offer much protection if the other facts in the case don't support you.

A significant part of the procedure for any corporation is the holding of certain *meetings* during the year. While all corporations are required to hold annual stockholder's meetings, public corporations must follow federal laws and private corporations must follow state laws that regulate their meetings. It is important that you follow the applicable laws, as a failure to do so can give a disgruntled stockholder or an outside creditor grounds for bringing suit.

Nevada corporate law requires only two meetings a year. They are the annual meeting of stockholders and the annual meeting of directors. These meetings can be held anywhere in the world, depending upon the Bylaws of your corporation. Nevada even allows these meetings to be held through teleconferencing or computer links, unless otherwise prohibited by your Articles of Incorporation or Bylaws.

The main purpose of your stockholders meeting is to elect the board of directors for the following year. If stockholders are unable to elect directors within eighteen months of the last election, a district court can order such elections. For most small, family-owned corporations, these elections are more a formality than anything else, but they must still be held. When outside stockholders exist, though, the Corporation Code has to be strictly adhered to.

Your corporate secretary, who monitors the election process, should be prepared with a current list of stockholders and, if applicable, a separate list of stockholders who are entitled to vote. The secretary is responsible for the proper execution of the voting plan adopted by the corporation.

A board of directors meeting is held annually (at least) to make all decisions that have been delegated to the directors by the stockholders. Typically, directors use this meeting to ratify all of the actions they may have taken by resolution (more on this later) since their last meeting. The directors also elect the corporate officers for the following year. Your Bylaws should contain all of the procedural directions necessary for the directors to conduct the business of their meetings, including the applicable definitions of a working majority and quorum.

WHAT PAPERWORK IS REQUIRED FOR INCORPORATING?

The following is by no means a complete list of all the corporate formalities, documents and operations that you need to follow in your corporate operations. Rather, it is intended to be a checklist of the minimum requirements for your corporation to follow to properly maintain your corporate status:

1. Follow your Articles of Incorporation and Bylaws in all dealings.
2. Hold your annual meetings of stockholders.
3. Give stockholders proper notice of any meetings.
4. Use appropriate waivers of notice for meetings.
5. Record proper minutes.
6. Include officer and committee reports in the corporate minutes.
7. Conduct important business *only* in meetings.
8. Record proper minutes to reflect decisions made during meetings.
9. Hold board of directors meetings at least annually.
10. Give proper notice of any and all board meetings.
11. Elect officers and conduct other business as per Bylaws.
12. Elect directors as necessary per state laws and Bylaws.
13. File returns for the corporation, even where no profit is shown.
14. File an annual list of officers and directors as required.
15. File an Annual Report with the Secretary of State.
16. Appoint a Resident Agent and be sure your agent gets state acknowledgment of status in return.
17. Notify agent of any changes in location of the stock ledger or any amendments to Articles or Bylaws.
18. Be sure all actions of stockholders are done by vote and recorded in the minutes of a meeting.
19. Be sure major decisions by directors are recorded in minutes.

20. Be sure that a properly executed contract exists for services contracted for by the corporation.
21. Be sure that funds and assets are properly conveyed between the corporation and other entities or individuals.
22. Never commingle corporate and personal funds.
23. Record all corporate loans in corporate minutes.
24. Maintain current records for the corporation.
25. Keep your stock ledger up to date.
26. Issue new stock certificates and redeem transferred certificates as such transactions take place.
27. Always sign on behalf of the corporation and indicate title.
28. Make sure the corporation looks and acts like a corporation.
29. Keep records proper and up to date.
30. Always maintain a traceable paper trail to prove that all actions were performed by a corporation and not just by an individual.

As you can see from this list, paperwork and the formality that goes with it are very important aspects in a Nevada Corporation. Corporate documents, including the Articles of Incorporation, Bylaws, resolutions, minutes, stock certificates and stock ledger *must* be handled correctly and consistently to maintain your corporate veil.

The role of the officers, directors, agents and stockholders in this process cannot be overlooked. That is particularly true in a one person corporation, where corporate paperwork may be the *only* thing that can prove an individual was *not* acting in place of the corporation or vice versa.

Without corporate records, a corporation cannot prove that its board of directors is acting properly when making decisions for the corporation. Without detailed and properly documented records, a court can determine that the board of directors failed to act at all, and since the board of directors was not functioning, neither was the corporation.

There are a million sad stories in the legal profession that start with some court attaching the personal assets of a director or stockholder where corporate records were improperly kept or reported. We're going to examine in detail each of these vital paper items so that you should never have to worry about that happening to your or your corporation.

The *Articles of Incorporation:* this is a document that your corporation must file with the Secretary of State to be legally recognized as a corporation. It is considered a binding contract between the incorporators, the state, and the shareholders regarding the functions, responsibilities, and duties of the corporation.

As long as the Articles you file meet certain requirements, the Secretary of State has no authority to mandate any changes in them. Outside the basic requirements, your Articles may contain almost any provision that is within the boundaries of Nevada corporate law.

The basic requirements include:

1. The name of the corporation,
2. The name and address of the person or entity that will be appointed as the resident agent for the corporation,
3. The number of shares the corporation is authorized to issue,
4. The series and number of shares of each class authorized,
5. The name and address of each board of directors member, and
6. The name and address of each incorporator signing the Articles.

In addition to these basic requirements, Nevada corporate code allows for the inclusion of a provision (discussed previously) that can eliminate the personal liability of a director or stockholder to the other stockholders. This provision is purely optional, but I can see no reason why a director or officer would *not* want this included in the Articles of their corporation.

Your Articles may (and should) include provisions that are needed by the incorporators to regulate the interactions between stockholders, directors and officers. These provisions can include limitations on the powers of individuals associated with the corporation, or even limitations on the purpose of the corporation itself. In some cases, the Articles may even limit the life span of the corporation to a specific period of time instead of allowing for perpetual existence.

When the Nevada Secretary of State receives your Articles of Incorporation and the appropriate fees, the Articles will be officially filed and a certificate of authorization to transact business in Nevada will be issued to your corporation. At no time before this authorization is the corporation recognized as a corporate entity by the state. Do *not* conduct business, even on a rudimentary level, before you receive your certificate.

Okay, let's take a look at a typical set of Articles. The Articles listed here will work for almost any state, but consult your state regulations if you are incorporating outside of Nevada.

ARTICLE ONE

The first section of the Articles of Incorporation should state the name of your corporation. This name should include the word "corporation," "company," "incorporated," "limited," or any appropriate abbreviation of these terms. One of these terms *must* be included if the corporate name resembles the name of a real person. The name of the corporation may not resemble the name of another corporation conducting business in the same state or in such a way that might cause confusion or a conflict of interest.

ARTICLE TWO

Your corporation must declare the period of its existence. The most basic corporate characteristic is to live in perpetuity. While the corporation can declare a specific period of life, such as 10 years, most corporations declare a perpetual existence. A corporation that declares a limited time frame can be subject to fines if the corporation operates after the stated expiration date.

ARTICLE THREE

Your corporation must state the purposes for which the corporation is being organized. Under the Model Corporation Act, a business corporation may be organized "for any lawful purpose or purposes, except for the purpose of banking or insurance," but you may choose more specific language in stating your corporate purpose. If, however, the corporation engages in any business activity outside of that limitation, it must amend the Articles of Incorporation or face penalties. For that reason, most corporations choose to be organized "for any lawful purpose."

ARTICLE FOUR

Your corporation must describe the corporation's stock, including the number of available shares, any classifications, preference or other rights, and the par values. It is usually preferable to organize your corporation with the largest number of shares that the Secretary of State will allow for the minimal filing fee.

In this article, you can provide for a certain number of voting and nonvoting shares if you want to. That way, if more investment is needed down the road, but maintaining control is a concern, your corporation could issue nonvoting shares. You can divide the corporation's stock into as many different classes of stock as you need in order to provide for future planning goals, but they must be stipulated in this article.

You can also declare a specific par value, such as $.01 per share or $100 per share in this section of the Articles. Many closely held corporations prefer to use no par value shares, which allow the directors to determine the selling price of the shares.

ARTICLE FIVE

In this section, your corporation is allowed to issue classes of stock in "series." That means that your Articles may provide for a portion of a class of shares to be issued with special dividend rates, redemption privileges, liquidation preferences, conversion privileges, or whatever. You may also stipulate that another portion of shares of the same class of stock may be issued with a whole different set of variables. The possibilities here are almost endless.

ARTICLE SIX

Here, your Articles may provide for "preemptive rights" for your shareholders. This means that certain shareholders have a right to buy a corresponding percentage of their current share holdings of any new stock of the same class. The corporation may offer to sell the shares to outside investors only if the shareholders with preemptive rights are not interested or can't afford to purchase the offering. This is often referred to as a "first right of refusal."

ARTICLE SEVEN

In this section, your corporation can provide for indemnification of its officers, directors, employees and agents for any liability to which they may be subject as a result of the performance of their corporate duties. The ability of a corporation to indemnify individuals this way may be controlled or limited by some state laws.

ARTICLE EIGHT

Your corporation must provide the street address of the registered office and resident agent located within the state of incorporation. The resident agent is responsible to receive service of process and official correspondence in the name of the corporation, and forward such communications to the appropriate corporate officer.

ARTICLE NINE

Here, your corporation must state the number of directors required. Nevada allows for only one director, while many states require at least three. The directors who will comprise the initial board of directors must be listed by name, with a complete street address included in the Articles of Incorporation

ARTICLE TEN

Your corporation must have at least one organizer or incorporator listed here. The incorporator(s) signs the Articles of Incorporation when they are submitted for filing. They will be re-

sponsible and liable if they have knowingly made any misstate-
ment of the facts in the Articles of Incorporation. Beyond that,
they have no responsibility to the corporation.

AMENDMENTS

The original incorporators may amend the Articles of Incorporation before stock is issued by filing a certificate with the
Secretary of State with the detailed changes. The opening para-
graph of the certificate of amendment must:

1. State that the signers of the certificate are at least two-
   thirds of the original incorporators.
2. State the date the original Articles of Incorporation were
   filed with the Secretary of State.
3. Certify that no stock has been issued to date.

The Secretary of State will file the amended version of the
Articles of Incorporation upon receipt of the certificate of amendment and any appropriate fees. All amendments made to your
Articles of Incorporation prior to the issuance of stock will be
considered as part of the original Articles of Incorporation.

If your corporation has already issued its stock, you are still
allowed to make amendments to your Articles of Incorporation.
However, there are only five areas in which the Articles of Incorporation may be changed.

1. The corporation's name may be changed.
2. The existing powers and purposes of your corporation
   may be either widened or narrowed.
3. Other powers and purposes may be substituted for the
   existing powers and purposes of the corporation.
4. Amendments may change the number or classification
   of the authorized stock, including changes to the par
   value, et cetera.
5. Optional provisions may be changed as desired.

Nevada corporate law dictates that the board of directors
meet in order to adopt a resolution to file for proposed amendments. The board then calls for a meeting of the stockholders to
vote on the proposed amendments. If the stockholders approve

(by whatever majority vote is required in the Articles or Bylaws) the secretary records all changes in the corporate record book and files for the amended articles with the Secretary of State.

CORPORATE BYLAWS

The Bylaws are a separate document from your Articles of Incorporation. They deal with internal corporate procedures that you establish for your operations. The Bylaws are considered a contract between the stockholders, directors, and officers. The Bylaws usually contain terms that are not required in the Articles of Incorporation regarding the regulation of rights and the affairs of the corporation.

Your Bylaws should state the place and time of annual meetings of the stockholders and directors, and detail the procedures for notifying these individuals of such meetings. The Bylaws should also define what makes up a voting majority and a quorum for meeting and voting purposes within the corporation. Procedures for calling special meetings are usually outlined in detail in the Bylaws, as are the standard orders of business. The Bylaws should also specify duties of the officers of the corporation.

Bylaws are drafted by the directors and adopted by the shareholders as their internal operating procedure. Directors may draft changes to the Bylaws at any time. Those changes must then be voted on by the shareholders. Neither the Bylaws nor amendments to them are filed with the Secretary of State.

Your Bylaws should do the following things:
1. Identify the location of the corporate offices.
2. Specify the date and time of annual shareholders meetings.
3. Provide for calling "special meetings" of the shareholders.
4. Define a voting quorum of shareholders.
5. Provide for the use of proxies.
6. Provide for informal actions, not requiring a formal meeting.

7. Provide for cumulative voting procedures.
8. Establish the number, tenure and qualifications of the directors.
9. Establish the date and time of annual directors meetings.
10. Establish director fees for meeting attendance.
11. Define what constitutes a quorum of the board of directors.
12. Provide for filling vacancies on the board of directors.
13. Establish procedures for removal or discharge of directors.
14. Describe the corporate officers and their specific duties.
15. Establish procedures for removal or discharge of officers.
16. Describe the share certificate.
17. Establish or define the fiscal year for the corporation.
18. Provide for the use of a corporate seal (no longer *required*).
19. Provide for the use of committees.
20. Provide for amending the Bylaws.

If your corporation functions without any Bylaws, the Articles of Incorporation become the only document that regulates the operations of the company. Since the Articles of Incorporation require more time, energy, hassle, and cost to amend, it is a good idea for your corporation to adopt good Bylaws as a way of maintaining flexibility in your operations.

CORPORATE MINUTES

The minutes of your corporate meetings provide an ongoing record of corporation business, and provide proof that the corporation has been functioning legally and properly. When you are too busy managing the business to attend to the detail of the corporate minutes, get someone else to do it for you. You *must* realize that accurate, written reports of corporate proceedings may be your last and only defense in litigation. Without accurate minutes, a judge or IRS agent can disallow major corporate actions, including such things as executive compensation, bonuses, retirement plans, and dividend disbursements.

The minutes of your meetings should show that the meeting was properly called, and that everyone there received adequate notice as required by the corporate Bylaws. If a written notice of the meeting was provided, then a copy of that should be included, and if no notice was given, the appropriate waiver of notice should accompany the minutes. The minutes should be signed by all those who attended, showing compliance that the minutes accurately reflect what took place in that meeting.

There are no standard formats for keeping minutes, but times, dates, and the location of the meetings, along with a list of all those attending, should be included. Any action by the board should be recorded. For every action that is taken during a meeting, the minutes should reflect that the issue was properly introduced (and by whom), seconded, discussed, and agreed to by a voting majority as defined in the Bylaws. The complete text of any resolution, contract, report, or other document adopted or ratified in a meeting should appear in the minutes.

Now, minutes don't have to include *every* word of discussion on every subject, but they should be comprehensive in scope. They should especially reflect any final decisions that were made, rather than the discussions that led to them.

Some particularly important meetings should be covered, *in detail*, by your corporate minutes. These would include:

1. Meetings to establish executive salaries. If the IRS feels that your salary or the salary of some of your employees is excessive, they may accuse you of trying to distribute profits through compensation instead of dividends. The IRS keeps a close eye on small corporations in particular, since it's easier to hide profits as deductible compensation when there are only a few employees or stockholders.

   If the minutes of your corporate meetings show that the company compared the salaries of similar executives at comparable companies, including their benefits, and considered an employee's training and experience *before* establishing their pay rate, then high compensation levels will be easier to justify. If these factors can't explain high compensation levels, the minutes should prove that your company's growth potential was a factor and that agreements existed for substantial bonuses if employees produced at a higher level to help the company grow. When the corporate minutes adequately reflect this posture in your company, the IRS might agree that increased compensation was warranted in a more profitable year.

2. Meetings to discuss accumulated excessive earnings. If your corporation accumulates over $250,000 in earnings, it may be penalized by additional taxes on top of those that apply to corporate profits. The IRS assumes that you are holding the money to avoid distributing taxable dividends. But, if for example, your corporation plans to make significant capital improvements, then reasonable grounds exist for retaining excess earnings. Your corporate minutes must record the reasons for the accumulation, though, including any cost estimates you've gotten for putting those plans into action.

3. Meetings to discuss a consolidation or merger. Detailed minutes are absolutely mandatory when corporate mergers or consolidations are in the works. You must outline the plan for selling or acquiring assets and for putting any new management control mechanisms in place. Such minutes are usually required to be filed with your corporate tax returns to properly validate disbursements made during the merger.

4. Meetings to discuss dissolution or liquidation. Minutes of meetings where liquidation plans are adopted are also filed with your corporate tax return. The tax consequences of such an action are very complicated. I suggest you seek counsel in drafting any minutes of this kind of meeting, as they will play a critical part in determining how the IRS looks at your cash and asset distributions.

5. Meetings to discuss dividends. When stockholders receive dividends as stock instead of cash, the dividends are not considered taxable until the stock is sold, that is, unless the stockholders could have chosen between stock and cash, in which case they can be taxable. The minutes of such meetings should clearly show whether the stockholders were given this option or not.

6. Meetings to discuss "step" transactions. When your corporation involves itself in several transactions that become steps toward a bigger transaction over an extended period of time, your corporate minutes should reflect that each of these steps was taken with the end result in mind. The progression of events should be clearly indicated.

7. Meetings to discuss qualified retirement plans. When your corporation decides to offer employee pension, profit sharing or stock bonus plans, the corporate minutes will likely be necessary to get IRS approval. If your plan meets the IRS requirements, employees won't be taxed on corporate contributions or gains until they actually receive the money. When the plan becomes operational, your minutes should indicate the amount of corporate contributions each year. If you decide to abandon your existing plan, the minutes should comprehensively document the reasons.

CORPORATE RESOLUTIONS

A corporate resolution is a document that records actions that the directors (or in some cases, stockholders) "resolve" to take on behalf of their corporation. The use of resolutions provides another easy way to manage the formalities of your Nevada Corporation. Resolutions can be included in the minutes of either directors or stockholders meetings, or they may be included separately in a resolution section of the corporate record book.

Nevada corporate law allows your board of directors to take action without an official directors meeting *provided* that all directors are willing to sign a formal resolution in support of the action, *and* that the action is fully ratified at the next directors meeting. Such resolution then has to be filed with the corporate minutes of that meeting.

Stockholders can take action without a meeting as long as at least a majority of the voting rights consent in writing to the action. In essence, a Nevada Corporation can conduct nearly all of its business with corporate resolutions. You *must*, however, keep your corporate resolutions in chronological order in your minutes, and maintain a complete record of all the corporate activities that result.

At the annual meetings, then, the shareholders should ratify all of the actions taken by resolution since the last meeting. Most people find this method of achieving corporate formalities much simpler and easier, and just as effective as holding special meetings and recording the minutes and all the problems inherent in that procedure.

A typical corporate resolution should contain the following:

1. The name of the corporation,
2. The state of incorporation,
3. A notation as to who originated the resolution (i.e., president, board of directors, shareholders, et cetera),
4. A notation that the resolution contains the direction of at least a majority of those empowered to make decisions at this level,
5. The text of the resolution,
6. The date the resolution was adopted, and
7. Signatures of all the individuals who approved the resolution.

CORPORATE STOCK CERTIFICATES

In most cases, every stockholder is entitled to have a stock certificate, signed by the appropriate corporate officers or agents, which certifies the number of shares the stockholder owns in the corporation. When the stock certificate is issued, the corporation is required to send to the stockholder a written statement that contains all of the information on the stock certificate. Most corporations confirm this information in writing to the stockholders on at least an annual basis.

If your corporation is authorized to issue different classes or series of shares, the stock certificates should reflect the kind and class of stock represented by each certificate. Other pertinent information on the stock certificate should include:

1. The state of incorporation,
2. The number of the stock certificate,
3. The authorized capitalization of the corporation,
4. The date the certificate is issued to the owner,

5. The name of the resident agent, and
6. Any terms that the Bylaws or Articles of Incorporation use to limit the issuance or use of the stock.

When you issue stock certificates, they will show how many shares the certificate is worth. Stock certificates have a stub that remains a permanent part of the corporate record, indicating the number of shares issued to that particular person on that date.

The backs of stock certificates are left blank. There is an area reserved on the back for when the certificates are endorsed and either transferred or redeemed ("cashed"). When shares are transferred from one individual to another, it is customary to record those changes in the official ledger, although that is not mandatory. However, Nevada case law holds that transfers of stock between individuals cannot be recognized by the corporation until such transfers are actually registered on the corporate books.

The significance of stock ownership is not the actual number of shares owned, but the percentage of ownership and voting rights those shares represent in the corporation. To determine this, the corporate secretary can tell you how many shares of stock are authorized by the state to be issued, and how many shares have actually been issued. Control of any corporation ultimately rests with the stockholders, and when a stockholder or group of stockholders control the majority of ownership and voting rights, they can do pretty much whatever they want with *their* corporation.

CORPORATE STOCK LEDGER

The stock ledger is the official record of the corporation showing the issuance and transfer of all shares. Transfers of corporate shares between individuals must eventually be registered on the books of the corporation in the stock ledger. Until that is done, all rights of ownership remain with the original holder of the shares. That includes the right to vote and the right to receive dividends. The purpose for this is to protect the officers of the corporation in determining these rights among the stockholders.

Your corporate stock ledger should contain the following:

1. Stockholder's name and address,
2. Date and time stockholders became owners of the shares,
3. Number and class of shares stockholders received,
4. Amount stockholders paid for their shares,
5. The number of the stock certificates stockholders received to evidence ownership in those shares,
6. The name of the person such shares were transferred from, and
7. The stock certificate number of the person from whom the stock was transferred.

In most jurisdictions, anyone who has been a stockholder of a corporation for at least six months is entitled to inspect the stock ledger either in person or by agent or attorney during usual business hours and on five days written notice. Some states require that the resident agent have a current copy of the corporation's stock ledger at all times.

Any corporation that cannot or will not open its stock ledger for inspection to a qualified stockholder may be fined by the state for every day access is denied. Additionally, the corporation can be held liable to the person for any damages resulting from the denied access.

Corporate stock ledger statement

Some states, including Nevada, allow that in lieu of keeping a copy of the stock ledger on hand, the resident agent must have on file a "stock ledger statement" that provides the name and address of the person who actually has the official stock ledger in their possession.

Under Nevada corporate law, the person responsible for the stock ledger can be located anywhere in the world. Thus, to find records of ownership for a Nevada Corporation might require a subpoena to the resident agent, which will only provide enough information for another subpoena, probably in another state's jurisdiction.

By the time the second subpoena is served, the stock ledger could have changed hands. A creditor would have to serve the resident agent all over again to find that new location, ad infinitum. The use of the stock ledger statement provides a real advantage to the privacy element for owners of Nevada Corporations.

THE CORPORATE SEAL

It used to be a standard practice for corporations to "seal" their formal documents or contracts. Now, the seal is no longer legally required in most states. The corporate seal may be required when executing documents from other countries, such as foreign contracts, but in most cases, it is not needed. Use of a corporate seal is completely voluntary, and should be written into the corporate Bylaws if you desire to use one. However, the legality of corporate documents that do not bear the corporate seal is not affected.

SUMMARY

The incorporation process is not difficult but it is certainly different. Many of the tasks involved in setting up your corporation can be done by an attorney or even companies specializing in these procedures. The key is to actually go through the process. If you are interested in establishing one of these corporations, a great place to go is Wade Cook Financial Corporation (WADE), a publicly traded company specializing in this area. For more information, call their offices at 1-800-872-7411 and ask to speak with someone about setting up a Nevada Corporation.

There are plenty of people out there banking on the fact that you will not be willing to do what it takes to implement the protection which you need. Don't play into their hands. Do what it takes.

XII THE SECRET MILLIONAIRE'S SECRET WEAPON

"He who can take advice is sometimes
superior to him who can give it."

KARL VON KNEBEL

Throughout this book, I have made reference over and over again to the importance of consulting with a qualified tax and/or other professional. This is perhaps the best advice I could possibly give you. Will this cost you some money? Absolutely. More importantly however, it will not cost you anywhere near as much money as it would had you not sought this advice.

Much of the work involved in setting up and running your own corporation is relatively straightforward and routine. Any knowledgeable and motivated businessperson can effectively accomplish much of this himself or herself. But one thing that you must realize is that you *will* need assistance from others from time to time. Some of the decisions you must make will involve complex areas of law and/or taxation and are best directed to qualified professionals. Other decisions

261

will require an integration of business, legal, and financial savvy and are best left to the assistance of a smart small business attorney.

WHAT IS A "MASTER MIND" TEAM?

As a "secret millionaire," one of the most important steps you could possibly take to preserve the wealth you have accumulated is to build your "Master Mind" team. This will consist of those professionals who will give you the much needed assistance in areas which require more specialized knowledge. This will include a vast array of different professionals, basically specialized tools for your toolbox. You will need several members for your team because you never know which one will be the best for any given situation. Just as you would not keep just one tool in your tool box, you cannot keep just one member on your "master mind" team. In building your team, here are a few suggestions on who you need:

1. Attorney
2. Accountant
3. Insurance Agent
4. Real Estate Agent
5. Stockbroker
6. Spouse
7. Pension Specialist
8. Others

While all of the above team members are important to your overall success, I want to pay particular attention to the two which will be most beneficial to you in establishing and operating your own Nevada Corporation: the attorney and accountant. Before we talk about this, you need to understand about an important pitfall that many people are exposed to. By understanding this, you will be less likely to fall into this trap.

Do not fall into the trap of thinking that you can just save the money and do it all yourself. As Wade Cook says in his best-selling books and seminars, *"Stop tripping over pennies on your way to dollars."* If you want to save the big money over the long haul, a "master mind" team can be the quintessential ingredient to your overall success. But the key is in setting up your team. I have included here a section on forming that team so that you can be further along on your mission to become a "secret millionaire" and so that you will be that much closer to having the things which you most want to have.

HOW DO I FIND A GOOD LAWYER?

The cost of placing a lawyer on retainer is cost-prohibitive for most small businesses. Even when dealing with an attorney on an issue-by-issue basis, fees can add up swiftly, sometimes too swiftly for legal advice to be affordable except for the most important and most pressing issues. Just as with individuals, more and more small businesses are trying to at least partially close this legal affordability gap by doing as much of their own work as possible. Oftentimes, doing this work yourself can save you some money. Other times, it makes sense to briefly consult with a lawyer at an interim stage, or have the paperwork reviewed upon completion. The key is being able to distinguish between what you should do yourself and what you should have someone help you with.

Depending on the size of your business and the complexity of your legal needs, the next step you are likely to take is to find a competent and cooperative attorney who can assist you with your various legal concerns. Obviously, you are not searching for a lawyer who will take over *all* of your decision-making and running of your business. That could cost an absolute fortune if you were paying this person on an hourly basis. Besides that, it would be unnecessary in all but the most complicated situations. What you really need is to find an attorney who can be a part of your overall team so that he or she can assist you with the more pressing concerns only.

It's important to understand when looking for a lawyer, that you do not need a high-dollar, big-firm corporate lawyer for all of your legal issues. For many of the legal needs, a lawyer is a lawyer is a lawyer. That is not to minimize the value of a good lawyer, but their services should be retained for only the most specialized legal work. In today's legal market, there is an abundance of lawyers who are more than willing to work with you, many times even in unorthodox payment situations. Generally, you may not want a lawyer who works with big corporations. Two main reasons for this are that they will probably deal with issues that are much different from your small business concerns and they will most definitely charge you big corporation fees.

When searching for a good attorney, refrain from starting off your search with advertisements, legal directories, or the phone book. Unfortunately, lawyer referral services operated by state bar associations are every bit as unhelpful. These sources too many times merely supply the names of lawyers who have signed up for that particular service. One of the inherent problems with this is that these services simply rely on the attorney's word that they have the necessary qualifications.

The better approach is to speak with people in the community who own or operate businesses which you respect or who have the same or similar needs. Many times at our seminars, we ask people to stand up and introduce themselves to the people around them. Later, we will ask them to go out and meet someone else that they have not had the opportunity to meet. One of the main reasons that we do this is so that they can learn from others in their area about valuable resources. Ask these people about their lawyer(s) and how they feel about the quality of their work. If you speak with five to 10 different people, it is highly likely that you will come away with some great information.

An additional source is to talk with other people such as bankers, accountants, insurance agents, real estate brokers, and others who may be able to provide the names of lawyers they feel comfortable and confident with in their own business dealings. One other source worth mentioning is to speak with friends, relatives, or even business associates within your own company who may also have names of possible attorneys to help you with your particular situation.

For most of your legal issues, you will not need to seek out an absolute specialist in their field. However, what if you do have a very technical legal question? Should you immediately seek out the services of a specialist? Generally, the answer to this is "no." One good approach is to seek out a sort of assistant for identifying your issues. An example of this may be a lawyer who specializes in general practice who could at least identify your issue(s) and then determine whether or not you need a specialist. There are some really good companies out there who hold seminars outlining various legal entities and assisting you with their implementation. Perhaps the best at doing this is Wade Cook Financial Corporation which holds seminars on business entities. They have a division of the company, a subsidiary, named Entity Planners International which specializes in setting up legal entities and assisting with questions about the operation of these entities. If you are interested in their services, you can call the company at 1-800-872-7411 and ask to speak with a member of the Gold Team. This is a great way to deal with your legal concerns in a very cost-efficient manner.

In the event that you decide to seek out a specialist for a more complicated legal matter, there are a few issues which you must pay particular attention to. After you have acquired the names of a few key prospects, don't wait around until a legal crisis occurs before establishing your initial contact with a lawyer. If you put the contact off until things are chaotic, you may not have sufficient time to find a lawyer who will work with you at an affordable price. In fact, it's extremely possible that you may end up settling for the first available person at a moment's notice. This almost always results in an unfavorable situation where you will pay too much for too little.

I learned this the hard way in a nonlegal area when I was building my home. I contracted the project myself and was responsible for lining up all of the subcontractors. After being strung along by one of these subs, I was left in a position where I needed the work done ASAP. I called around and found the first available person to handle the job and was rather dissatisfied with the end result. I blame myself for this unfortunate situation because I let myself get into a situation where I had almost no choice but to take the first person available. In retrospect, it seems logical that I would not get the optimal results. If this person was available immediately, this should have told me something. They don't have any work. Why is that? Even if you are able to get a top-notch professional to do the job, if you wait until the last minute you will certainly pay for it.

When you do contact a lawyer, state your intentions in advance. Tell them that you are looking for someone who is willing to give you guidance, get you pointed in the right direction as needs arise, and to tackle those important legal issues which you may find yourself faced with. In exchange for this, let the attorney know that you are more than willing to pay in a fair and prompt fashion. If they seem agreeable to this arrangement, ask to come to their office for a face-to-face meeting to get acquainted. Many lawyers will not charge you for this initial consultation. However, I have always found that it is a good idea to at least offer to pay them for their services. You want to establish from the get-go that while you only need them for specific issues, you are certainly not looking for a free ride. As an attorney myself, I can assure you that most attorneys don't mind talking to you briefly about inconsequential matters, but when it starts interfering with their making a living, it becomes a different matter.

Once you go in to meet with the lawyer, state your intentions again that you are looking for more of a legal advisor, a coach if you will, to assist you with legal concerns. Let me warn you right now that many lawyers will find this a bit unattractive, this whole idea of helping you in piecemeal fashion. If they seem especially uninterested, thank them for their time and move on. At this meeting, you will also want to discuss additional issues such as fees. It is sometimes an uncomfortable subject to bring up, but let me assure you that it is nowhere near as uncomfortable as bringing it up too far down the road.

Dealing with the issue of fees, it is always best to get a clear understanding of how fees will be imposed and calculated. An example of this might occur when your lawyer gives general legal advice from time to time or perhaps steers you in the right direction for a good legal source. The question now is: how will you be billed for this information? Some lawyers will bill a flat amount for a call or conference. Others will bill to the nearest time interval. Common time intervals are six, ten, or twenty minutes. When I was with a private firm, the standard practice was to bill in six minute increments. The premise with this practice was that it takes at least six minutes to do anything once you document it in detail for billing purposes. The most important thing is to understand whatever billing system is in place.

The beginning of your relationship is the most critical time to develop the understanding of the billing process. To do this, ask the attorney specifically what it will cost for the job. If you feel that the amount is too much, don't hesitate to negotiate with the attorney. Ask for some alternative scenarios as well.

It is always a good idea to get all fee arrangements in writing. Any lawyer should understand this completely. The reason for this is that the written document will evidence a clear meeting of the minds on the issue. This becomes especially important when dealing with a larger job. The fact is, in many states the law requires that agreements between lawyers and clients be in writing if the fee is expected to be in excess of $1,000. I personally feel that it is advisable to get the agreement in writing even if the amount falls below this level. As I stated earlier in the book, there is a simple rule which I like to follow which is: *I would rather have it and not need it than need it and not have it.*

There are a few standard methods which lawyers use to bill their clients. To better equip you in your dealings with attorneys, it is important for you to understand what these methods are. The primary methods are as follows:

1. By the hour,
2. Flat fee for a specific job,
3. Contingent fee based upon settlement amounts or winnings, and
4. Retainer.

To give you a better understanding of these methods, let's take a look at them on an individual basis.

BY THE HOUR

In most parts of the country, competent legal services are available for your business at a rate of $150 to $250 per hour. Some of the newer attorneys who are still in the developmental stages of their practices may be available for paperwork review, legal research, and other types of legal work at lower rates. The only way to find out for sure is to ask.

Flat fee for a specific job

In this type of arrangement, you would pay the agreed-upon amount for a given project. The amount you pay will be regardless of how much or how little time is spent on the project by the lawyer. When you first begin working with a lawyer and are concerned about hourly costs soaring out of control, it is perhaps a good idea to negotiate a flat fee for a specific job. An example of this might be in a situation where a lawyer draws up a real estate purchase agreement for a set fee, or reviews and finalizes a buy-sell agreement for a flat fee, for instance, $500.

Contingent fee based upon settlement amounts or winnings

This is the type of fee predominantly used in personal injury, products liability, fraud and discrimination type cases, where a lawsuit is likely to be filed. In this instance, the lawyer would receive a percentage of the recovery in the event that you win the case, but would receive nothing in the event that you lose. You may ask yourself why an attorney would take a case knowing full well that he may not get paid if you were to lose. You must understand that in the event that you do win the case, the lawyer will be paid handsomely. This pay will be in the neighborhood of 33 to 40% of the amount of the judgment. Since most business legal needs involve advice and assistance with drafting documentation, a contingency normally makes little sense. Notwithstanding this, if your business becomes involved in a personal injury claim or a lawsuit involving fraud, unfair competition, or an infringement of a patent or copyright, you may decide to explore the possibility of this type of fee arrangement.

Retainer

Many corporations can afford to pay relatively modest amounts on a yearly basis to keep a business lawyer on retainer for ongoing phone or in-person consultations or routine business matters during the year. This may run anywhere from $1,000 to $2,000. Of course, you must realize that your retainer won't cover a full blown legal crisis. It may however, take care of any routine contract and other legal paperwork preparation and review throughout the year.

If you ever have any questions and/or concerns about an attorney's bill or the quality of his or her services, it is important that you voice those concerns. Acquiring legal assistance is just like purchasing any other consumer service. If you feel dissatisfied with any portion, you should seek a reduction in your bill or make it clear that the work needs to be redone to your satisfaction. Be reasonable about this. If you are in the wrong and feel that the attorney should have been able to get results for you that are simply unrealistic, deal with it. You should voice your concerns in the event that you feel that you were not given adequate representation, not for failing to accomplish your desired results. If the attorney operates a well-run business, they should have no problem whatsoever dealing with your concerns in a positive and timely manner. If you are unable to get an acceptable response from that lawyer, find another one as soon as possible. If you do change attorneys, you are entitled to get your important documents back from the first lawyer.

In the event that you are to discharge your attorney, you may still feel that you have been unjustly wronged. If you are unable to come to an acceptable resolution to your problem, write to the client grievance office of the state bar association for the state in which the incident occurred. Another tip is to send a copy of the letter to the attorney. Oftentimes, a phone call to the attorney from this office tends to bring about the desired outcome.

I want to leave you with one final thought in regard to choosing an lawyer. It is crucial that you pay special attention to the rapport between you and your attorney. Keep in mind, you are looking for someone to guide and assist you in a manner that shows they are working *with* you. In many instances, it is best to trust your instincts and find a lawyer whose personality and business philosophies mesh with your own.

How do i find a good tax advisor?

Becoming proficient in the area of taxation is a huge task. To truly master all of the tax information applicable to you is almost impossible. Besides that, after you spend all your time trying to learn everything there is to know, you won't have time to be effective in your business. The good news is that you don't have to become an absolute expert in the field of taxation in order to significantly reduce your tax bill. Once you are equipped with a firm base level of knowledge, it is more advisable to find a good tax advisor. This person will become a key ingredient in your overall success and should become a part of your master mind team.

There are many different types of tax advisors out there to choose from. The tax field is somewhat unregulated which suggests that you need to be careful. You need to find someone who really *is* an expert rather than someone who merely claims to be an expert. What you are really looking for is someone who is experienced in helping small businesses rather than someone who specializes in rapid refunds who took a two month course advertised through the newspaper. At the same time, there is seldom any need to seek the assistance of a CPA with one of the Big Six public accounting firms for your small business issues.

Ideally, you need a professional who understands the type of business in which you are involved. The following is a list of some of the tax professionals who may be of assistance to you:

1. A TAX RETURN PREPARER

Persons who refer to themselves as tax return preparers are not licensed through the IRS. The reason for this is that there is no requirement for such license. You can think what you want about the lack of formalized testing or licensing program. Some states impose their own requirements but most simply allow anyone to do it. This refers to both private individuals and also to the larger tax return preparation chains. These folks may be extremely knowledgeable about the subject of taxes or they may not be, you take your chances. As such, be careful.

2. An enrolled agent

An enrolled agent is a person who is licensed by the IRS as a tax preparer and advisor. In order to obtain this license, the person must pass a test administered by the IRS or by having at least five years of experience working for the IRS. In the United States, there are over 20,000 enrolled agents who provide not only tax assistance but sometimes even bookkeeping and accounting services as well. Of the tax pros available out there, enrolled agents are typically the least expensive.

3. A tax attorney

A tax attorney can oftentimes be the most expensive source of tax assistance but can also be the most valuable. A tax attorney is one who has attained an advanced law degree in the area of taxation or one who has received a tax-specific certification from a state bar association, though many states do not specifically grant this type of certification. These professionals should be retained in the event that you find yourself with a serious tax problem, require legal representation in court, or have a legal problem with the IRS. They may also be of great assistance for complex tax and estate planning issues.

4. A certified public accountant (CPA)

Finally, we have our friends, the CPAs. CPAs are licensed and regulated by each state and are required to pass an extensive examination prior to obtaining their license. While this is similar to attorneys, I like to think that the bar exam is much more difficult than the CPA exam. This may have something to do with the fact that I passed the bar exam but never took the CPA exam. In any event, these are licensed professionals who perform sophisticated accounting and business tax work and tax preparation. They can be some of your greatest allies when it comes to business tax advice but are generally not as aggressive as tax attorneys when dealing with the IRS. It is my personal opinion that a CPA should be a part of your team as well as an attorney.

Tax professionals can be of tremendous assistance in many key areas. For this reason, it is important to choose a good member for your team. While there are several ways to choose a good tax professional, asking someone from the IRS for their suggestion is not your best resource. One of the best possible ways to find a good tax pro is to ask other people if they know someone. Obviously, there is more to it than simply asking someone else but this is a great place to start. If you can get the names of at least four or five to speak with, you can take it from there. The information you learned in choosing an attorney is applicable here as well. Make sure to find someone who you feel both comfortable and confident with.

In addition to asking others for referrals, look for advertisements. You should take these advertisements with a grain of salt. As with all advertisements, those promoting the services of a tax advisor will paint a picture of a top notch professional whether that is the case or not. Another source will be the local bar associations and CPA societies. These names are usually given on a rotation basis from their list so you need to understand that this is not a recommendation or certification of competence. It is your responsibility to decide who you will use for your tax needs so make sure that you feel good about your decision.

Another item which needs to be addressed is the fees associated with tax advice. Tax professionals aren't cheap, but neither is the lack of tax advice. It is important to realize that the fees involved in obtaining sound tax assistance is a part of your investment in your business. A good tax professional can save you far more than they ever charge you. With that in mind, let's take a look at tax fees.

It is always a good idea to develop a clear understanding of how any fees will be imposed as soon as possible. Specifically, you need to know if fees will be charged on an hourly basis or whether services will be performed on a flat fee basis. The most common type of billing practice amongst professionals is to charge hourly. These fees can range anywhere from $25 to $250 per hour, depending on what type of tax professional you use (enrolled agents as the low, top CPAs and tax attorneys as the high).

You will remember that we said it is important to get things in writing when establishing your relationship with your attorney. This is also the case when dealing with your tax professional. You should ask for a written agreement *before* any work is done so that all parties know exactly where they stand. This will become especially important should a dispute arise.

Remember also, that expenses are almost always negotiable. If you don't want to pay a large fee, voice your feelings. This is a problem that many people find themselves in. They don't want to pay so much but they never ask to pay less. Trust me, no one is going to reduce the bill for someone who seems happy paying the current fees. If you don't like the situation you're in, you have to do something about it.

SUMMARY

Building your master mind team is one of the most critical ingredients to your overall success. When dealing with an issue of this importance, it is essential that you spend a little time making the decisions as to who will become a part of this team. Top legal and tax professionals are not cheap, but they can be worth their weight in gold when used properly. Above all, make sure that you find members for your team who you feel both comfortable and confident with. Always remember, the money you spend on top tax and legal assistance is not an expense, it is an investment.

XIII The Secret Millionaire's Call to Action

"Use all your wisdom, all your learning, all your knowledge, and move forward."

I n many ways, I believe this is the most important chapter in the book. Not because it has the most crucial information on Nevada Corporations, but because it covers the most quintessential ingredient to your success. If you lack this final portion, your success will be greatly limited. That essential element is *action*.

Understand, I am in no way minimizing the importance of learning about specific subjects. Gaining this knowledge is one of the most important undertakings a person could apply themselves to. But I need to ask you a question. If you have all of the information, yet fail to act on it, how much good does it do you?

Think about it. What does that tell you? Does that mean that there is no need for knowledge? Of course not! The thing you need to get a handle on is the way to balance these issues.

The best way to illustrate this point is to take a look at an example that I go through in my live seminars. During the seminar I will ask the students to raise their hands if they: 1) have children in college, 2) have put their children through college, or 3) put themselves through college. I have the students keep their hands up through the next question which is: "How many of you deducted that expense?" Invariably, nearly every hand in the room goes down.

The next question is one of the most telling. Why not? Why aren't you deducting these expenses? Understand that there are specific restrictions on whether or not these expenses are deductible. Too many times however, people fail to deduct things that they could have deducted.

When I ask people why they neglected to take the deduction, the answer is usually because they didn't know about it. They simply did not know that they could take this deduction. This is the first problem which comes up, lack of knowledge.

Lack of knowledge is a major hurdle for many people. It is very difficult to take advantage of benefits when you don't know about them. That should show you how I feel about the need for knowledge. It is crucial, but you need to be careful as to the knowledge you are receiving. Let me give you an example.

After I ask the question about deducting the educational expenses, my next question is: "Why not?" The response I get is important because it demonstrates the type of information being disseminated out there. I have many people who tell me that they didn't deduct this expense because their accountant told them that they couldn't take that deduction.

Let me begin by saying that the accountant is right. *They* can't take that deduction. The problem is that they didn't ask the right question. The accountant answered the question which was asked. Do you sometimes feel like you're getting the wrong answers out of life? Perhaps you're asking the wrong questions.

Asking the right questions falls under the category of knowledge. You need to know the right questions to ask if you are looking for the answers that you want. I want to show you how I experienced this.

When I was in law school, I had a course on federal income taxation. One day during class, I asked the law professor whether the expense of law school courses was deductible. The professor's response was that these expenses were not deductible. Actually, he went into great length to explain that there are few instances in the entire tax code as clear cut as the nondeductibility of these expenses.

I must admit that this is not the answer I wanted to hear. But wait a second. I did get the correct answer to the question I asked. Fortunately, I recognized the problem and immediately asked a follow-up question.

This follow-up question relates to a question I ask at the seminars as I mentioned earlier. Basically, I was in the exact situation that my students find themselves in. I had asked a very well-respected tax expert an important question and I got the wrong answer. Not the wrong answer to the question, but the wrong answer from the one I was looking for.

Do you suppose that this could stop a person dead in their tracks? Sure. The key is that we must have enough knowledge to get to the next step.

At the seminars, after I hear about what the accountants have told the students, I ask a new question. The question is: "How many of you work for a corporation who will either reimburse you or pay for college courses which you take?" All of a sudden, hands shoot up all over the class. I then ask those students whether they think that that corporation deducted that expense. Their answer is a resounding yes!

But wait a second, I thought that our accountant told us that we can't deduct that expense. I thought that my law professor said that these expenses are not deductible. How is it then that the corporation can deduct these expenses? What's the difference?

The difference is that those companies are corporations. As corporations, things work a little differently. Corporations can deduct things which individuals simply cannot. Why can't people take those deductions? Lack of entities.

That is the second hurdle which people must overcome. If you do not have a corporation, you cannot receive the benefits of corporations. Entities do you no good whatsoever if you don't have the entities.

The thing you need to understand is that there are two stumbling blocks which people are faced with out there. These are:

1.   Lack of knowledge, and
2.   Lack of entities.

One important point is that both of these must be mastered. If you have knowledge of entities, but you don't have the actual entities, what good does this do you? Conversely, if you have entities but don't have the knowledge to effectively use the entities, how much better off are you? In essence, one cannot work without the other.

The real issue is how to overcome these areas which we are lacking in. Which should be tackled first? That can be rather tricky but it needs to be addressed if we plan on achieving any sort of meaningful results.

Setting up entities is easy. Anyone can go out and find an attorney to set up any type of entity that they want. It reminds me a little bit of the stock market. Is it difficult to purchase stock? No. Once you go out and purchase the stock, does that mean that you will automatically achieve the optimal results? Not at all. It works the same way with entities. You need to know what to do with it once you purchase it. You need the knowledge.

While knowledge alone will not make you successful, lack of knowledge can certainly make you unsuccessful.

Once you determine that you need the knowledge, where do you go to get it? Do colleges teach you how to actually implement strategies or do they teach theory? Remember that college course, How to Operate Corporations 101? It's not there is it? Do books really take you step-by-step through the actual day-to-day workings of your corporation? To truly understand how to do these things, you need to learn it in a way where you can really *learn*.

It was with this thought in mind that I developed an intensive hands-on training program for operating your corporation and actually implementing the strategies. It is the cream of the crop when it comes to interactive workshops.

We call it the Secret Millionaire's Corporate College. It is not a seminar, but more of a workshop. When I say workshop, I mean that you will be *working*. This is no lecture setting, but an actual interactive environment where people get things done. We show people how to make sense out of legal requirements and understand technical legal jargon. It is a literal buffet of knowledge.

The workshop is a course designed as a step-by-step process for accomplishing corporate objectives. Specifically, we go through how forms need to be filled out. We spend a great deal of time on how records need to be kept, not only the minutes of your formal meetings, but specific resolutions which must be documented for implementing corporate policies. People will get more accomplished during their time at the Corporate College than they may have accomplished during any other period of their entire life.

The Secret Millionaire's Corporate College is a two-day event which is structured in a way to enable graduates to hit the ground running, fast. I'd love to be able to say that it is the best workshop of its kind, but in terms of effectiveness, it is the *only* workshop of its kind. It is an absolute learning revolution.

My goal is to provide a setting where people have the opportunity to make things happen. I learned a long time ago that you have two choices. You can either *wait* for things to happen, or you can go out and *make* things happen. You and you alone are in control over what type of person you are.

As I conclude this book, I'm excited. I'm excited about the opportunities available for you to go out and really make things happen. I'm excited about what you can do, not only for yourselves, but for your families.

When all is said and done, you have a decision to make. You are the one responsible for what you do with what you've been presented. You can go on doing things the same old way which will produce the same old results. Or, you can do things the way millionaires do things. If you want to get different results, you must do things differently. You must become a "secret millionaire."

APPENDIX I:
NEVADA LAWS

*"Knowledge is of two kinds. We know
a subject ourselves, or we know where
we can find information upon it."*

SAMUEL JOHNSON

Throughout the book, I've made reference repeatedly to the great benefits offered by Nevada's laws. It's one thing to talk about how great these laws are, but something of even greater importance can be the actual reading and understanding of the actual laws. While most people never take the time to read the statutes pertaining to corporations, I wanted to include the following resource material for you to use in case you decide to delve into the specific laws. A complete list of each of these Nevada Corporation laws is available at wwwleg.state.nv.us. Following is the relevant contents pages of the Nevada law book.

CHAPTER 78
PRIVATE CORPORATIONS

GENERAL PROVISIONS

FORMATION

POWERS

CHAPTER 78A
CLOSE CORPORATIONS

GENERAL PROVISIONS

FORMATION

SHARES OF STOCK

POWERS AND DUTIES

TERMINATION OF STATUS AS CLOSE CORPORATION

CHAPTER 80
FOREIGN CORPORATIONS

NRS 80.010   Requirements to do business in Nevada; filings; limitations on name; certification of authority to engage in certain businesses.

NRS 80.012   Reservation of corporate name; injunctive relief.

NRS 80.015   Activities that do not constitute doing business in Nevada; persons not doing business in Nevada exempted from certain provisions.

NRS 80.016   Determination of whether solicitation is made or accepted in Nevada.

NRS 80.025   Modification of corporate name to qualify to do business in this state: Requirements; procedure.

NRS 80.030   Filing of amendatory documents after qualification.

NRS 80.040   Qualification: English translations to accompany documents in foreign language.

NRS 80.050   Fees payable by foreign corporations.

NRS 80.060   Resident agent: Appointment.

NRS 80.070   Resident agent: Revocation of appointment; resignation, death or removal from state; filing new certificate of acceptance of appointment.

NRS 80.080   Service of process on foreign corporation in this state.

NRS 80.090   Limitations of actions.

NRS 80.100   Authority of directors and representatives: Contracts and conveyances.

NRS 80.110   Annual list of officers and directors and designation of resident agent: Filing requirements; fee; forms.

NRS 80.120   Certificate authorizing corporation to transact business.

NRS 80.140   Contents of annual list: Names and addresses; penalties.

NRS 80.150   Defaulting corporations: Identification; penalty and forfeiture.

NRS 80.160   Defaulting corporations: Duties of secretary of state.

NRS 80.170   Defaulting corporations: Conditions and procedure for reinstatement.

NRS 80.190   Publication of annual statement; recovery of penalty.

NRS 80.200   Surrender of right to transact intrastate business.

NRS 80.210   Penalties for failure to comply with requirements for qualification; enforcement.

Appendix II: Resource Information

The Secret Millionaire Series:
The Secret Millionaire Guide To Nevada
   Corporations
The Secret Millionaire Guide To Living Trusts
The Secret Millionaire Guide To Pension Plans
The Secret Millionaire Audio Tape Set on
   Nevada Corporations
The Secret Millionaire Demo CD-Rom on
   Nevada Corporation Maintenance

Other books by John V. Childers, Jr.
Million-Heirs

Seminars available from
Wade Cook Seminars, Inc. (1-800-872-7411)
   BEST—Business and Entity Skills Training
   Wealth Institute

Entities available from
Entity Planners, Inc. (1-800-706-4741)
   Nevada Corporations
   Living Trusts
   Pension Plans
   Limited Partnerships
   Charitable Remainder Trusts